HAYNES MODERN SPORTS CARS

MGF

Other books by this author:

MGB Including MGC & MGB GT V8

MG V8: 21 YEARS ON From MGB GT V8 to RV8

MG PHOTO ARCHIVE 1945-1964

MG PHOTO ARCHIVE 1965-1980

MG THE UNTOLD STORY

HAYNES MODERN SPORTS CARS

MGF

DAVID KNOWLES

First published in 2000

British Library cataloguing-in-publication data:

A catalogue record for this book is available from the British Library.

ISBN 1 85960 637 7

Library of Congress Catalog Card Number 00-131890

Haynes North America Inc.
861 Lawrence Drive, Newbury Park,
California 91320, USA

Published by Haynes Publishing, Sparkford,
Nr Yeovil, Somerset BA22 7JJ, UK
Tel: 01963 442030 Fax: 01963 440001
Int. tel: +44 1963 442030 Fax: +44 1963 440001
E-mail: sales@haynes-manuals.co.uk
Web site: www.haynes.co.uk

Design by Simon Larkin, layout by Jill Gough

Printed and bound in Great Britain by J.H. Haynes & Co. Ltd

Introduction

The period in MG history following the launch of the Metro was a time of renewal for a company that had been battered by controversy but nevertheless weathered the storm. Whereas pessimism had been the watchword prior to 1980, new generations of management moved forward with greater optimism in the years that followed. Casting off unwanted baggage from its past, the new banner of 'Rover Group' took the place of 'BL' in the summer of 1986.

The return of the company to the private sector in March 1988 saw Rover Group freed from the shackles of state control, but the ambitious plans that ensued all had one thing in common: they had to achieve the maximum amount from the minimum investment. One such idea was a particularly bold but logical one: to re-enter the sports car market, which BL had once called its own but had allowed to fall away through under-investment and environmental politics.

What began with the germ of an idea swiftly took root as the 'Phoenix' programme – a mission to build a new sports car within the impossibly tight budget of £40 million. It was clear from the outset that this would not be an easy thing to achieve, and so some very clever lateral thinking ensued, using contractors and partnerships to the best commercial and engineering advantage.

Within five years of the bonfire being lit, the Phoenix finally flew – and gave rise to what arguably is the best MG sports car ever built. Of course few gestations as complex as this are ever straightforward, and that of the MGF certainly saw some fascinating twists and turns; indeed the roller-coaster ride continues as I write, five years after the launch.

What John Towers, Nick Stephenson and their colleagues did not know when they embarked on Project Phoenix was the fact that Rover Group would be sold to BMW a year before the MGF's launch. There were understandable fears that BMW – planning a sports car of its own that would emerge as the Z3 – might not look too kindly on the MGF. Fortunately for MG fans, BMW ensured that the MGF was not stillborn, although the new proprietors were always slightly wary step-parents. In 1999, the MGF received a mild facelift, and BMW spoke confidently of an MG future tied to the all-important new Mini. Then, in the spring of 2000, the whole apple-cart was overturned, and first one bidder and then another was announced as BMW rushed to divest itself of MG and Rover, victims, it was claimed, of European exchange rates.

This prolonged crisis occurred just as the text of this book was being finalised, and so thoroughly did events change direction within days that the final chapter had to be re-written three times!

MG, however, is now back in British ownership, with a familiar team at the helm, and plans for a bright future released from the internal marque conflicts that seemed to hold it back under BMW. Surely now, the second-generation Phoenix deserves to soar free, bearing the MGF aloft with it. This book tells the story of how it all happened…

Acknowledgements

Without the help of a great many people, writing this book would have been an impossible task and I am truly indebted to all of them. The groundwork for this book actually began before the MGF was launched and then, within days of attending the launch at Geneva, I was ensconced in the company of Brian Griffin at Longbridge. He took time out of his busy schedule to ply me with copious quantities of black coffee while he filled his ashtray to overflowing. I already knew that Brian was the man to speak to, as while trying to speak to him in order to contact his father (former BMC Chief Engineer Charles Griffin), the helpful lady on the Longbridge switchboard explained in broad 'brummy': 'Oh yes, you mean the Chief Engineer for PR3...'

Another key player, of course, was Gerry McGovern, alumnus of the Royal College of Art, whom I have had the pleasure of meeting on many occasions. After his highly regarded work on the MGF, Gerry moved on to mastermind the Land Rover Freelander with equal aplomb, being rewarded with the position of Chief Designer for Land Rover. 'MGs are much more interesting than Land Rovers,' he admitted. Gerry's talent was obviously spotted from afar, for in the autumn of 1999 he was 'head-hunted' by Ford Motor Company to take charge of the Lincoln Design Studios in Detroit and California. For the time being, therefore, Gerry's involvement with MG has ceased, but then who knows what the future may hold?

Before Griffin and McGovern there were others, notably Richard Hamblin (initiator of the Phoenix project) and Don Wyatt at Rover Special Products. Richard left Rover in late 1991 to set up an independent design studio, so I was pleased to hear from him how thoughts of an MG sports car revival first took shape, even before Mazda's MX-5 wowed the crowds at Detroit in January 1989.

Don Wyatt invited me into his inner sanctum at Gaydon, and kindly arranged for some of the photographs you see in this book to be taken specially for me – even if a few of them did appear elsewhere first! The fact that the prototypes themselves survived to be photographed is due in no small part to Wyatt and his colleagues, tucked away in a corner in their slightly decrepit accommodation at Gaydon (before the superb modern design centre was ready).

At MG Cars, I owe a great debt of gratitude to spokesman Kevin Jones, as well as Kevin's erstwhile boss Denis Chick (not to mention Denis's predecessor Ian Elliott), and the many people involved in revitalising the MG marque from time to time. I am also grateful to those brave souls who were prepared to share with me their recollections of the darker period of MG history. During the dramatic sequence of events in the spring of 2000, I was also fortunate to be able to interview Jon Moulton and Nick Stephenson, representing in turn Alchemy Partners and Phoenix Consortium. If any names are missing from the list below, please accept my sincere apologies for the omission.

Greg Allport, Nick Argent, Roy Axe, Ian Beech, David Blume, Denis Chick, Tom Conway, Steve Cox, Ian Elliott, Nick Fell, Mike Ferguson, Phil Gillam, Brian Griffin, Richard Hamblin, Vincent Hammersley, Mark Hughes, Kevin Jones, Don Kettleborough, Chris Lee, John Lindsay, Tim Martin, Gerry McGovern, Mike McHale, Mark Mansfield, Wynne Mitchell, David Morley, Graham Morris, Jon Moulton, Harold Musgrove, Robin Nickless, Mike O'Hara, Guy Pigounakis, Tony Pond, Tom Purves, Phil Raby, Paul Ragbourne, Andrew Roberts, Mike Satur, Steve Schlemmer, Gordon Sked, Nick Stephenson, Michael Whitestone, Dave Woodhouse and Don Wyatt.

David A. Knowles

Origins of the mid-engined MG

Ask anyone with a vague interest in motoring to identify the quintessential British sports car and it is quite likely that they will answer MG. The chances are that even those not professing a particular interest in cars will still recognise MG and the rose-tinted aura that surrounds it.

EX-E, revealed in 1985, was a spiritual landmark in the long gestation of the mid-engined MGF.

After the demise of the MGB and closure of the Abingdon MG factory in 1980, for about a dozen years MG's existence was precarious – reduced to the role of a 'GT' badge on warmed-over mainstream saloons. Yet, when MG's custodians began to consider its renaissance in the 1990s, their market research showed that the name had been undamaged by its time in the automotive doldrums: people still had a warm feeling about the little sports car with the octagonal badge. The concept of a mid-engined MG, however, began some 20 years earlier.

In the aftermath of the 1968 merger of MG's parent company, by then British Motor Holdings, with the aggressive Leyland Motor Corporation (including Rover and Triumph) run by Sir Donald Stokes, it was Leyland men who took all the top jobs. Soon various teams were looking at model duplication and an obvious area was sports cars, where Triumph and MG were deadly rivals, particularly in the important North American market. At Triumph, work was already quite advanced on the Bullet/Lynx project, intended to spawn a family of cars to replace the classic TR roadster as well as adding a 2+2 coupé. An engineering programme was already in hand and prototypes had been built. At MG, work on replacement models had concentrated more on the Midget than the MGB.

The mid-engined ADO21 prototype

At the end of the 1960s, Don Hayter, who had been a key figure in the development of the MGB, found himself engaged in various forward-looking exercises. Soon after the formation of British Leyland, he was summoned to see the new Austin Morris engineering supremo, Harry Webster. 'Harry had decided that Triumph would work on a front-engined rear-wheel-drive TR6/MGB replacement and that MG would work on a mid-engined Midget/Spitfire replacement,' Hayter recalled. 'He asked me to come up with a packaging layout, which soon came to include both E4 and E6 engine options.'

Hayter still has a copy of the 'blue book' (a small top-secret pamphlet that set out the basic parameters of the design brief) in which ADO21 is defined as a small mid-engined sports car with a choice of the 1,275cc (78cu in) A-series engine or two versions of the new E-series Maxi engine. Before long, however, Hayter's designs sidelined the A-series, and added the possibility of the totally new E6 engine which first saw the light of day in the Australian Austin Kimberley of 1970 and in 1972 would appear (with a slightly shorter block) in the Austin/Morris 2200 and Wolseley Six.

Experiments with mid-engined sports car concepts began soon after the formation of British Leyland in 1968. This is Harris Mann's Maxi-based Austin Zanda of 1969.

Rob Owen, one of Harris Mann's colleagues at Longbridge, produced this 1970 sketch of a possible mid-engined sports car.

This sketch, by Paul Hughes of Austin Morris Styling, forms part of the original 'Blue Book' proposals for ADO21 – a concept for a new mid-engined MG sports car.

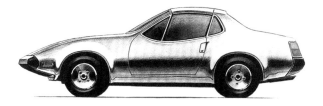

Unfortunately the launch of the Austin Maxi in April 1969 with its 1,485cc (91cu in) version of the engine showed the new unit's shortcomings and a longer-stroke 1,748cc (107cu in) derivative was rushed into production in 1970, just as ADO21 was being developed.

With the official 'nod' from Longbridge, the engineering team at Abingdon began designing and then building the first test 'mule' – uncannily presaging the activities of the PR3 team over 20 years later. The design took three months to progress to the start of build, followed by another six months to complete the engineering exercise.

The starting point was a blue ex-development left-hand-drive MGB GT, which was converted to right-hand drive and adapted to accept the mid-mounted E4 engine. A vertical firewall with a rectangular Perspex window was installed just behind the driver, while various components in the way of the engine, such as the battery and fuel tank, were relocated under the bonnet in the former engine compartment.

The MGB's front suspension was retained for the 'mule' but adapted as necessary, while at the back an all-new de Dion set-up was fabricated specially. 'The de Dion tube pivoted at the rear of the tunnel, level with the heelboard,' recalled Rod Lyne, one of the ADO21 team. 'Initially, this was accomplished by a rubber bush but this was found to make the car steer at the rear and so it was replaced with a solid universal joint.' Externally, the mule looked slightly Heath Robinson as it was fitted with 13in (330mm) wheels at the rear (with a wider track, necessitating wheelarch flares) while with the tailgate missing and the firewall fitted, the result would have seemed very peculiar to the casual onlooker.

An early bugbear of the Maxi was its abominable cable-operated gearbox, later replaced with a superior rod system. Unfortunately for ADO21, the convoluted gear linkage ruled out the rod set-up and so the cables had to be adapted as well as possible. To make things even worse, gear selection positions were transposed: first, third and fifth gears were back, while second and fourth were forward. Driving the 'mule' must have been an interesting experience!

While the engineering team at Abingdon was concentrating on the greasy bits, Austin Morris Styling at Longbridge took Hayter's concept drawing as a starting point and began to develop a modern sports car style for ADO21. In charge of the team was Harris Mann, fresh from penning the concept sketches for the Allegro. He recalls that the tall E-series engine, mounted in the Issigonis style above its transmission, was a particular headache in terms of packaging.

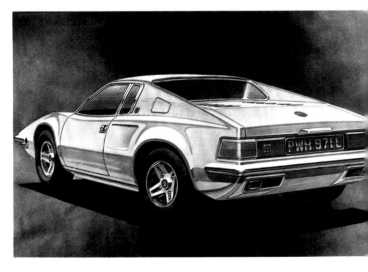

The solution arrived at by Harris Mann and his colleague Paul Hughes, whom Hayter credits with most of the styling work on ADO21, was to use flying buttresses between the roof and rear end to disguise the height of the engine cover. Carefully contrived styling creases in the wings gave the

One of Paul Hughes's
renderings of AD021 (left)
shows a 'DGT' badge on
the rear.

The AD021 proposal
became a full-size wooden
model (above) in November
1970 – a month before the
project was cancelled.

This AD021 packaging
drawing, by Don Hayter,
was used by Harris Mann as
the basis of the 'definitive'
style for a full-size model.

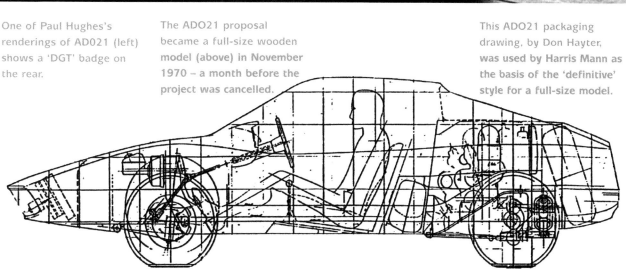

illusion (from the side) that the whole car was low and sleek. It was only from the rear that the height of the rear deck became apparent and even then Hughes had introduced a slope to hide the effect, while the narrow letterbox-shaped rear window was similar to that of the Lotus Europa.

Austin Morris Styling had already shown the potential of a mid-engined sports car design of the future with the Zanda concept car, which was unveiled on the Pressed Steel Fisher stand at the 1969 Earls Court Motor Show as a fully-finished glass-fibre mock-up. Zanda was clearly designed before ADO21 but it undoubtedly set the scene for a practical production car in a similar image. Like Zanda, ADO21 was a coupé, partly because of the packaging problems but also because noises from the USA seemed to indicate that the open sports car had a limited life ahead of it there.

Having developed the style of ADO21 using the traditional tape-drawing approach (where full-size elevations are created with black tape on large white boards), a full-size wooden model was constructed. A management viewing of the model took place on 4 November 1970, a year after the project had begun, but by this stage priorities were shifting elsewhere and within a matter of weeks work on ADO21 ceased. Presumably the mock-up was destroyed and, a few months later, Charles Griffin instructed that the MGB GT 'mule' should suffer the same fate.

Unbeknown to Abingdon, a British Leyland fact-finding mission to the USA (by Spen King and Mike Carver, both Triumph men at the time) had found that the Americans did not want a mid-engined sports car. They wanted a modern-looking car wrapped around a traditional mechanical package, with the option of a 2+2 version – something very much akin to the Triumph Bullet/Lynx programme.

Another nail in ADO21's coffin was its reliance upon engines which were not only untested in the US market but which were likely to prove difficult to develop for the burgeoning US emissions legislation. ADO21 was an interesting experiment that used far too many unique components and as the original brief had been to develop a car to replace the Midget, it had grown potentially too expensive for its intended market sector. Add in the innate hostility to an MG-developed sports car project from well-placed Triumph men at Longbridge and the fate of ADO21 is easier to understand. If circumstances had been different, the MGF would certainly not have been the first mid-engined production MG.

Some may argue that the prospects of any real long-term future for Abingdon died with the cancellation of ADO21. In the main, future sports car engineering would be the preserve of Triumph, although Austin Morris had shown with ADO21 that it could produce a striking state-of-the-art style for a sports car, even with the most unpromising of components.

A question that still puzzles some enthusiasts is what

ADO21 would have been called had it gone into production; some styling drawings show MGD badging, but these badges are merely 'jewellery' used by the designer for effect. There is little doubt that had it been built, ADO21 would have become the MGD but nobody involved in the project ever called it that (for fairly obvious reasons of security).

A new British Leyland sports car: birth of the TR7

In the spring of 1971, two teams of British Leyland designers were working on submissions for a viewing by top management planned for July of that year. Neither team was based at Abingdon.

Sir Donald Stokes had set the small Triumph engineering and design team to work reviewing its Bullet proposal. At Longbridge the Austin Morris Styling Department set to work with a rather more open brief: to develop a strikingly modern corporate sports car which had to accommodate a relatively mundane mechanical package.

Taking its old Michelotti-designed Bullet proposal as a starting point, Triumph grafted on impact-absorbing bumpers front and rear, the then-fashionable pop-up headlamps and a fixed roof. The result, not unlike the VW-Porsche 914, was not exactly an aesthetic masterpiece. Austin Morris, however, did not have the baggage of an existing design to work from, other perhaps than having quite recently developed the ADO21 style with a sharp-nosed, almost wedge, shape. Working under the direction of Harris Mann, the Longbridge designers set to work creating a pair of full-size clays: one intended to be a Triumph and the other an MG, the difference being down to an entirely different exterior body on a common interior body structure. While it was most likely that both MG and Triumph versions would have emerged from the massive new Triumph plant at Speke, there remained the faint possibility that the MG version could have been built at Abingdon.

By July, both the Austin Morris and Triumph teams were ready; the latter had also asked William Towns (designer of the later Aston Martin Lagonda) to produce some scale model studies too. At the management viewing, Stokes was enthused by one of the Austin Morris clays, insisting that its avant-garde styling was just what he wanted – for the Triumph TR7. Ironically, Stokes chose the clay wearing MG badges over the alternative, which Mann had badged as a Triumph. However, the new corporate British Leyland mid-range sports car would be engineered by Triumph and would use the slant-four engine similar to the unit already developed for Saab. At the same time, serious MG development work on future products was curtailed.

At Abingdon, an ADO21 test mule (left) was built using an ex-development MGB GT, with a Maxi engine mounted behind a firewall.

At the same time as MG's ADO21 studies, Triumph worked on the Bullet programme to replace the TR sports car line. This is a quarter-scale model photographed in 1969 against a Coventry background by Triumph Engineering's Norman Rose.

Last days of **Abingdon**

By the time BL's sports car strategy began to unravel, there were some fairly desperate exercises – such as the MG Boxer of 1980. This last-ditch attempt to make an MG out of a TR7 mercifully failed.

By 1979 BL Ltd, as British Leyland had become the previous year, was in trouble. The new Chief Executive, ex-Chloride Chairman Michael Edwardes, planned to refocus the company on core areas of business. While the sports cars were good earners for the company in times of favourable exchange rates, they were also seen as a drain on resources and, in the case of the MGB and Midget, were exceedingly long in the tooth.

The Triumph TR7, launched in 1975, had swallowed an enormous capital investment and incurred additional manufacturing costs and its supporters argued that there was more potential in keeping the TR7 and scrapping the rest of the small and mid-size sports cars. Once the new convertible TR7 was available, one of the main reasons for keeping the MGB had disappeared and it was killed off. After 1980 there was no longer an MG sports car.

Within Edwardes's recovery plan, there was little room for such fripperies as new sports cars and the prospect of a new MG in the mould of the MGB, TR7 or even ADO21 seemed pretty remote; by 1981 the TR7 was also dead. In that context, it is easy to see why Austin Rover decided to apply the MG badge to the Metro in 1982 and subsequently to the Maestro and Montego in 1983 and 1984 respectively. The move was not without its critics (both inside and outside the company) but the general feeling among most MG enthusiasts – who were still coming to terms with the failure of an Aston Martin bid to rescue MG – was that applying an MG badge to a Metro was perhaps better than oblivion.

Richard Hamblin
The famous Ogle Design studios, where he became Transport Design Director, were the starting point for Richard Hamblin's automotive design career. While still at Ogle,

Hamblin had numerous contacts with BL Cars and later Austin Rover, including a proposed Triumph Acclaim face-lift programme and the ECV3 research vehicle (working with Spen King at BL Technology). In April 1983 Hamblin was head-hunted by Roy Axe to run the new Austin Rover Interior Design Studio, with Gordon Sked in charge of the complementary Exterior Studio.

Hamblin's first significant programme within Austin Rover was to develop the interior for the new Rover 800,

working in conjunction with Honda, although the interiors of the two versions were quite different. Then, in April 1986, as Gordon Sked changed from being Director of Exterior Design to Director of Production Design (Exteriors and Interiors), Hamblin switched from Interior Design to Concept Design (Exteriors and Interiors). Hamblin explained: 'Concept Design is normally known as Advanced Design in most companies, but not so at Austin Rover.'

During this changeover period, Hamblin ran the MG EX-

E and Rover CCV interior design programmes. Working for him were Graham Lewis, Richard Carter, Jeremy Newman, Ian Beech, Derek Anderson, Gerry McGovern and an excellent team of modellers. In Concept Design, Hamblin and his team produced the Rover R8 200 cabriolet, an R8 coupé concept model (with a removable rear roof section), the MG F-16 and 'forward visions for future Rover models'.

The Concept Studio also produced a number of paper studies, including the first concept for an updated MGB (see next

The **mid-engined**
Metro: MG 6R4

The Metro (launched as an Austin in 1980 and as an MG in 1982) was such an important car for BL that there were moves afoot from an early stage to produce a motor sport derivative. The MG Metro Turbo, introduced a few months after the basic MG 1300, was a fine starting point. During development some very powerful cars had been built, with frightening power outputs that would never have been feasible for everyday road use. There was also an interesting experiment to build a full-race version of the A-series engine, complete with a twin overhead cam conversion and a prodigious power output. This car was displayed at the same motor show that saw the debut of the Austin Mini Metro itself. However, although a Metro racing series was soon under way, boosted by the MG name, there were bolder plans afoot.

Austin Rover PR man Ian Elliott had dinner with BL Motorsport Director John Davenport prior to the Metro launch and Davenport told him of plans being formulated for a mid-engined Austin Rover rally supercar. Working in great secrecy (even at BL Motorsport itself many were unaware of the project) before the MG Metro even appeared, Davenport laid the plans for the Metro-based 6R4 to be built by Formula 1 constructors Williams Engineering of Didcot.

Patrick Head of Williams was given a brief to build a mid-engined rally car out of the Metro (no mean task in itself) and initially the engine used was to be a cut-down V6 based on the venerable ex-Buick Rover V8. In the meantime, a special all-new Austin Rover race and rally engine, dubbed

the V64V (for vee six, four valves per cylinder), began development. The Rover V6 was referred to as the V62V and generated some 260bhp (257PS), which was transferred to the road through an advanced purpose-built four-wheel-drive transmission incorporating a centre differential.

The prototype MG Metro 6R4 (six cylinders, rally car and four-wheel drive) broke cover in February 1984. Austin Rover's Commercial Director, Mark Snowdon, announced that although there was no definite commitment to international rallying, that was the ultimate aim. Tony Pond drove the red and white car in the York Rally on 31 March 1984, where it easily set the fastest times for the first eight stages – a very auspicious beginning. Throughout 1984 the 6R4 performed well, showing the potential for the version in the pipeline.

Of course, MG enthusiasts were excited about the car and hoped that it foreshadowed great things for the marque but as far as Austin Rover was concerned, the primary function of the 6R4 was to lift the image of Metro rather than the MG marque. 'Metro was our life's blood,' former Austin Morris Chairman Harold Musgrove told me in 1995. 'MG was very interesting and we were delighted to put the badge on the 6R4 but as far as we were concerned it was Metro which was crucial.'

The MG Metro 6R4 had a promising start in 1985 but before long events would overtake it. Austin Rover had decided to eschew the screaming turbochargers of the opposition, relying on natural aspiration for its custom-designed engine, but as time went on this decision was found to have been ill-judged. The opposition (in particular the barnstorming Peugeot and Lancia teams) never sat still and the little 6R4 gradually found itself outpaced.

Then, in the summer of 1985, FISA (the body in charge of international rallying) decreed that two years hence, the Group B class into which the 6R4 had been pitched would be abandoned in favour of a new Group S, with power output limited to 304bhp (300PS). This might have made a more level playing field in which the 6R4 could have regained a competitive edge. However, a year later a tragic fatal accident (in a Lancia) led to FISA announcing the very next day that Group B would end in January 1987, six months earlier than planned, and that Group S would not happen. Suddenly the MG Metro 6R4 had no future and, perhaps even more unfortunately for MG fans, an even more exciting mid-engined four-wheel-drive MG had its development curtailed.

---

chapter) that Hamblin would later resurrect as Adder 'to fill a particular marketing need... This concept preceded the Heritage story by a number of years.'

Like many of his colleagues, Hamblin noted that a lot of their work appeared to lead nowhere: 'Most of the models we designed and built were shown around to much interest and then disappeared into a very large storeroom, due mostly to lack of development funding. It was mainly this fact that led me to become interested in low-cost delivery methods and an almost

desperate wish to get some exciting product into the Rover range.' So when Roy Axe moved out to set up the Advanced Studio at Tachbrook, Hamblin had no interest in staying in mainstream design. 'I started manoeuvring to create a new MG Car Company and/or a Special Vehicles Division.'

Eventually, as described in the following chapter, Hamblin became a Director of Rover Special Products, partly fulfilling his aim. However, in late 1991 Hamblin left Rover to run his own consultancy, Omni Design, in Coventry.

MG concepts
for the future: EX-E

With Roy Axe firmly established at Austin Rover, work swiftly got under way to develop the Rover part of the Austin Rover/Honda large car, Project XX in Austin Rover parlance. With new £5.2 million design facilities at Canley sanctioned by Harold Musgrove and a revitalised team of designers (including Gordon Sked, Richard Hamblin and Gerry McGovern, each of whom would eventually play crucial roles in MG's future), Axe was able to begin to explore and map out the renaissance of Austin Rover.

Gordon Sked (Director of Rover Design by the time of the MGF launch) had been with British Leyland through the tough years, joining the company in 1970. Sked's name appears on a number of ADO74 and ADO88 styling sketches, while a tenuous link with the MGB was the design of the MGB GT rear pillar trim flash, which appeared on production cars from 1974 in order to hide a previously leaded joint. Under Roy Axe, Sked became Director of Exterior Design, while a new recruit (from the famous Ogle Design studios) was Richard Hamblin, who similarly took charge of Interior Design.

With the new design focus centred on Project XX and yet a frustratingly long gap before the public could see the result of their efforts, Axe and his more than one hundred-strong design team were keen to let the world know about their new-found confidence. As with any design studio, many 'what if?' exercises were undertaken but all stayed under wraps.

Gerry McGovern in the Advanced Concepts Studio began work on studies for a series of new Austins ('Roverisation'

During 1984 a new 'MG Midget', seen below with the old version, was proposed as a spin-off from studies into a next-generation Metro. MGF designer Gerry McGovern was involved in this concept exercise.

Gordon Sked
Originally Gordon Sked wanted to be a doctor but changed his mind and decided to become a car designer, his real ambition! So in 1966, aged 19, Sked joined Rootes and began

sandwich course studies while moving, as a trainee, from one department to another. It was Roy Axe who helped him get into design. 'I had been working in places like the foundry, the production line and many other vital areas of experience but it was design that I wanted and I kept badgering Roy until he spoke to my training officer and agreed to give me a three-week trial in the design office.' Those three weeks would prove crucial. 'I sat down alongside one of the designers and did my best to evolve a

technique, one that served me in good stead.'

A move to British Leyland in 1970 saw him working alongside Harris Mann and others in the Longbridge studio. 'My first job was to work on the replacement for the Mini, still a relatively young design in 1970. I got deeply involved in looking at ways forward with the design of the Mini.'

During his time at Longbridge, Sked worked on various projects to face-lift the MGB. Changes in the British Leyland structure, prompted

by the Ryder reforms of 1975-6, saw David Bache appointed overall Design Director with several studios reporting to him. In 1977 Sked moved to the Rover studio at Solihull, where he was responsible for the SD1 face-lift and Vitesse as well as ADO88 (leading to the Metro) and a lot of work on the abortive Triumph Lynx and Broadside projects.

In 1981 David Bache left BL Cars and for a time there was no overall Director of Design, until Roy Axe arrived. 'We had already begun working with

Honda on the XX programme and so *pro tem* I guess I was the interregnum between David and Roy,' explained Gordon Sked.

Sked then became Director of Exterior Design, with Richard Hamblin as his counterpart on interiors. 'The EX-E project was basically under Roy Axe; Richard had overall responsibility for the interior and I had the same for the exterior. Gerry McGovern had been working with Richard but at that point he switched over to work under me on the exterior of EX-E. Gerry and I

worked in total concert on the exterior of that car.'

When Roy Axe moved out to set up his semi-independent studio, Sked took charge of mainstream Rover design and oversaw the period when the Rover grille made a comeback. Meanwhile, at Rover Special Products work on the Phoenix programme began to take shape – but that story belongs to the next chapter. Gordon Sked remained at Rover until 1995, when he left and set up Gordon Sked Design Associates in partnership with his wife.

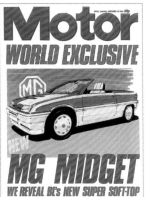

Somehow photos of Gerry McGovern's 'MG Midget' leaked out and *Motor* ran a 'scoop' story which claimed that the car was being readied for production on a Honda Civic CRX platform. The sketches were accurate but the facts were wrong.

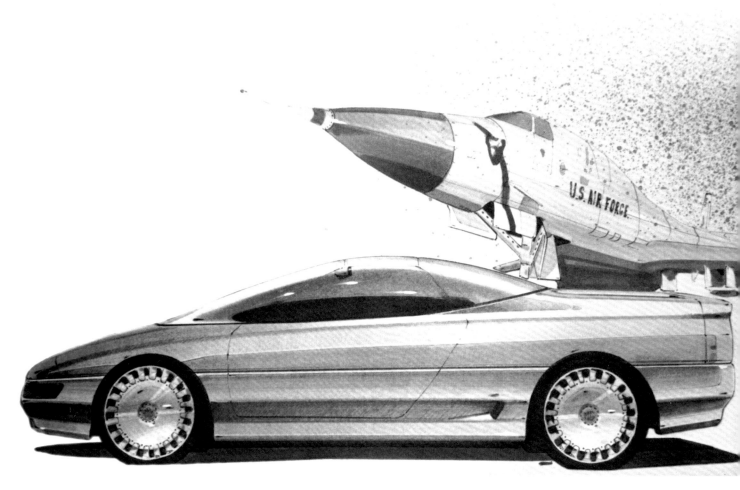

This sketch is close to the definitive style of EX-E. Note the fighter aircraft theme: the 'F-16' connotation would resurface with the next phase of MG sports car studies.

Gerry McGovern

If there is one person who has become inextricably linked in the public eye with the MGF it is Gerry McGovern, the flamboyant designer with the luxuriant curly locks and cheeky grin. McGovern attended Lanchester Polytechnic (now Coventry University) after which he studied at the highly regarded Royal College of Art in Kensington. Support for the young designer came from Chrysler, which at the time maintained a well-staffed design studio at Whitley, near Coventry, and before long McGovern came to the attention of Roy Axe.

There followed a period at Chrysler's US design studios, where McGovern was able to acquaint himself with the latest design techniques, prior to a

Two of the various ideas sketched for the MG EX-E. All emphasised a modern cab-forward stance modelled on contemporary sports racing cars.

was a thing of the future) and one of them was AR6, a predecessor of R6 and known in the studio as Joe 90. 'AR6 was my three-door concept which had been influenced by Giugiaro's Medusa concept car, with its novel side section,' McGovern explained. 'It was simply a studio concept and we developed a Midget as an offshoot from it.'

A remarkably accurate colour drawing of the result made the front cover of *Motor* magazine's 19 January 1985 issue. Motor proclaimed its scoop as depicting BL's 'new super soft-top' and said that it was to be based upon the floorpan of the Honda Civic, a logical but totally false deduction. (*Road & Track* had already featured a Honda CRX privately turned into a convertible, including one with an MG badge provocatively glued on its nose, in its July 1984 issue.) Gerry McGovern remembers the fuss over security that the *Motor* leak engendered, for the magazine claimed that its accurate sketches were based upon photographs – and cameras, of course, were not allowed in the Advanced Concept Studio for obvious reasons.

However, the McGovern Midget was little more than a pretty styling model looking for a chassis. Yet there was a growing mood within the company that it would be nice to take an MG concept a step or two further, bringing in some proper engineering feasibility and exploring future developments in the automotive field. Roy Axe decided around the end of 1984, just as the MG Metro 6R4 programme was given the green light, that it would be a good idea to produce an MG sports car concept based on the state-of-the-art 6R4 running gear. 'Remember that there was no MG sports car at that time and that although some thought had been given to the idea there was nothing in the pipeline,' Axe explained. 'The Rover 800 would be following on in 1986 and so the idea was to

probable return to the UK. However, at this point, Chrysler decided to unload its European operations (selling the bulk of them to Peugeot) and McGovern found himself returning to Peugeot and Talbot products. Roy Axe, meanwhile, had moved to Austin Rover, where McGovern soon joined him.

The following years were exciting ones for the young designer, for he felt himself to be very much a part of the creation of a brand new, almost clean-sheet, image for Austin Rover, or Rover Group as it

became. By the time Roy Axe had created the Concept Studio, McGovern was ready to become its Chief Concept Designer. Many projects ensued, such as the AR6 Midget and of course the EX-E prototype, for which McGovern clearly retains much pride and affection. After EX-E came the similarly well received Rover CCV coupé, and the MG F-16.

By this time, however, McGovern was beginning to share the frustration of some of his colleagues, and indeed the world at large, that great concept cars were not making

it into production. Work on production cars followed, McGovern by now working with Gordon Sked, who was in charge of Product Design. McGovern's first product was the R17 Rover 800 face-lift, followed by the sporting coupé and cabriolet versions of the R8 Rover 200. Then, in 1991, the MG PR3 project came back in-house from RSP and McGovern was tasked with making it into a modern but clearly identifiable MG.

There is no doubt that McGovern was a good ambassador for Rover with the

MGF – even if, as a designer, he tended to be accorded all the credit for the whole thing (an impression he is always keen to correct). By the time that the MGF was in production, however, McGovern was already busy on something new, which eventually emerged as the Land Rover Freelander and saw his appointment as Director of Land Rover Design. Other eyes in the industry were clearly stalking his progress, however, as in September 1999, Ford appointed McGovern to head up its Lincoln Design Studios in Detroit and California.

provide a showcase of the talents within the company ahead of the new Rover. We wanted to avoid a direct conflict with the Rover 800 – a very important model – but we also wanted to generate some interest and excitement ahead of its launch.'

In fairness the 6R4 platform was not the only one considered at first but it swiftly became the obvious focus. Thus began what would become the MG EX-E concept, which brought together Axe's designers and their counterparts in forward engineering. The exciting plan was to build a fully-feasible car which, if the will was there, could eventually be taken through to some form of limited production.

Inspiration was easy to find (Roy Axe was an unashamed Ferrari enthusiast with a 308GTB at the time) but beyond that there was enthusiasm within the Exterior Design Studio, headed by Gordon Sked, for the exciting forms of the latest fighter aircraft, with their forward-mounted and sleekly rounded cockpit canopies. In the time-honoured fashion, there followed an intensive bout of sketching – much of it by Gerry McGovern, who tackled the challenge with relish. For the interior, studio head Richard Hamblin and his staff (notably Gerry Newman who later was involved in the MG RV8) settled on a cocoon-like theme, again modelled loosely on a fighter aircraft and packed with forward-looking technology.

On the engineering side, meanwhile, several themes emerged. Plastic panels were proposed for the bodyshell construction. Austin Rover's Gaydon Technology offshoot had been working on this and indeed had already demonstrated its work in the one-off ECV-3 concept car. In the case of the prototype, the shell was moulded from the finished clay master by Specialised Mouldings of Huntingdon, while the complex glazed canopy was polychromatic plastic, with a near-opaque tint at the top.

The suspension and running gear were closely based upon those of the 6R4, making the task of engineering them into EX-E much simpler, but even so, with a longer wheelbase and other packaging differences, a great deal of effort was required. Leading players in this part of the project included Spen King and Roy Brocklehurst, who had both had experience of mid-engined sports car concepts in the 1960s (King with the Rover P6BS and Brocklehurst the MG ADO21) in the 1960s.

Building on the 6R4 base, the engineering team carried out work on new features such as driver-adjustable ride height (adapted from the forthcoming Project XX's double-wishbone suspension) and, as Brocklehurst told me late in 1985, there was a great deal of impetus to build a fully-working prototype. However, despite enthusiasm for the project within the company, there was never any certainty

EX-E was at one stage finished in red (left), in which guise it closely resembles the products of a certain Italian sports car marque.

Austin Rover photographed EX-E in its familiar silver hue (above) outside the Cambridge Technology Park – a suitably modern setting.

After its sensational show début at Frankfurt in 1985, MG EX-E took over the front cover of *Autocar*.

EX-E made its British debut
at the Earls Court
Motorfair, a month after
appearing at Frankfurt. Roy
Axe, who led the design
team, is seen with the car

that it would be revealed to the public; indeed, the decision to unveil it at the Frankfurt Motor Show in September 1985 was very much a last-minute affair.

As Gerry McGovern has related to automotive historian Jonathan Wood, Harold Musgrove came into the Canley studio just days before the car was due to be sent to Germany, along with its purpose-designed stand. Musgrove was 'like a bear with a sore head,' according to McGovern, and angrily asking: 'Why are we sending this? Why should we do this?'

Despite this last-minute panic EX-E appeared at Frankfurt, where it stunned the world press and even made the BBC main evening news, with a report by William Woollard of BBC Television's *Top Gear*. The British weekly motoring magazines *Autocar* and *Motor* both splashed the silver car over their front covers in the next issue. Naturally questions were asked about the origins of the EX-E name and the official answer was that the EX was an echo of the old MG experimental register, while the choice of the E suffix was because D had already been used for a previous prototype version.

I had thought that this was nonsensical PR-speak, designed to cover the marketing-led decision that EX-E was more euphonious and visually elegant than EX-D. Ian Elliott put me right: 'I remember it well. I was preparing, with the usual great haste, the text for what would become the EX-E poster and there was a session in Roy Axe's office in which we discussed what the beast should be called. Having been in styling as an apprentice when the ADO21 was under way and having seen the Paul Hughes drawing that clearly showed an MGD badge on its rump, I suggested that we could legitimately jump the letter D – not that there was any overwhelming sense of obligation to follow the production

car sequence with a one-off EX car anyway. So without any great agonising, this decision was taken up. And, yes, it does look and read better than EX-D but that was very much incidental.'

Harold Musgrove was cagey about the future of EX-E, saying at the time: 'I believe that the EX-E is a superb illustration of the talent and technology within Austin Rover, qualities upon which our future as a significant world car manufacturer depends...as a car enthusiast I would dearly love to build it. But as a businessman, well that could be a different matter. At this moment, I don't know the answer but it does have manufacturing feasibility. One thing I will confirm is that our future studies with the car will include further assessment of its production viability. We must consider whether to make some prototype runners.'

Sadly, those prototype runners were never sanctioned and although EX-E went on to appear at the British Motor Show the month after Frankfurt and throughout the world thereafter, it became a dead-end. Roy Axe believes that sensitivity from management about the company's continuing public ownership was a strong factor in this: 'The EX-E project officially died because of lack of funds but there was more to it than that. The paymasters (the Government) would, it was felt, have thought such a car frivolous, particularly when they were hoping to sell the company.' Of course, another factor might have been the cancellation in 1986 of the Group S rally class. There were enthusiasts within the company, incidentally, who would have liked to have seen a competition role for EX-E (*Cars & Car Conversions*) magazine, indeed, speculated along these lines), but a limited run of 200 cars for homologation was sadly never to be...

After EX-E, Austin Rover only revealed one more design concept in public. This was the elegant Rover CCV (Coupé Concept Vehicle) unveiled at the January 1986 Turin Motor Show, in the heart of glamorous European car design territory.

More MG exercises: **Gerry McGovern** and the **F-16**

Even though EX-E never made it beyond the concept stage, it certainly served its primary purpose, to stimulate interest in a re-born Austin Rover ahead of the July 1986 launch of Project XX as the Rover 800. There is also a belief shared by several in the car design industry that EX-E served as inspiration for Giugiaro's Nazca show car that followed in its wake and that the Honda NS-X took several design cues too; the design from Austin Rover was that good. What EX-E certainly did was to reinforce the message that there remained an enormous amount of untapped potential for a new 'proper' MG. Whenever senior Austin Rover executives were interviewed by the motoring press you could almost sense them squirm as, halfway through delivering an up-beat message about the MG Metro, Maestro or Montego, the interviewer would interrupt and say: 'Yes, but what about an MG sports car?'

'Of course, 90 per cent of the old MG sports cars had gone to the USA,' Harold Musgrove acknowledges, 'and we considered that the best way to get a sports car would be to use the interior structure of a mass-produced base. People would say "why not do one off the Metro – it would be lovely", but they didn't appreciate the practical problems. For example, the Metro had a four-speed gearbox, used single-piece door-skin pressings, and wasn't sold in the USA.'

At the same time, Austin Rover had been determinedly championing the development of its advanced K-series engine – a decision challenged by Mrs Thatcher and some senior civil servants, who saw no reason why the company should not buy Honda engines. In the end support from Norman Tebbit (then Secretary of State for Trade and Industry) helped to secure the money needed.

So advanced was the K-series engine, with its novel through-bolt construction, light weight and low coolant requirement, that it was logical that the Concept Studio should look at possible applications for it and a natural choice was a small sports car. EX-E had been all very well but the prospect of it sitting in Austin Rover showrooms alongside the rest of the Austin, MG and Rover ranges would have been a rather strange one. A smaller MG would have been more feasible, closer to mainstream engineering and closer to MG's tradition of affordable fun.

Gerry McGovern and colleague Richard Carter accordingly began work on a fresh MG sports car concept although at first the actual powertrain was not defined. Graham Lewis explained: 'It was to have a front engine but this could have been an A-series, K-series or the 2-litre (122cu in) M16. None of these were particularly specified, we were just exploring the

Photographed in December 1987, the MG F-16 followed in the wake of EX-E. Gerry McGovern and Graham Lewis were responsible for this proposal, taking some styling cues from EX-E but producing an MG of more traditional size.

Front view of MG F-16
mock-up shows clean lines
with pop-up headlamps.
Graphics on the flanks are
aircraft-inspired.

concept.' The result was a neat red sports car with pop-up lights, with many styling cues drawn from the successful EX-E.

The car was much admired but for quite some time sat in the studio alongside other studies, the marketing department being unconvinced that it needed further attention. After about six months (by which time Graham Day was in charge of the renamed Rover Group and the Rover 800 was being readied for a 1987 US launch) interest reawakened and the red sports car began to be planned with a K-series engine, possibly using the Metro's Hydragas suspension.

With the EX-E behind them, the designers decided to choose F as the model letter for their new prototype. The F-16 fighter plane remained a powerful source of inspiration and the combination of F (with connotations of fast, Ferrari etc) and 16 (for 16-valve engine) had some conceptual appeal. A small amount of concept engineering ensued, under Derek Anderson, to the point in the late summer of 1986 when further decisions would be needed by the Rover board before the project could go much further.

At the same time there were ructions throughout the company. Harold Musgrove 'retired' (along with Peter Regnier and Mark Snowdon) during a management *putsch* in September, while Land Rover was pitching for funds for 'Project Jay' – which would emerge as the Discovery. It was felt that the Land Rover project, closely based on the existing (and highly profitable) Range Rover, would provide a simpler and faster return. Roy Axe was frustrated, but explained to me: 'If you look at sports cars purely from the point of view of profits and margins, they would never get off the ground. But low-volume cars – especially open-top ones – can provide a massive boost to a company's image despite being unlikely to become major earners in themselves.' For the time being, therefore, the MG sports car had to remain a dream for the future.

'Roverisation' and a return to the private sector

A process of 'Roverisation' was initiated by BL's new Canadian Chairman, Graham Day, within two months of his arrival in May 1986. His philosophy was to try to take the whole Austin Rover range progressively upmarket and in so doing he tried to focus increasingly on the Rover name, with MG hanging on rather precariously as a 'GT' badge.

What we did not know at the time, of course, was that within Rover Group there was a determined band of enthusiasts for the development of the MG marque. At the top of the pile was Graham Day himself, who repeatedly acknowledged the value of the MG name. Day told *Car* magazine that the MG name had been 'under exploited and under developed and allowed partly to change character over the past five to eight years'. There is little doubt that Day had seen the various MG design exercises in the studios at Canley (including EX-E and Gerry McGovern's Midget) and he recognised that these were truer to the spirit of MG. Day also realised the importance of good design; he sanctioned an £8 million cash injection into Roy Axe's studios, which saw staff numbers climb to over 300.

By the spring of 1988, Graham Day fulfilled one of the main objectives of his appointment when the Rover Group was finally returned to the private sector. Rover was now accountable to a financially astute board at British Aerospace rather than a government keen to divest itself of the company. It was at one and the same time a refreshing and a daunting challenge.

Two studio concepts that did not see light of day were an open version of the Rover 800 (this page) and an MG-badged Rover 200 coupé (facing page).

Last chance at the MG saloon: **MG Maestro Turbo**

In the midst of this process, however, something peculiar happened. Most of us had given up the idea of a turbo version of the MG Maestro as a lost cause; the MG Montego Turbo had proved to be a frightening handful and the prospect of a lighter, shorter wheelbase car based on the same mechanical components now seemed incomprehensible. There had been Maestro turbo development vehicles in the past and even though some had used a non-intercooled (and hence lower powered) version of the engine, they had all proved extremely fast.

So the rather low-key introduction at the October 1988 Motor Show of the MG Maestro Turbo (referred to in the sales literature just as the 2.0 MG Turbo) was quite a surprise. It swiftly transpired that this was effectively (although not overtly) a limited-edition model, built with the assistance of Tickford Engineering, who did much of the engineering development and built the finished car. With an engine output of 154bhp (152PS), a top speed of 128mph (206kmh) and an impressive 0-60mph (0-96kmh) time of 7.0 seconds, this would prove to be the fastest MG until the advent of the MGF VVC.

Just as the MG Maestro Turbo was making its first public appearance, a possible role for the MG marque was being debated back at Rover Group headquarters. The three Rover-Honda joint project cars – the Bounty (Acclaim), Rover 213/216 and XX (Rover 800) – had all proved highly successful and Rover was hard at work on the fourth (YY) which had been ratified by the British Government back in June 1985.

By the autumn of 1988, project YY (rechristened R8 to avoid media puns about 'why? why?') was just a year from launch as a neat hatchback and saloon range with closely related Honda counterparts. This time round Rover had been determined to ensure that its small car range differed visually from the new Civic, with which it shared a great deal, echoing the successful visual differentiation of the larger XX and Honda Legend.

For the R8 project, Rover was even more ambitious and was laying tentative plans to extend the range beyond the expected basic three-, four- and five-door family models into niche models, such as coupés, cabriolets and sports estates, and the car would see the debut of the company's much-heralded K-series engine. There was some soul-searching, however, when it came to choosing the badge for these additional models (in particular the convertible version) for there was no recent tradition of open Rovers and there was an obviously strong argument in favour of using the MG badge.

Gerry McGovern became involved with the niche models, known as the Tracer (open) and Tomcat (coupé), and remembers the debate about badging. An MG-badged R8 coupé prototype, initiated in Rover's Concept Studio under Richard Hamblin, was photographed in the Canley studios in December 1988, just two months after the debut of the MG Maestro Turbo. The motoring press, frequently fed by fairly reliable leaks from within the company, was full of rumours of an MG-badged coupé in the pipeline.

'When we started on Tracer, we had the usual arguments about volume,' Hamblin explained, 'so I went away and put an add-on roll bar and removable rear window on the convertible. Together they seemed to make some sense, although when the product when into 'main-line', they decided that they wanted to do the coupé differently.' Hamblin was not too keen on applying the MG badge to the coupé in case it led to arguments that a sports car would no longer be needed but he points out that with the MGF, MG eventually would end up as a one-product brand.

However, the idea of glueing an MG badge on a car which was clearly based on something else was on the way out; badge engineering would die with the last MG Maestro and Montego models in late 1991, the MG Metro having passed away in 1990.

If the seed of doubt about using the MG badge on humble saloons had been taking root, it positively flourished after February 1989, when an event took place at the Chicago Auto Show which would help to nudge MG back into its rightful role. Mazda's launch of the MX-5, which went on to become an outstanding success, was truly the catalyst that the MG enthusiasts within Rover needed.

MG sports cars
back on the agenda

The design 'think tank' within Rover – which had generated the MG EX-E and numerous other studies, most of which never saw the light of day – was inspired by the launch of the Mazda Miata/MX-5 to explore the idea of an MG sports car afresh. In doing this, Richard Hamblin (head of the

From various prototypes, the mid-engined PR3 was the one selected for development into the MGF.

Concept Studio) knew that he had the tacit support of Chairman Graham Day. It was clear that a new sports car could take any one of a number of forms but Hamblin admits that he was fascinated by the re-creation of the MGB bodyshell and its possible basis of something new.

In addition to the F-16, the Concept Studio naturally developed a number of paper studies. 'Amongst these was one where I noticed that the Porsche 911 had been launched at about the same time as the MGB and yet the Porsche was still on sale,' Hamblin recalled. 'Asking myself what the MGB would look like if it too had stayed in production and been continually refined, I posed this question to my designers. This produced the first concept which I later resurrected as the basis of what became known as Adder, to fill a particular marketing need.'

The Adder proposal, which led to the MG RV8 and is described later, was all very well but if MG had a real future as a sports car marque, it would certainly need new material in the long term rather than a reheated classic. So in July 1989 a board meeting at Canley, chaired by future Rover supremo and post-BMW saviour John Towers (then Director of Product Development), explored various options for a return to sports car building. By this stage, the Rover 800 was being sold in the USA as the Sterling and the dealers were clamouring for additional models; an MG sports car might fit the bill nicely.

While the Rover executives debated the viability of a new MG inside the offices at Canley, David Bishop, of British Motor Heritage, was arranging a display outside that included 'TAXI' (the first MGB rebuilt into a Heritage bodyshell) and the last MGB Limited Edition from the Heritage Collection. Bishop had a trick up his sleeve, however, for he had invited MG enthusiast Roger Parker to bring his home-converted MGB V8 roadster, fitted with a recent fuel-injected 3.5-litre (215cu in) Rover engine.

Their meeting over, the Rover executives came out to view the assembled trio of MGBs. There was polite interest in Parker's car, leading to him lifting the bonnet and, before long, being asked to fire the engine. Parker told the author: 'When the engine started, all conversation stopped.' There then followed a test drive within the factory, resulting in enthusiastic discussions about the viability of producing such a car using available Rover components.

David Bishop, unsurprisingly, was already convinced of the merits of this idea, having also considered and rejected the idea of a 2-litre (122cu in) four-cylinder MGB (using the M16 engine from the Rover 820i). In the aftermath of that Canley meeting, therefore, David Bishop went away with tacit approval to build a development car of his own, although it was not certain how far he would be allowed to take the project.

Bishop harboured a desire for Heritage to take charge of the whole enterprise, building a modernised MGB V8 which he anticipated selling for around £17,000. The problem was that whilst Heritage had achieved miracles in reintroducing the MGB bodyshell, the leap from there to full car production, sales and marketing would be enormous; it was a step that the Heritage directors were not prepared to take. A prototype (registered LFC436S and dubbed DEV1) was nevertheless built with a brand new Rover V8 EFi engine and was ready by May 1990.

By that time, however, Rover was pushing ahead with its own studies and so the Heritage V8 became part of a bigger programme, out of David Bishop's control. The story of the part that the MGB V8 (code-named Adder) would take is described in the next chapter.

Roger Parker's home-brewed MGB V8 EFi roadster inspired the MG Adder programme, which saw light of day as the RV8.

Parallel lines:
the **beginning of a new era**

Although naturally Rover would never have admitted as much at the time, it is a fact that public interest in the MG marque, fuelled to a great extent by the automotive press, played some part in the thinking that eventually led to a new MG. Of course, it is one thing to wax lyrical about the idea but quite another to put a serious business case together. The fact remains, however, that all the vibes were right. The Mazda MX-5/Miata was an important part of the equation; Richard Hamblin acquired an early Federal-specification 1.6 as soon as it was available, and, when the 1.8 version was launched, shipped one straight from Japan.

The Japanese, of course, had quietly moved in to take over a market that British Leyland had once called its own. In 1982, there had been the striking mid-engined Toyota MR-J concept, translated a year later into the MR2, while Mazda was doing very nicely with the Wankel-engined RX-7 coupé. Nissan had moved in early with the Datsun 240Z in 1969 but subsequently had rather lost the plot as subsequent Z-types grew bloated and meanwhile Honda had done well with its sporty CRX coupé, based on the Civic.

British Leyland had talked many times, internally, of building a joint sports car with partner Honda but this had never come to fruition. Honda was not convinced it needed its British partner's help in that field and in any case British Leyland had been going through so many changes of plan that the Honda/MG ideas always fell through the cracks first. Gordon Sked told journalist Ian Adcock that he felt 'absolutely and utterly frustrated' when he saw the MX-5.' On the one side we had tremendous respect and regard for

what Mazda had done. They had the balls to do it; they got on and did it. As designers we all felt that, but on the other side, it should have been us up there.'

The public debate about MG was addressed during the course of a management conference (or 'scrum' as insiders called it) on 18 September 1989, attended by Graham Day (by now Chief Executive) and numerous other directors. Richard Hamblin recalls Graham Day saying of a new MG sports car: 'If someone can show me that we could do this for £40 million, we could do it.' Richard Hamblin's response was to say: 'Can I take you at your word?' Day retorted that he simply didn't believe that it could be done; typical new car programmes cost many times as much, even then.

Spurred on by Day's challenge, Richard Hamblin decided to pursue his own study into a new MG. 'Knowing the pent-up desire for a true MG in the market, understanding that such a market's volumes were product-led, unlike mainstream segments, and believing in the need for Rover to recapture an exciting image and finally, having nothing more pressing to do, I set out to work alone using Graham Day's words as authority.'

Hamblin swiftly came to the view that he needed a 'carry-over' base if he was to reduce both time and budget and he began to recruit converts to his cause. One of these was Mike Donovan, the Land Rover engineer who had led the Discovery programme, whom Hamblin approached because of his obvious knowledge of working with an existing platform. Next, Hamblin was able (through David Blume of Rover Japan) to get to see the Pike Studio which had

**A change in
the wind direction**
In the story of how a new MG sports car came to be, it is important to consider the changing political climate, not

only in terms of who owned Rover but also in terms of the people within the organisation. Richard Hamblin commented: 'You need to appreciate the shifting power base and product plan; what made this proposal work when others had failed; how such an exciting car came to fruition.'

An undoubted factor was the change of management. In 1986 Harold Musgrove retired, soon after the arrival at Austin Rover of J. Graham Day (pictured left), a Canadian who had successfully run the nationalised British

Shipbuilders. Musgrove was a 'hands-on' manager, with a lifetime in the motor industry behind him, but Day was very different. He lacked automotive knowledge but knew that it was important to 'love your customer to death'. So he was perhaps more receptive to new ideas and was keen to explore as many avenues as possible with the ultimate objective of returning the Rover Group (as he renamed the company) to private ownership.

'Harold Musgrove ran the company with a rod of iron,' Hamblin said, 'and some things

that happened later would never have got off the starting blocks in his day. I can just imagine trying to get a 'skunk' project up and off the ground, with no approvals and no approved budget whatsoever (as I did in the early days of Phoenix). I would have been on the carpet in Harold's office just for thinking about it.'

Musgrove had seen the company come through a very difficult period and although an MG sports car would have been nice to contemplate, it was hardly at the forefront of management plans. 'We were developed fashionable niche cars such as the Be-1, Pao and Figaro for Nissan from humble Micra running gear.

'It took some effort to find the factory,' grinned Hamblin. 'We went to see Autech, a subsidiary of Nissan, but found that the cars were not built there; they were being produced by Takada Kogyo. That, like many Japanese businesses, was independent from its prime client but totally dependent upon its patronage. They had batch production processes very well set up and they were handling all the specialised processes such as painting polymer mouldings within this batch procedure. This was all especially interesting as it was quite alien to what was going on in most Japanese car factories at the time.' Hamblin was sufficiently impressed with Takada Kogyo to invite a tender for designing and engineering a new MG. Perhaps Takada was wary of upsetting Nissan, for after a series of talks it politely declined.

Having completed his fact-finding mission, Hamblin returned home and presented a report to colleagues Nick Stephenson (Director of Small Cars), Fred Coultas (Chief Engineer for the Metro) and Mike Donovan. So by October 1989, a month after the 'scrum' and three months after the meeting at which Roger Parker's MGB V8 had been seen, Rover had agreed to sanction fresh MG sports car studies. At this stage, all manner of ideas were in the melting pot. Fred Coultas remembers: 'We even toyed with the idea of buying TVR, not as a serious study, and we gave some thought to Reliant, with their excellent chassis; no idea was too crazy.'

Design Research Associates and the 'DR' projects

With the successful launch of the Rover 800, Roy Axe had successfully achieved the first part of his goal to revitalise Rover. However, it was felt within the company that if Rover was to have a real long-term future as master of its own destiny, then serious 'think tank' studies were needed away from the day-to-day headaches.

Accordingly in October 1989 (as Richard Hamblin's report was being considered) Axe established a separate design studio called Design Research Associates in a small unit at Tachbrook, Warwick. In so doing, Axe effectively took back control of the Advanced Design Studio from Richard Hamblin, who was immersing himself in specific projects, and made himself available for corporate British Aerospace design activities. Gordon Sked continued to oversee the Canley studios.

Tasked with looking at what was meant by 'Britishness' – a major part of any export strategy involving the USA – Axe and his team, drawn from the Concept Studio, began to look at two themes: a British saloon and a British sports car. The brief was a very open one; there was no need to confine the thought processes to existing Rover components or platforms and there were consequently wonderful projects such as a KV8 engine for both the saloon and the sports car, the latter being known as DR2. Ian Elliott is keen to emphasise that the KV8 was a very real project that (had the BMW take-over not happened) could have replaced the classic Rover V8. 'It was always there as an option for the future,' Richard Hamblin said of the KV8, 'but the trouble was that like so many things it had been

thinking about a sports car,' Musgrove told me, 'but we hoped to be able to achieve this through our growing relationship with Honda. We had a deal with Honda whereby if either party developed a new model, it would offer a version of that model to the other partner. In this way, we could have had a closely related Honda and MG sports car but, of course, it never happened.'

Richard Hamblin is also firmly of the opinion that another important factor was what he perceived as a 'power vacuum' inside the company at the time that he started Phoenix in 1989. He took advantage of this vacuum at the top in Design, after Roy Axe's move, and in Product Planning, which had been decimated. 'There were detailed, thorough and approved product plans for the company,' acknowledged Hamblin, 'but an all-new viable and realistic MG sports car featured on none of them, could not be funded and was the least of the 'main line' concerns.

'Product plans went through an annual cycle, starting with a giant 'wish-list' and ending with a minimum position. 'Main line' replacement strategies for small, medium and large cars, in themselves, were difficult to fund and execute with the limited cash and manpower resources, and moreover Honda was influencing Rover's product plan by its own plan, which allowed Rover an easier way forward than stand-alone development.'

However, MG kept rearing its head, explained Hamblin: 'There was a good deal of pressure and speculation by the press; there were people who knew what an MG was and knew what it could do to lift the parent company's rather dowdy image... A few people inside the company would not just roll over and accept the downward spiral, and there were still a few Product men left who retained a 'can-do' attitude – people like Fred Coultas, Mike Donavan, Nick Stephenson and David Blume.' These people, and others like them, ensured that the Phoenix project survived and was developed to its exciting discussed for several years and was regularly in and out of the forward programme.'

Roy Axe was an unashamed fan of the 'big Healey' and he freely admits that this was an influence in the development of DR2. The full-size green styling model that evolved was larger than most traditional MG sports cars but then it was intended to be an evocation of 'Britishness' rather than specifically an MG. There was a fully-styled interior and although there was no chassis or engine, it was considered feasible that a production version of DR2 would have shared its running gear with the big, smoothly-styled saloon. I have seen a photograph of the saloon – and it certainly was stunning – but to date Rover has not released the photograph for publication; it was that good.

Other than serving as inspiration, these concept exercises were intended purely as 'future-casting' without fully-engineered prototypes. In the case of DR2, however, there would be further studies (within another programme that began around the same time), which would ensure that DR2 received a fresh lease of life.

Project **Phoenix**

Richard Hamblin and his colleagues listed (in no particular order) the obvious layout options for a new sports car:

A transverse-mounted front engine with front-wheel drive
An in-line front engine, driving the rear wheels
A transverse mid-mounted engine driving the rear wheels

It was a short step to christening these three options Routes 1, 2 and 3, becoming in due course PR1-3 (the initials PR standing for Phoenix Route).

According to Hamblin, even more ideas had been looked at from time to time: 'We had no rear-wheel-drive platform left in the Rover range but we did have Land Rover. A 'gentleman's 4x4 sports carriage' in the manner of a Blower Bentley (with a high driving position) off a Land Rover chassis did occur and indeed was looked at a number of times. However, at this stage I concluded that such a proposal would be too 'off-the-wall' to stand the political and marketing battles...' Route 2 was conceived as a plastic-bodied car and there was a related Route 4 with steel panels. At the time Route 5 was conceived as an exotic sports car rather in the mould of EX-E; the later PR5 would be quite different.

There were mixed feelings within Rover about the idea of using plastic body panels. Richard Hamblin mounted a display with a Pontiac Fiero, Renault Espace, BMW Z1 and

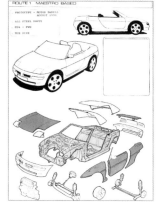

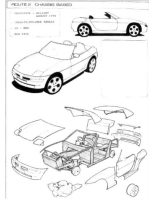

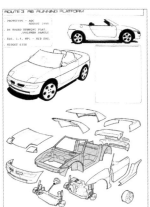

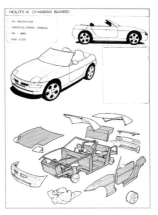

Concept layout plans for the four 'routes' examined in the lead-up to the Phoenix programme: notes at top left show who would build each prototype, its method of construction, the engine and the overall size. 'Route 3', which would become PR3, was at this stage seen as a plastic-bodied MG Midget.

Roy Axe's DR2 prototype in its original guise, photographed in February 1991, by which time it had been integrated into Rover Special Products' PR5 exercise. Side crease was inspired by the Austin-Healey 3000 – Axe owned one!

even a Mazda MX-5 (which had an SMC plastic-covered bonnet panel) but he recalls that there were doubts about adopting such materials other than for bumpers.

Brian Griffin, who had been intimately involved in the face-lifted K-series Metro, was used to working with Nick Stephenson (in his capacity as Director of Small Cars) and he soon found Stephenson's and Hamblin's sports car enthusiasm infectious.

Griffin recalls that John Towers (Product Development Director) kept asking if a way could be found for Rover to do a new MG – but not an MG at any cost; it had to be financially feasible and buildable, either inside the company or by subcontracting some of the work. Nick Stephenson had a great deal of respect for Harold Dermott's Midas Cars operation, which produced extremely professional low-volume sports cars using Metro running gear. Unfortunately, there was a serious fire at the Midas factory in April 1989 and the business never recovered.

Nevertheless, there was scope in using an outside company to come up with ideas. It was realised that it would be logical to try three different companies, one for each Route, thereby not only ensuring that one contractor was not overloaded but also to benefit from a maximum spread of lateral thinking.

Brian Griffin was in Nick Stephenson's office when the latter was on the phone to John Towers in September 1989 and remembers the conversation. 'Nick said that the normal tender procedure would take too long and suggested that we should offer a cash deal to each of the three companies to do the work on a 'take it or leave it' basis. John agreed there and then and so that is what was done.' Towers had just agreed to £750,000 of expenditure over the telephone, so Stephenson knew he had to deliver.

Three **Phoenix Routes:** PR1, PR2 and PR3

The plan was settled quickly: the three companies would each be supplied with an identical GRP bodyshell, moulded from Gerry McGovern's earlier F-16, along with a package of mechanical components and would build a running prototype within their different briefs. Initially five companies were asked to provide paper proposals; Abbey Panels and the French company Société Anonyme des Usines Chausson, both known for their very professional prototype work, narrowly missed the final short-list. Rover selected three companies from the British specialist car industry: Motor Panels (well known for high-quality prototype work), Reliant (chassis and GRP expertise, seen in its Scimitar SS1) and Automotive Development Centre Ltd, formerly part of GM-Vauxhall. Richard Hamblin placed the contracts in October 1989 (not March 1990, as has been written elsewhere), deliberately allowing each company 27 weeks to come up with the goods. He commented: 'The longer the time, the more opportunity there is to spend money and find problems. These were planned to be (and indeed they were) real hands-on, no-drawings prototypes.' The table on the facing page shows, in essence, how each car differed.

Richard Hamblin admitted to some personal satisfaction in conceiving the three original alternative packages, obtaining the necessary budgets (with Nick Stephenson's help), placing the orders with the contractors and ensuring that the resultant prototypes were assessed properly by the top people in the company. Hamblin explained the reasons for his sense of

The Motor Panels PR1 prototype was closest in proportions to Gerry McGovern's original MG F-16, which is pictured on page 25.

The three **Phoenix Routes**

Code	Contractor	Drivetrain layout	Design philosophy
PR1	Motor Panels	Front engine, front-wheel drive	Maestro based with M16 engine
PR2	Reliant	Front engine, rear-wheel drive	Scimitar chassis, 3.9-litre (241cu in) Rover V8 engine
PR3	ADC	Mid engine, rear-wheel drive	Metro based, 1.4-litre (85cu in) K-series engine

PR1 was based on the floorpan and running gear of the Maestro, but fitted with the new M16 twin-cam engine from the Rover 800.

Slightly odd proportions of Reliant's PR2 prototype result from the nose of the F-16 having been stretched to accept in-line installation of a Rover V8 engine.

satisfaction: 'In the case of PR1, we knew that the Maestro was the basic floorpan used by the company at the time and so it was an obvious choice. There was also a thought that it could be bought by younger people who had only ever driven front-wheel-drive cars. For PR2, we knew the appeal of a big rear-wheel-drive V8 but we realised we would probably have to have a separate chassis and use Land Rover parts, as Rover was now essentially a front-wheel-drive company. For PR3, we wanted to try a car with more excitement deriving from its rear-wheel-drive mid-engined appeal. There was no point in doing a 'me too' Miata copy; others tried and failed but we had to look at all three options (PR1, 2 and 3) with fairly open minds and consider them in the context of the company. The only thing certain in my mind was that there had to be a proper MG once more.'

Hamblin dealt on a one-to-one basis with the chief executives of the three contractors, including Merrick Taylor of Motor Panels and Patrick Twemlow of ADC. 'I personally supervised the build of all three,' Hamblin added. 'Most of this took place during a period after Roy Axe had taken on the Advanced Concept Studio that I had been running and before RSP became involved; it was a great experience.'

When the three prototypes first arrived at Rover's Gaydon research centre, they naturally caused a great deal of interest. Any engineer worth his salt would be keen to see just one prototype, but to see three in one go was a real treat. By the time that PR1, 2 and 3 all came along, however, Rover's exploration into niche activities was about to move up a gear with the formation of a special subsidiary charged with exploring the whole gamut of production-feasible, as opposed to wish-list, concepts.

Rover Special Products

In the middle of the previous decade, Land Rover had established a small internal group (known as the Swift Team) to develop what would emerge as the Discovery, which was designed in the remarkably short period of 23 months. From this exercise, Rover learnt a great deal and it seemed logical to create a small unit along similar lines in order to brainstorm and bring to fruition some of the niche-model ideas that everyone was talking about but no one could find the time to do.

The idea in essence was to bring a similar role to that of the Concept Design Studio (now under Roy Axe) in dealing with more down-to-earth projects and tying them in with some engineering feasibility, so that whole vehicles could be brought to pre-production stage. At that point, if desired, they could be handed over to the relevant production business unit. Rover's board took the view that this idea was worth trying and so a three-month study was commissioned at the beginning of 1990, under the wing of Sales and Marketing Director Kevin Morley, and culminated in the approval of a Special Projects Activity on 28 March 1990.

The result was the formation of Rover Special Products (RSP), under the joint management of four directors: Steve Schlemmer, Richard Hamblin, David Wiseman and John Stephenson (all reporting to Morley). Their headquarters was at Rover's Gaydon test centre, well away from prying eyes. Schlemmer, who remained when the others later departed, readily acknowledges the important part that Richard Hamblin, in particular, played in getting the process going; it was Hamblin, after all, who had done much of the groundwork.

The group successfully brought forward and handed over

Brian Griffin

An engineer of the old school, Brian Griffin will find the solution to a problem more through his years of hands-on experience than from reading the latest textbook. The son of

BMC's Chief Engineer, Charles Griffin, young Brian clearly had a tough act to follow. Cars were in his blood, however, for in September 1960 he joined BMC at Longbridge as an apprentice. The usual apprentice's lot of six months here and six months there followed but by 1964 he found himself on chassis engineering in the design drawing office, working with Fred Coultas.

There followed many challenging jobs throughout his time at BMC and, in due course, British Leyland, including the E6 engine

installation for the ADO17 Austin/Morris 2200, installation work on the O-series engine and prototype development of the Metro and Maestro. After a spell at the, then new, Gaydon research facility, Griffin headed up the engineering team working on the 1990 Metro face-lift, for the K-series engine, and therefore became fully acquainted with the R6 Metro and its running gear.

Plans for a more thoroughly updated new Metro, codenamed R6X, were suddenly dropped in 1989, and with the consequent gap in the

small cars programme, Griffin and his boss, Nick Stephenson, were able to look at less pressing projects.

By 1991, Brian Griffin found himself being drawn into the Phoenix programme, as he was asked to do a review of PR3. In due course, he became Chief Engineer for the PR3 (later MGF) and continued his involvement for some time after the MGF was in production. Subsequently he became Chief Engineer for another, equally exciting project, the all-new Mini, which will see the light of day in 2001.

to the main business groups a number of early projects. Its main goal, however, soon became management of the studies for an MG sports car, for the pressure to do something was mounting. However, Richard Hamblin explained that in the early days he had some trouble getting the MG project accepted into the RSP plan as it was seen by his fellow directors as 'too big and personal a project'. Thankfully, such concerns were soon overcome.

The **Phoenix** prototypes

In the summer of 1990 the three Phoenix Route prototypes at Gaydon were studied intensely by a small team of engineers and managers: Robin Nickless (chassis), John Burton (body) and Richard Hamblin (overall design), the latter assisted by Dick Bartlam and Don Wyatt.

It was clear from the RSP team's first look at the finished PR1 prototype in July 1990, that Alan Scholes and his team at Motor Panels had excelled themselves. Taking the F-16 plastic shell solely as a reference aid, they had preserved the same proportions but had formed steel panels into a complete monocoque. They used a Maestro floorpan from which 70mm (2.75in) had been removed in the seat area, so that the end result seemed for all the world as though it had emerged fresh from a production line.

The battery was relocated in the boot (not only for packaging reasons but also to improve weight distribution) while nice touches included well-engineered pop-up headlamps, a completely enclosed metal tonneau (*à la* BMW) and a serviceable but neat interior using an R8 Rover 200 facia. Of course, styling was only of secondary importance in a prototype intended to explore an engineering and packaging concept, but good impressions certainly count. PR1 clearly impressed many people, notably Robin Nickless and Richard Hamblin; both felt there was a compelling argument for following this route to production. Hamblin told me: 'The wheelbase and track were almost identical to the original F-16 model. At that time, we felt that this just had to be the answer...' A handicap, though, was the Maestro floorpan's limited future life.

Even had Rover switched to the Rover 200 platform, with a 2-litre (122cu in) turbo version in the offing, there remained a deep-seated resistance to front-wheel drive in a sports car. 'I wouldn't say that the PR1 excited me as a sports car but it was the concept that seemed most deliverable for the company,' Hamblin commented.

PR2, which arrived at Gaydon in February 1990 (well ahead of the others), was very different to PR1; it was closer in concept to a TVR, with its longer nose and big-engined V8 grunt and it drew many fans. The interior was basically lifted straight from the Reliant SS1 and was therefore simple and unpretentious, while the pop-up headlamps were similarly adapted from those in the SS1.

Reliant's Peter Slater and his team had taken the bodyshell and very neatly stretched the engine area to fit over a lengthened Scimitar chassis, to which MG Maestro front suspension and brakes had been fitted in place of the normal Reliant wishbones. The expertise of the Reliant men in working with GRP was self evident in the quality of the conversion.

Of course, PR2 excited the real sports car enthusiasts at Gaydon (particularly those who were keeping an eye on the V8-engined Adder project) but even they recognised the pitfalls; Rover had no rear-wheel-drive platform and so a production version of PR2 would have required a new chassis. The engine might not have been too much of a problem but there would have been clear cost implications in engineering

Opened rear lid of PR3 reveals the engine and a small luggage compartment. The car also had luggage space in the front, but this feature was abandoned during subsequent development.

Models show that the mid-engined PR3 prototype, built by ADC, was a diminutive design. The proportions and overall style were a great success. The removable hard-top was neat.

the car for the market where it would be most warranted – the USA. Nevertheless, PR2 would give rise to further projects, including PR4, PR5 and a host of other avenues, described later.

Meanwhile PR3 probably generated the greatest amount of interest for, in crude terms, Ernie Cockburn and his team at ADC had 'cut-and-shut' a Metro floorpan. The front suspension was retained but another Metro front subframe (with bolted steering arms) and a 1.4-litre (85cu in) K-series engine were squeezed in behind the driver. The body had been 'quartered' (both shortened and narrowed) in US customising parlance by 150mm (5.90in) and 100mm (3.94in) respectively).

As a packaging exercise, overall it was not very efficient, but the potential was clear to all and indeed many were convinced that the styling of the ADC PR3 was very effective, even though the objective had been solely to explore the engineering aspects. The use of Metro components, including the Hydragas suspension, was a stroke of genius but this was not certain at the outset. Richard Hamblin explained: 'Looking back, the mid-engine configuration may seem obvious for the third alternative but it wasn't so at the time. This solution came to me last after struggling to find the third alternative with ADC. Moreover, it would not have been possible had the Metro not had independent subframes.'

A detailed report was prepared for the Rover board by Richard Hamblin in July 1990, setting out the case for and against each of the three options, described in the report as MGF-1, MGF-2 and MGF-3 rather than PR1-3. In his report, Hamblin postulated that production was feasible within three years from the 'go-ahead'. However a report on its own was not enough; with three exciting prototypes lurking in the hangars at Rover's Gaydon test facility in Warwickshire,

a management ride and drive was the obvious answer.

One evening in August 1990, the Rover board swept into Gaydon and made its way to the test track. According to Richard Hamblin, all three prototypes impressed but 'everyone fell in love with the PR3 – in particular John Towers, who emerged from it wearing a big grin.'

However, if US sales were to be a priority then a Midget-sized car was not going to be the answer. As PR1 faded from the picture (for the time being) attention focused on PR2, with PR3 playing second fiddle. After viewing and driving the three, David Blume (Vice-President of Rover Japan) declared there was only one choice and it had to be the mid-engined car. Japanese market considerations would soon prove especially important. Also in July, a report was produced by Rover's internal Product Assurance section at Gaydon into the issues to be addressed if PR3 were to be sold in the USA. 'Project Phoenix: Product Assurance Submission for Vehicle Certification in Europe and the USA' summarised the eight main issues:

1 No airbags.
2 Not a lot of crush space at the front
  for 30mph (48kmh) impact.
3 No demist ducts; new facia design required.
4 Engine not full catalyst specification for USA.
5 Illegal front bumper for US pendulum test
  (front is 'all holes') also lamp damage is inevitable.
  and displacement may be inadequate.
6 Windscreen frame strength.
7 Visibility; current condition is very tight.
8 Not a lot of car for rear impact.

Could these issues have been addressed? 'Yes, they could, if the money had been there,' considered Hamblin.

No idea was too wacky to explore at Rover Special Products – hence this very 'retro' idea for a new MG harking back to the MGA.

PR3 was also photographed inside the studio for the records on 26 February 1991. By now the car carries MG badges on the wheel centres and the nose. The view of construction at ADC shows that PR3 was finished to a very high standard – even the concealed structure was painted.

Roy Axe's green DR2
prototype (see pages 31-33)
was used as the basis for
the red-painted PR5/DR2,
which utilised a TVR donor
car – as the interior
confirms. Frontal styling
was particularly smooth,
and somewhat redolent of
the Jaguar E-type.

The bigger picture: an MG **sports car** for the USA

If a bigger sports car was what the Americans wanted, the question remained as to what the company should and could do to satisfy the latent demand. Clearly PR2 was closest to this ideal but as it had only been intended as an engineering concept, there would have to be a lot more work before a feasible car could emerge. A significant problem was the lack of a suitable Rover platform but the idea was felt worthy of further study. One of the first exercises was to look at PR4, which was a desk study into giving the PR2 type of car a steel rather than a plastic bodyshell. Also it seemed logical to take stock of what Roy Axe and his team at Design Research Associates had developed.

Axe's DR2 had been purely a concept model (just as Gerry McGovern's F-16 had been four years earlier) and to turn it into a 'runner' would require a certain amount of lateral thinking. Rover clearly had no suitable chassis and so rather than continue with the hybridised Reliant unit of PR2, it was decided to marry GRP panels taken from the DR2 clay to the chassis and sub-structure of a TVR 'S', to create PR5/DR2. A second-hand TVR was purchased and next day the RSP team at Gaydon set to with a chainsaw to hack the unwanted bodywork from the hapless TVR. The interior that Roy Axe had envisaged for the original DR2 was a smoothly styled luxurious one-off but, for the purposes of the hybrid PR5/DR2, it was decided to retain the TVR's slightly incongruous interior. This is exactly how the car appears in the Heritage Motor Centre at Gaydon today.

The end result was an instant hit. With its smooth curves, elegantly rounded proportions and Healey-inspired side swage, PR5/DR2 had the sort of presence which could have stood it in good stead alongside the best that Jaguar or Porsche could offer. However, there remained the problem of how to build a V8-engined rear-wheel-drive car, when the only other such vehicle in prospect was the Adder limited edition. Clearly a PR5 V8 could share some running gear with the Land Rover range and as the Discovery was due to get a new gearbox in 1993 (shared with the Adder RV8), this seemed a possibility.

It was clear, however, that to be a success, a large V8-engined sports car needed to be sold in the USA. US sales and marketing would be one thing but the cost of homologation, certification and dealer service back-up (Sterling was Rover's only model on sale in the USA) would have been considerable. That made larger production volumes a necessity, with consequent greater investment in that area too and frankly the position of the whole Sterling operation was looking unsteady.

DR2 had been well received in US styling clinics organised by Product Lab (unlike the F-16 model, seen as being too small), so it was agreed that it was the right way to proceed. The obvious, if slightly unpalatable answer, was to base the new car on the same platform as the Rover/Sterling 800 with a 2.7-litre (224cu in) front-wheel-drive Honda V6. Rover was also working on its own K-V6 engine derived from the K-series four and so there would be the future prospect of making the PR5 more British. 'Several people championed the idea of basing PR5 on the Rover 800,' Hamblin explained, conceding that the many shared mechanical parts would help the dealers. He thought it was 'a bit of a dead end' but others disagreed so he had to try to make it work.

The new problem would be ensuring that as much of DR2's style as possible could be retained using a very different platform, for the proportions of a large front-wheel-drive saloon are quite unlike those of a traditional long-nosed British roadster. Don Wyatt at RSP produced a couple of composite pictures, using photographs of the current Rover 800, to illustrate the point. PX1 retained the standard Rover 800 wheelbase, while PX2 had about 200mm (7.87in) removed. These were both desk studies, however; no prototypes of PX1 or PX2 were built.

To some extent this was old ground, for in 1986 an open two-door Rover 800-derived model had been shown at US clinics alongside Gerry McGovern's F-16. However, with the best will in the world, it was not easy to produce a convincing sports car using the standard 800 wheelbase and so PX1 swiftly proved a dead end. PX2, however, was a more promising prospect for further consideration.

With the decision to go for a shorter wheelbase, there remained the problem of producing a style which emulated the long-nose look of Roy Axe's DR2 – not an easy task if the engine compartment architecture of the Rover 800 was to be retained. John Stephenson (RSP's Commercial Director) came up with the ingenious idea of a second firewall, set back some 300mm (11.81in) behind the main bulkhead. This would allow the dashboard, windscreen and door hinges to be set further back within the body, giving the sort of proportions needed for a traditional sports car.

There remained an economic case, however, for simply going with the short wheelbase and sacrificing some of the 'retro' appeal of DR2 in favour of a more modern design theme. Accordingly PX2 in turn split into two alternatives, known as Adventurer 1 and Adventurer 2, the former being the cheaper modern-styled route and the latter the clever 'double-wall retro' version. Don Wyatt produced renderings for both Adventurers and wire frame packaging models (shown to me on a visit to Gaydon in 1995) were built at Motor Panels.

Development of the Phoenix Programme

PAPER STUDIES

Route 3
Mid-engined
Rear-wheel drive
Steel body

PR3
Prototype built
by ADC of Luton
in 1990

Route 1
Front-engined
Front-wheel drive
Steel body

PR1
Prototype built by
Motor Panels of
Nuneaton in 1990

Route 2
Front-engined
Rear-wheel drive
Plastic body

PR2
Prototype built by
Reliant Motors of
Tamworth in 1990

Route 5
Exotic sports car,
possibly like EX-E.
Not necessarily the
PR5 concept

Route 4
As Route 2, but steel
or aluminium panels

PR4
Never built

ROY AXE'S DESIGN STUDIES

DR2
Styling model that
emerged from
various studies
into British-style sports cars by Roy Axe's
Design Research Associates

A POSSIBLE 'BIG' MG

PR5/DR2
Larger front-engined
prototype built 1990,
initially rear-wheel drive

Revived PR1
philosophy

**Heritage
MGB V8**

Adder
First model, developed
by Styling International,
spring 1990

Results of the July 1991 clinic

On 18 June 1991, the results distilled from the Manchester clinic were to hand. They make interesting reading and are summarised below:

PR5

'This is a 'whoosh' car as the XJ-S should have been. At £40,000 it is probably too underspecified and too cheap to be in the same segment. It is a two-seater, is intrinsically different from the XJ-S and it is less practical and therefore even more of an expensive 'supertoy'. Given that it is both 'whoosh' and a 'supertoy', it should probably be priced nearer to £45,000 with an even 'whooshier' specification; ie electric everything, super ICE, less basic instrumentation and a bit of room behind the seats. As a Rover one can see it positioned halfway between R17C (the Rover 800 Coupé) and the XJ-S convertible in a sector where there is very little obvious competition. It is not a German supercar; it is a somewhat timeless almost classic British feeling;

everything is silky and feline. It is a car for posing and cruising in – a car for the successful who wish to make a more educated and elegant statement. It is mainly a toy for men but also for rich women. The market positioning would be Jaguar traditional; nothing to do with the super-modernity of the Honda NSX or the mechanismus of the Porsche.'

MG and Rover brand names in a sports car context

'The major opportunity for this car is that it would make a surprising statement about Rover but it is also a long shot unless it has the 'whoosh' specification, superb quality and follows a successful R17C. As an elegant classic British offering, PR5 could potentially occupy unique ground at £45,000. MG is a brand in suspension; heritage and emotion are in the mind and in old MGs. Therefore the future of MG is up for grabs. The only carry-on required is emotion and 'sportscarness'. Rover, on the

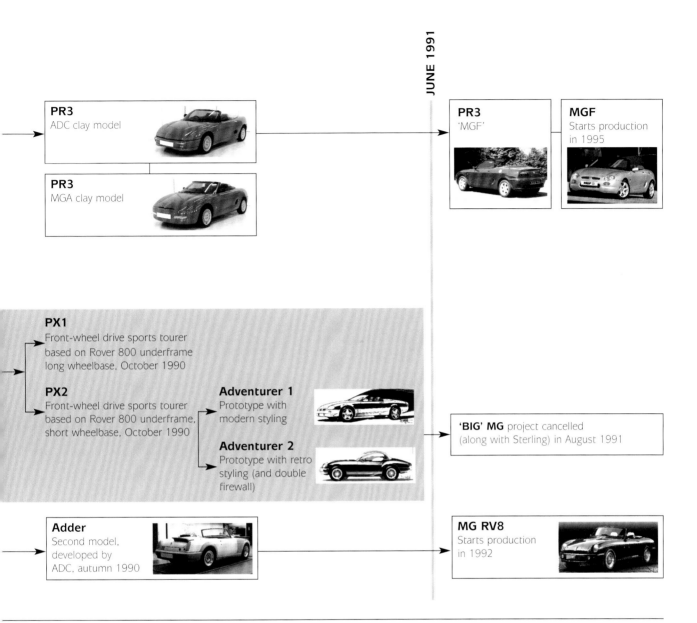

PR3
ADC clay model

PR3
MGA clay model

PR3
'MGF'

MGF
Starts production
in 1995

PX1
Front-wheel drive sports tourer
based on Rover 800 underframe
long wheelbase, October 1990

PX2
Front-wheel drive sports tourer
based on Rover 800 underframe,
short wheelbase, October 1990

Adventurer 1
Prototype with
modern styling

Adventurer 2
Prototype with retro
styling (and double
firewall)

'BIG' MG project cancelled
(along with Sterling) in August 1991

Adder
Second model,
developed by
ADC, autumn 1990

MG RV8
Starts production
in 1992

---

other hand, has no sports car
heritage or top-end credibility
and as such it is far from
being a brand for a sports car
of any type.'

Adder retro-MG
'There is a market for Adder
as a rich man's 'celebratory
toy'. It needs to be 'authentic'
and not a direct carry-over. It
is not a 'classic' and not an
original; it is a special
'celebration'. Top speed is
Adder's main emotional
problem; there is some
concern about 3.9 litres
(241cu in) but the Morgan

Plus 8 seems to be okay.
Adder is an MG – an MGB-ish
MG. It does not have any
restricting influence on future
plans; it would help PR3 as it
would begin to 'thaw' the
brand.'

PR3 (the MGA and ADC clay models)
'PR3 is all about positioning
and credibility: 1,400cc
(85cu in) would be a major
threat to competency and
1,600 (97cu in) was seen as a
minimum. The MGA clay is a
potential product of the
future but it needs more

engine performance to be
credible for a wide enough
market. The ADC clay is more
mainstream, more a 'car of
today' and more closely
positioned to the MX-5.
Positioning on the A-C axis
(vehicle size category) is a
major issue. PR3 could be a
Rover but would have more
credibility as an MG if MG is
resurrected. PR3 as a Rover
would lead to the death of
MG as a brand and would also
need much more reassurance
for product credibility and
image. The Rover brand is not
very sexy. Future MG and

Rover styling would seem to
have little in common.'

Conclusions
'PR5 has little credibility as an
MG or a Rover; it is too big
and luxurious to be an MG
particularly if PR3 is to be an
MG. It also has little credibility
as a Rover; PR5 as a Rover
could significantly enhance
the brand if it could be made
credible. Total quality and
engineering competence and a
more luxurious specification
would be needed. Is there a
large enough market for PR5
at £45,000? Probably not.'

'Adventurer 1' was a wire-frame full-size model built by Motor Panels to simulate the packaging of a sports car based on the Rover 800 platform, and retaining that car's overall proportions. Don Wyatt then produced a concept rendering of a modern style somewhat removed from the DR2 origins of the PR5 programme.

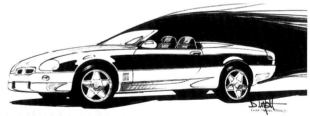

Rough seas ahead:
a change of course

All the time that RSP was working on the three sports car projects – Adder, PR3 and PR5 (now Adventurer 1 and 2) – there was a faction within the mainstream Rover organisation which wanted to see PR3 given more of a focus. There was no doubt that a small nimble mid-engined sports car was closer to the traditional idea of an MG than a large luxurious front-wheel-drive tourer, no matter how beautiful. PR3 also had some powerful allies in John Towers and Nick Stephenson and with their assistance PR3 was taken back in house from RSP.

Key players in exploring the route to production feasibility for PR3 were product engineer Brian Griffin and manufacturing engineer John Doyle. In the early months of 1991, they began to assemble a team to carry out serious engineering studies, including the creation of engineering prototypes. Before long, a curious beige Metro van was doing the rounds of the Warwickshire countryside. Dubbed Sim-1 (for Simulator 1), or more commonly 'pizza van', the Metro had been cannibalised to take a 1.4-litre (85cu in) K-series engine in the rear; the top of the van ingeniously lifted to expose the engine compartment.'

Meanwhile Sivert Hiljemark, and subsequently Roland Bertodo, and their team at Rover Powertrain were developing future versions of the K-series engine. Larger capacities, turbocharging and innovative valve control systems were all on the cards and naturally these were of considerable interest to Griffin.

To take the PR3 concept a stage further, fresh styling models were commissioned. 'We had identified the packaging hardpoints,' Griffin explained, 'and we were going for an MGB-sized car. We never wanted to do a Midget.' Some design work had been carried out by RSP's Richard Bartlam (who had worked on Adder) and Richard Hamblin had then passed these sketches to ADC at Luton with a brief to create a clay model on a wheelbase some 100mm (3.9in) longer than the PR3 prototype. ADC was told to look for inspiration to cars like the EX-E and the more recent European and Japanese sports car opposition.

Hamblin was then approached by MGA Developments (MGA standing for Michael Gibbs Associates) at Coventry who 'told me that they were not very busy... So we were able to take advantage of their services at marginal cost and let them work on a clay too.' The designer in charge at MGA at that stage was Peter Horbury, nowadays better known as Volvo's Director of Design. John Sowden at ADC was responsible for that company's effort, which included an interior model. The latter, Hamblin considers, was 'not too far off the final MGF article'.

In May 1991, Nick Stephenson (in his capacity as Forward Programmes Director) presented a report on PR3 to the Rover Group board's executive committee, who met and reviewed both the ADC and MGA Developments models. A customer clinic was due to be held in Manchester the following month for an appraisal of PR5 and Adder and it was agreed that the original PR3 (now nicknamed 'pocket rocket') and the two new styling models would be put on show in Manchester alongside PR5 and Adder.

PR5 was very well received at the clinic (see pages 44-45) but was seen as a £45,000 sports car, and not therefore really in MG territory, but people could see where Adder was coming from. Views on the PR3 styling clays reinforced the opinions expressed by Rover Group's mainstream

Similarly, 'Adventurer 2' – with a secondary firewall and relocated seating position – was turned into a wire-frame full-size model. Don Wyatt's rendering shows how he saw the PR5 style evolving: a very elegant car could have ensued, but would it have worked as a front-wheel-drive MG? Before long, the debate would become academic.

designers: engine capacity was thought of as of 2.0–2.5 litres (122–153cu in) rather than 1.6 litres (97cu in) and, whilst both were attractive, neither's character was as clearly identified as 'MG' as would have been liked.

At research clinics direct questions ('Does this look like an MG?') are not asked. Richard Hamblin explained the approach. 'People would be asked questions such as: "What sort of engine should be in that car?" or "What would its top speed be?". It is true that people thought that the engines would be larger than planned, and we would have struggled to cope with that. We didn't get as many people identifying the car as an MG as we would have liked – but to say that the clays were seen as being 'insufficiently MG' would be unfair.'

The exact words of the clinic summary (in a hand-written fax from RSP's Mike O'Hara on 18 June 1991) make interesting reading. On the PR3 clays, it was concluded that 'MGA is a potential product of the future – but it needs more engine/performance to be credible and have a wide enough market.' The ADC clay was thought 'more mainstream – more of a "car of today" and more closely positioned to the MX-5'. PR5 was a problem, for it was not clear what Rover could do if the MG badge did not suit it; there were tortured analyses of how the Rover badge would sit on the Roy Axe shape but hardly anyone really believed this was the answer. 'Even so,' Hamblin maintains, 'the badge debate concerning PR5 only served to strengthen the case of those who wanted to base it on the front-wheel-drive Rover 800.' This was a logical strategy because Rover lacked a suitable rear-wheel-drive platform, but the various 800-based styling ideas that emerged had heavy and not particularly sporting proportions because of the constraints of the largely Honda-sourced running gear beneath.

'At this point,' Brian Griffin explained, 'Gordon Sked agreed that it would be sensible for the mainstream Rover design studio to look at PR3 and he appointed Gerry McGovern to oversee the work.' McGovern's brief was to take the same basic packaging but to ensure that the design was obviously an MG.

Meanwhile, Rover withdrew from the North American market in August 1991. Graham Morris, who had headed the US operation, returned home to a new job as Managing Director of Rover Europe. One of the responsibilities he assumed was overseeing Rover Special Products, by then deeply involved in the Phoenix project.

The news that Sterling was to die and with it Rover's presence in the US market (other than the separate and highly successful Land Rover franchise) dealt a fatal blow to PR5. It had already been decreed as too expensive-looking for an MG, but now without a means to sell it, it was dead in the water. Suddenly all attention was on Adder and PR3.

The whole family of Phoenix prototypes survives within the Heritage collection. Seen outside the museum in 1999, they are (from left) PR5/DR2, PR1, PR2 and PR3.

Two of the various concept sketches for PR3 produced by Rover Special Products designers. The aim was to evolve a cohesive design to replace the adapted F-16 style of the engineering prototype.

Sports cars on the march again

The 1980s had been as turbulent an era as any in the life of MG's parent company but, as we saw in the last chapter, the launch of the Mazda MX-5, unashamedly modelled on the classic British sports car, had not gone unnoticed at Rover Group headquarters. Even before its debut, however,

Glorious studio photograph for the definitive MG RV8 brochure shows the lithe lines to good advantage.

Rover's British Motor Heritage subsidiary had staged a minor coup of its own.

BMH had been formed to police the burgeoning industry associated with classic cars and had established a network of some 55 Heritage Approved suppliers. Beyond that, there were thoughts of licensing or participating in the manufacture of quality components to the original specification, using the considerable resources that the parent British Motor Industry Heritage Trust could tap into.

In 1983 David Bishop had joined BMIHT to run its small museum at London's Syon Park. In October 1986, Bishop (a Triumph sports car enthusiast) heard that the dies and tooling for the Triumph TR7 had been destroyed and realised something had to be done about the MGB tooling before it was too late. He had started work at Pressed Steel as an apprentice in 1961 and so, by the time he left Swindon 22 years later as Materials Control Manager, he knew the body manufacturing system inside out. There followed an exploratory visit to Swindon, where Bishop found that thanks to others before him (notably Swindon's Production Controller David Nicholas, an unsung hero of the MGB story), a remarkably complete set of tools and jigs survived either at Swindon or at known locations elsewhere around the country.

With an investment of just £100,000, Bishop collected all the tools and jigs together at a small industrial unit at Faringdon, roughly halfway between Swindon and Cowley and a similar distance from Abingdon. The location was no coincidence; Bishop relied on his contacts in the industry to secure the invaluable assistance of a team of workers, many nearing retirement or retired and most with some prior experience of MG bodyshell production.

Between Christmas and New Year 1987, Bishop studied the 250-page Pressed Steel parts book, listing and cross-referencing all of the Pressed Steel/BL parts and sub-assemblies for the MGB. This enabled him to determine the corresponding Pressed Steel tooling die numbers and as these are invariably marked on the dies themselves he would be able to locate them in the masses of stored press tools at Swindon. The search took until the end of March 1987, after which Rover was asked for permission to remove the tooling and proceed.

'There were some 800 press tools in all, weighing over 1,000 tonnes, which meant 50 lorry loads to be moved to the operation we set up at Faringdon,' Bishop recalled. Even though it was normal to store tools and dies outside (coated in thick preservative grease), some of the older MGB tooling had been outside for 20 years. Some could be repaired at Faringdon and others at the pressing plant, while just four lost dies had to be remade.

The Faringdon facility was fitted out with equipment largely salvaged from nearby Cowley, which was undergoing redevelopment, and the new MGB bodyshell was launched on 13 April 1988 at Rover Group's central London headquarters, just a fortnight after Rover's dramatic acquisition by British Aerospace.

At the end of the month, visitors to the Classic Car Show at Birmingham's National Exhibition Centre were treated to the spectacle of a team of MG specialists transferring the guts of a rusty old MGB roadster (registration number TAX192G) into a gleaming Tartan Red Heritage bodyshell. The result of their endeavours was a splendid 'good as new' MGB (swiftly dubbed 'TAXI' on account of its registration number), which now forms part of the Heritage collection and is frequently on display in the museum at Gaydon.

Important RV8 development cars lined up at Gaydon are (from left) 'DEV2' (the second Adder development vehicle), KAE 868P (a 1975 MGB GT V8 bought for comparison work) and 'DEV3' (the third development vehicle).

A left-hand-drive MGB followed in September 1989 (built by MG specialists Brown & Gammons) and was driven across the USA, where it was tried by a series of dewy-eyed journalists who raved about it, noting that this was the genuine article. Peter Egan wrote in *Road & Track*: 'A British Motor Heritage MGB is a labour of love that just happens to work quite nicely as an automobile. It is also a sports car whose character and subtle charms have to be experienced before you can understand why so many people worked with such enthusiasm to save it.'

It was a promising story for MG enthusiasts and, of course, did absolutely no harm to the subtle campaign for a new MG sports car.

Developing the MGB V8: Project Adder

While the Heritage MGB V8 project attracted a great deal of interest at Rover Group, it was recognised that if the company was going to create an all-new MG sports car, and effectively reinvent the brand, a warmed-over MGB might cause difficulty. Richard Hamblin's inspiration had led to a sketch by Jerry Newman at RSP for a modern 'evolved' interpretation of the MGB and before long this gelled into Project Adder (a tongue-in-cheek reference to the AC Cobra). It was a short step from there, via a number of coloured renderings by Newman's colleague Bruce Bryant, to Hamblin commissioning a full-size mock-up from Styling International at nearby Leamington Spa.

Hamblin sent a Carmine Red MGB roadster to Styling International, a subsidiary of internationally renowned prototype specialists Hawtal Whiting. There, Jonathan Gould took charge of interpreting Bryant's drawings and applying clay direct to the MGB. Budget constraints precluded any significant changes other than to the front end, while alterations to the rear panels were confined to flaring the wheelarches to match the new front wings. The bonnet remained standard MGB; the problem of fitting the Rover V8 inlet manifold beneath the bonnet had yet to be addressed.

By July 1990 the Styling International car, surfaced with bright red Dynoc film, was ready and was shown to Kevin Morley. According to Don Wyatt, working with Dick Bartlam within RSP, Morley was not over-enthused: 'He said it was a great car and he liked the V8 concept, but didn't see that there was enough to form the basis of a programme.' However, Adder had some strong champions within the unit in Richard Hamblin, David Wiseman and John Stephenson, while David Blume of Rover Japan also lent support. 'In fairness to Kevin Morley, he didn't exactly say "stop work",' Hamblin pointed out.

Accordingly, Hamblin decided to try a second time, but this time he sent a bare MGB bodyshell to ADC, the company that had made the PR3 running prototype, together with the Styling International car as reference. In the usual manner, opposite sides of the ADC model were treated differently: one side was very similar to the Styling International car, with substantial flared round wheelarches, while the opposite side built upon a more square-shouldered theme as depicted in an alternative rendering by Richard Bartlam. He acted as the RSP liaison man, working with ADC's John Sowden and his staff at Luton virtually full time on the project.

As ADC's version of Adder took shape, the nose became stronger with distinctive twin round lamps mounted in the

Bruce Bryant of Rover Special Products produced this rendering (derived from an earlier sketch by colleague Jeremy Newman) that led to Styling International's theme for the first Adder prototype.

Richard Bartlam's sketch shows a chunkier version of Adder, with rounder headlamps and square shoulders to the wheelarches, in many ways closer to the definitive MG RV8.

The first phase of the Adder programme was developed at Styling International in May 1990, using a Carmine Red MGB with panels over-laid in clay. The completed model is displayed with heavy-looking wheels and a tail spoiler.

A second Adder clay was developed at ADC using a bare MGB shell. It received different wheelarch and wheel treatments on either side, and a spoiler was modelled for the offside rear.

bumper unit. Some debate continued over the 'nostrils': should the grille divider be solid, as per the old rubber-bumper MGB, or should it be left as a half-height feature on which to mount the MG badge? This issue was not resolved until some time later, as the removable 'block' in some photographs of the Dynoc-finished green car indicates. The obvious headlamps to use came from the latest Porsche 911, although Wyatt and his colleagues tactfully referred to them as 'brand X' units. As an insurance policy against these units not being licensed for use in the MG, one side of the model was fitted with conventional 7in (178mm) round units under glazed covers, similar in style to those of the classic Jaguar E-type.

Whereas budget limitations had restricted work on the Styling International car to a face-lift of the nose, a spoiler had been fitted on the boot lid to balance the effect; indeed Jerry Newman's original sketch had shown such a feature. The same idea was tried again on the ADC car, along with a variety of proprietary rear lamps including Metro units, which looked unbelievably hideous. The spoiler was a love-it-or-hate-it feature and, although the idea was followed through to final viewing, in the end it was dropped. The conclusion was reached that special rear lamps would be needed and these were tooled at considerable cost.

If there was one criticism that could never be levelled at the MGB it was cockpit length, for the classic roadster had been able to accommodate 6ft drivers in reasonable comfort; indeed the MGB was superior to many more recent sports cars in that respect. However, the windscreen was very shallow (deliberately on account of Abingdon's motor sport aspirations for the MGB), hampering forward visibility when the hood was erected.

Unfortunately the height of the windscreen governed the design of the hood mechanism, which could not be redesigned for the new car within the time and budget available; so although a new one-piece windscreen frame was designed, it was of the same proportions as the MGB item. Seat mounting height was determined by legislation and so the seats themselves, new and nicely padded, could put the top of the screen in a taller driver's lines of vision. Don Wyatt admits this caused a degree of anguish at Gaydon but there was little that could be done other than hope that the seat cushions would settle with use.

As the ADC clay took shape, Kevin Morley approved the creation of a glass-fibre reinforced plastic model, which would provide a better indication of the finished article. 'Doing this can often destroy the clay model,' Wyatt explained. 'The combination of curing heat and the suction when removing the GRP moulds can pull the clay to pieces. If you have time, this can sometimes be avoided but we didn't have the time, or the budget for another clay, and so the original clay was destroyed. From this stage on, therefore, we had to rely upon a GRP model for all further development.'

Rather than making a complete model, GRP wings and bonnet were made from the moulds taken from the ADC clay and transferred to the Heritage MGB V8 (DEV1). The whole ensemble was painted metallic British Racing Green and had a full leather and walnut interior. This time, when Morley saw the car, he was clearly more convinced, for he sanctioned the project for further development as a 'celebration of the MGB'. The idea was to launch the car in 1992 (30 years after the MGB had made its debut) and use it as a link to the all-new MG which, at that time, was seen as coming in 1994.

By now it was June 1991, however, and with a clinic planned for the other MG sports car projects, Adder was made ready for an outing to see if potential customers shared RSP's enthusiasm.

Seen in Rover's Canley studio, the finished ADC clay – resplendent in British Racing Green – looks very elegant.

RV8's frontal aspect has
styling hints of the MGF
that was to follow.

The first production RV8
(facing page) at Cowley in
April 1993, and a pre-
production version (left) at
the Birmingham Motor
Show in October 1992.

The 'Celebration MG':
Adder prepares to strike

At the June 1991 Manchester clinic Adder had been well received by the carefully selected 'customers'. The issue of the grille aperture and 'brand X' headlamps was finally decided. Within a month, the Rover board had seen the car and approved the £5 million necessary to produce Adder as a limited edition of 2,000 – for launch in the summer of 1992. All that Richard Hamblin and his crew had to do was turn the car into a production reality – simple really...

By August 1991 the development of Adder was in full swing but in the meantime the effects from the withdrawal of Sterling from the USA began to ripple through the company. The need for PR5/DR2 had suddenly evaporated and although the two PR3 clays had been received favourably at Manchester, there were some concerns about their style and stance.

This was all the ammunition that Gordon Sked and Gerry McGovern at Rover's main Canley studio had needed to regain control of PR3, although Adder remained as essentially an RSP programme. Then, during August, RSP directors Richard Hamblin, David Wiseman and John Stephenson all left the company; Don Wyatt, John Yea and Mike O'Hara effectively took their roles in non-executive positions. Steve Schlemmer remained in charge of RSP but he now reported to Graham Morris instead of Kevin Morley.

Meanwhile Dick Bartlam and Don Wyatt proceeded with the task of preparing the tooling patterns for the unique bodywork, to be pressed by Abbey Panels. To assist in the this process, the Abbey Panels subsidiary Descartes Design was commissioned to work with Rover Body & Pressings to create a master die-stack of production-ready tooling. However, it swiftly became apparent that this would not be a simple task as the Heritage MGB V8 prototype (to which the ex-ADC GRP panels had been fitted) was based on an ex-Florida MGB which, it transpired, had been involved in an accident. The front end, forward of the windscreen, was twisted by 20mm (0.78in) and, with no clay model to refer back to, there followed an intense programme of work by Don Wyatt and Dick Bartlam, who restyled the car right on the die-stacks over Christmas 1991.

By the summer of 1992, Rover Group was ready to issue a 'teaser' brochure to the press and public. The modified DEV1, complete with its GRP wings and wearing a proposed rigid tonneau cover (later abandoned because it could not accommodate the new double-skinned Tickford hood), was photographed at the Ealing film studios in West London. The resulting photographs were retouched to remove the rigid tonneau, and as the nose of the prototype showed the alternative headlamp treatments on either side, only a side view was published, along with some detail shots.

MG reborn:
the launch of the **MG RV8**

In September 1992, with the RV8 just a month away from its public unveiling, Rover invited a group of MG Car Club, MG Owners' Club and selected MG writers and publications to Canley to see a pre-production prototype. I was one of those present and, following the unveiling, was intrigued to be told in confidence by a Rover executive that not one but three rather interesting MG prototypes lurked behind the large oak doors at the end of the room. I know now that these were the PR1, 2 and 3 prototypes.

In October the green-shrouded form of an RV8, mounted on a turntable within a circular Perspex-walled enclosure, took centre stage on the Rover stand at the British Motor Show. Photographers and journalists packed the stand as Rover Chairman John Towers gave the customary launch speech. Then, with a flourish, the cover was removed and a Le Mans Green RV8 was unveiled to strong applause: MG was back and this was only just the beginning...

During the following months, the initial euphoria faded slightly. When the RV8 had been conceived, the classic car market was buoyant, and target customers with sufficient money to spare were felt likely to be tempted to acquire an RV8 as a toy with investment potential. By late 1992, however, the classic car market had collapsed and so the new MG RV8 was no longer seen as an investment. Sales were very slow and some people within the company began to ask awkward questions. Salvation came, however, from the Japanese market following the unveiling of the Japanese-specification RV8 at the 1993 Tokyo Motor Show. Far-East orders flooded in and resulted in over 65 per cent of the total build being shipped to Japan; most were finished in either Nightfire Red or Woodcote Green, the latter being the colour of the Tokyo Show car.

Production of the RV8 continued into 1995, by which time nearly 2,000 had been built. At the time of writing, a number are still rumoured to be stored unused in a warehouse in Tokyo, while many have slipped back to the UK on the 'grey import' market as second-hand cars. They are easily identifiable by the standard air conditioning (with intakes replacing the front fog lamps of home market cars), small front wheelarch lips, Rover badging on the front wings, metric speedometer and the fact that nearly all seem to be finished in Woodcote Green paintwork.

By 1995 the RV8 had arguably achieved its mission to revitalise MG as a sports car marque (rather than an alternative 'GT' badge) and to bridge the gap to the MGB. Now it was time for the interim car to move over and make way for something much more modern, a car that would carry the MG identity successfully into the future.

The RV8 was a great success in Japan. These pictures show the launch at the Tokyo Motor Show in 1993, and the final shipment of cars – together with the first batch of MGFs – at Southampton in 1995.

A new lease of life for the MG badge

Throughout the early years of the MG badge, the style and shape hardly altered, while the colour remained Kimber's favourite combination of chocolate and cream. In 1953 Nuffield decided that black and white would be more appropriate. A more lively effect was wanted for the MG Midget in 1961, so the black enamel in-fill in the octagon and letters was dispensed with and the cream background changed to red; this became the MG theme for the next 14 years.

In 1975, for the MG Golden Jubilee celebrations, BL decided to change the badges on the Midget, MGB and MGB GT V8 to gold, with a black infill in place of the red. This black infill was retained from 1976–1980 even though the gold finish reverted to chrome. For the final MGB LE models, however, BL reverted to chrome and red again and this colour scheme was passed on to the MG Metro, Maestro and Montego.

By the time that Rover was looking at bringing the MG

The interior of the RV8 was undoubtedly one of the grandest ever seen in an MG sports car.

Line drawing is Don Wyatt's proposal for the new MG badge, with radiused characters giving a 'fuller' appearance. DCA Design Consultants then produced various coloured renderings.

name back on a sports car, there was a strong feeling that something should be done to disassociate the new car from the 1980s saloons and at the same time build a bridge to the 'good old days'. Steve Schlemmer of RSP credits Don Wyatt for the groundwork: 'His skill and sensitivity to what was required and his pragmatic approach to what was possible led to the result that we had on the car and all the associated material.'

According to Wyatt himself, the redesign was something of

a rush job, necessitated by pressure from the advertising agency charged with designing a corporate MG style. Wyatt could only tell the agency that he felt there was a need to leapfrog the 1960s and hark back to the traditional MG badge, and so on that basis, the new badge was developed to the form in which it appeared on the preview brochure for the RV8. This design reverted to the original style, although a translucent jewel-like bronze replaced the brown infill to the characters and frame of the badge, while

instead of a solid white or cream background, there was a golden theme with horizontal graphic lines.

Although this was moving in the right direction, Wyatt felt that more was needed, so he engaged the services of DCA Design at Warwick to produce a number of badge mock-ups. A rounded theme emerged, moving away from the flat badge and straight lines and giving an enhanced sense of depth. This produced the desired result and was adopted as the badge for the RV8 and, in due course, the MGF.

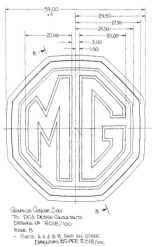

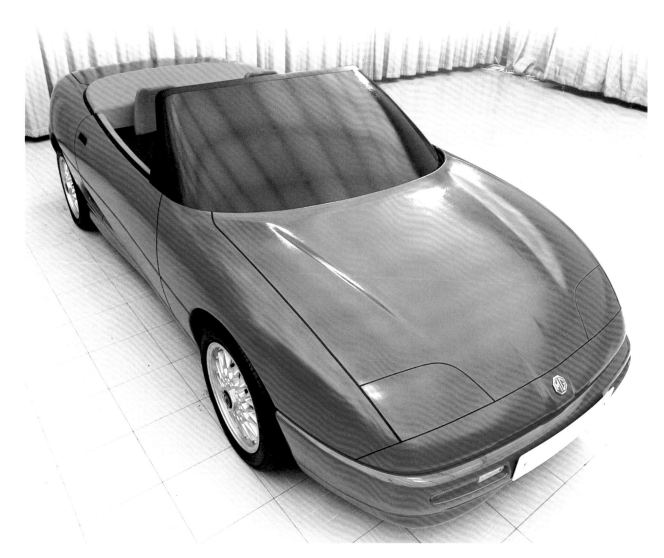

PR3 becomes MGF

Development of PR3, the small mid-engined prototype that led directly to the MGF, had been returned to Rover's main design and engineering units in August 1991. Both disciplines naturally had to work closely together: packaging and production feasibility require synergy between those concerned with aesthetics and those tasked with making the car function and buildable. The car that was developed also had to be marketable and viable in business terms.

Normally, the co-ordination of these aspects of a project would need a single overall project director but, as PR3 was not really part of the core programme back in 1991, such

The ADC clay – known as 'PR3/8300' – was fitted with MG badges and chunky cross-spoke alloy wheels for this studio shot.

MGA's styling clay for PR3 (upper two pictures) shows some features – such as the shape of the side air intakes and doors – that graduated to the MGF.

ADC's styling clay (lower two pictures) was subtly different; the nose is less successful. Note the idea for engine bay venting around the tail lights.

an appointment was not made. Brian Griffin and his team dealt with the engineering while Gordon Sked and Gerry McGovern looked after what may be termed the styling/packaging.

Several issues were identified at the outset, using the running PR3 prototype as an engineering starting point and the ADC and MGA clays as a design base reference. On the engineering side, the diminutive size of the PR3 prototype created several packaging problems that would have been unworkable or undesirable in production. The limited space meant that on the prototype a small fuel tank had been inserted and this was identified as a fairly common defect in contemporary sports cars.

Making the wheelbase slightly longer, by about 4in (100mm) brought benefits in terms of cockpit space and handling. The early PR3 was entertaining to drive but the quirky handling (inherent in short-wheelbase cars) was felt to be undesirable in a car that was supposed to be driven easily by anyone. Then there was the question of engine size. The original car used the standard 1.4-litre (85cu in) K-series engine in 16-valve guise but, while this was an excellent power unit with quite a high specific power output, it was less able to give the performance required if the car's size was increased significantly.

From the styling perspective, McGovern and his colleagues were not convinced about either the ADC or the MGA styling clays. Both had stuck to the original concept of concealed headlamps, taking their lead from the PR1-3 engineering prototypes, which in turn had their roots in McGovern's original F-16 of 1985. The MGA and ADC clay mock-ups both featured pop-up headlamps while those on the running ADC-built PR3 prototype had been clever pop-down units but, according to McGovern, 'they gave a disproportionate look at the front and rapidly became dated'. However, there were fans of the running PR3 prototype, complete with those pop-down lamps. Richard Hamblin commented: 'When I left Rover two years later there were still people telling me that this style was for them the best of all!'

When it came to the MGA and ADC PR3 styling clays, Gordon Sked 'didn't feel that they were either particularly British or MG in character'. McGovern is also firmly of the opinion that the designers had veered too strongly in the direction of aping the EX-E prototype, with its high and massive rear end. That was suitable for a powerful sports car of the type EX-E was intended to represent but less appropriate for an affordable sports car, which is what an MG should really purport to be.

Gordon Sked suggested that EX-E was a sensible starting point for these studies: 'Like Gerry, I felt that we needed to overlay maybe a little more of the MG heritage on PR3. And

Once the main Rover design studio took PR3 back in-house, work began on what would become the definitive MGF clay. Here the task has only just started, and there are hints of both the ADC and MGA clays. From behind, there are cues from the ADC clay coupled with Gerry McGovern's engine vents.

Evolution of the K-series engine

There was never really much doubt about what engine should power the new MG sports car. The all-new K-series engine was unveiled in the Rover 200 range launched in October 1989 and at first was available in just a 1.4-litre (85cu in) guise, with a choice of eight or 16 valves. By May 1990, the Metro range was extensively face-lifted (and renamed Rover 100 outside the UK) and adopted the K-series in both 1.4- and 1.1-litre (85 and 67cu in) guises. It was

clear that the new engine would be a major part of Rover's plans.

The K-series engine (not to be confused with an earlier prototype Mini engine of the same designation!) was notable for its exceptionally compact lightweight five-layer 'ladder' construction with ten long through-bolts that gave the engine block additional strength by compressing the whole structure. From quite early on, therefore, studies ensued into extracting more performance out of the 1.4-litre (85cu in) 16-valve

version and experiments took place with forced induction.

Brian Griffin recalls being asked by his colleague Roger Stone to blast an anonymous-looking Rover 216 Vitesse (of the 1984-9 generation) round the Warwickshire back roads. This car had been fitted with a supercharged 1.4-litre (85cu in) K-series that produced a frightening 200Nm (147lb ft) of torque and 152bhp (150PS). 'I found that I could easily get wheel-spin at 90mph [145kmh] on the north bend of the Gaydon test circuit in the wet,' Griffin

remembered with a grin.

Tests of both the Volkswagen G-Lader and Sprintex superchargers took place and showed promise, albeit with some penalties in terms of fuel consumption and engine durability. For the time being, however, supercharging seemed to be an unlikely option; this was before PR3 had even been thought of.

Although 1.4 litres (85cu in) had originally been foreseen as the largest feasible size for the K-series, some imaginative engineering saw the limit opened out to 1.6 and 1.8

we wanted to recapture that affordable wind-in-the-hair motoring aspect of MG.'

The lack of an MG identity also persuaded Sked and McGovern to give the new car something of an MG 'personality'. 'We decided that it should have a definite link to the MGB – the combination of grille aperture and lamps was fundamental – but nevertheless it had to be a modern interpretation,' McGovern stated. The design team set about rationalising the way forward in three key stages; firstly they established the proportions and stance of the car, ensuring that its cab-forward mid-engined design was thoroughly contemporary rather than a pure nostalgia trip. Secondly, they defined the design rationale for the car, and lastly they ensured that it contained the essential elements of that MG personality – features that could tie the new car into its heritage, without becoming a crude pastiche.

Typical of the features defined at this stage were the exposed rounded headlamps with just a hint of a scalloped recess in the wings, the small plinth moulded into the forward edge of the bonnet, and the transverse panel gap between bonnet and bumper. The latter feature was perhaps most closely associated with the rubber-bumper MGB. 'The rubber-bumper MGB was an unfortunate marriage of a plastic nose and a car not originally designed for it,' pointed out Gordon Sked, '... but by the time that we were looking at PR3, plastic noses were *de rigueur* in the motor industry and it would be quite a different thing to design the nose as part of the car from the outset.'

There was a conscious decision to eschew the traditional chrome grille (something the team knew would upset some traditionalists), which had been absent from the last MGBs, to distance MG a little from the Rover brand, where the chrome grille was poised to make a comeback.

These two sketches by Julian Quincey are close to the MGF style.

litres (97 and 110cu in) for an investment of about £200 million. The principal justification was to reduce the company's dependence on partner Honda for the bought-in 1.6-litre (97cu in) engines that powered a large proportion of the high-volume Rover 216 and 416 models.

The use of 'damp' cylinder liners (wet at the top for maximum cooling and dry into the cylinder block at the bottom) allowed bore sizes for both the 1.6 and 1.8 to be increased by 5mm (0.197in) to 80mm (3.15in) while

maintaining the same overall block dimensions. The stroke of the 1.8 was longer, at 89.3mm (3.52in), but otherwise the 1.6 and 1.8 are broadly similar, although the latter's crank is stiffer and the big end fixings are stronger.

The similarity with earlier MG history is uncanny; BMC engineers saw the mainstream B-series unit grow from 1,489cc (91cu in) in 1953 to 1,622cc (99cu in) in 1961 for the saloon cars (and MGA) and to 1,798cc (110cu in) for the MGB in 1962. In the case of the K-series, capacities grew

from 1,396cc to 1,589cc (85 to 97cu in) for the Rover 200/400 range and ultimately to 1,796cc (110cu in) for the MGF. The similarity in bore and stroke dimensions between the MGB and MGF is even more intriguing: 80.26x88.9mm (3.16x3.50in) and 80x89.3mm (3.15x3.52in) respectively.

The 1.8-litre (110cu in) B-series engine for the MGB had come about largely because testing of the early prototypes with 1.6-litre (99cu in) units had indicated that an MGB so equipped would be slower than the MGA. To a

great extent, the 1.8-litre (110cu in) K-series came about for much the same reason: as PR3 grew in size and the competition moved on – a 1.8-litre (110cu in) Mazda MX-5 was on the stocks – so did the need for a bigger engine. Standard on the MGF applications are 16 valves and Rover's latest MEMS 1.9 (Modular Engine Management System) controlled fuel injection, the latter boasting extra control features and improved circuitry yet benefiting from reduced size and cost.

Variable valve timing

Although the base model MGF would provide ample power for many owners, it was recognised that there would need to be a more powerful top-of-the-range model. It was possible to extract a lot more power from the K-series, as competition experiments would prove, but for everyday motoring a more sophisticated approach would be needed.

Rover had begun exploring the development of Variable Valve Timing (VVC) in 1989, under the code-name Hawk, resurrecting a patent idea

abandoned over ten years previously by piston manufacturer Associated Engineering. By Easter 1993, a development engine (the first of 120 prototype engines) was running on the test bed. This would be followed by some two million test miles and over 50,000 hours on the test bed, including severe rig tests and fatigue test cycles to prove the reliability of the VVC system.

The remarkably clever and complex system that evolved provides variable valve control over the whole range of engine operation, with continual

Early renderings show a car of low, mean stance. One Gerry McGovern sketch (top) has a hint of Porsche about the nose, while a simple drawing (centre) carries an 'MGF GT' number plate.

adjustment that can be applied smoothly in a linear rather than a crude stepped manner. This achievement actually places the VVC engine ahead of both the highly regarded Honda VTEC-E and BMW Vanos systems. The complexity is such that even within Rover's Advanced Powertrain division, VVC soon came to stand for 'very very complicated'.

Rather than being a single piece, the inlet camshaft is broken down into four semi-independent camshafts – one for each cylinder and each with two lobes. As the camshafts for

cylinders three and four are separated from the others, a separate drive is arranged by toothed belt from the back of the exhaust camshaft. Twin control mechanisms at each end of the inlet camshaft control the respective pair of cylinder camshafts. A control shaft, running inside the inlet side of the head, has gears engaging each twinned control mechanism and is turned either way by a rack and pinion, driven by the hydraulic control unit (HCU). The accompanying photograph shows a cutaway of the VVC control unit for

cylinders one and two.

VVC provides infinite variation of the inlet cam period between 220° and 295°, with a constant lift of 9.5mm (0.37in). The corresponding variation of inlet/exhaust valve overlap is between 21° and 58°. A special new version of MEMS, known as MEMS 2J, provides the additional electronic control required to send the correct signals to operating solenoids on the HCU. The MEMS 2J also accommodates two other special features on the 1.8 VVC engine: full sequential fuel injection with adaptive control

and a distributorless direct ignition system with one coil per cylinder.

In order to exploit the enhanced breathing capabilities of the VVC cylinder head, larger valves are fitted, the inlets increased from 27.3mm to 31.5mm (1.07in to 1.24in) and the exhausts from 24mm to 27.3mm (0.94in to 1.07in). A special matching inlet manifold and plenum chamber with increased flow capacity is made from two aluminium castings.

The MGF was available with both the basic and VVC versions from the outset.

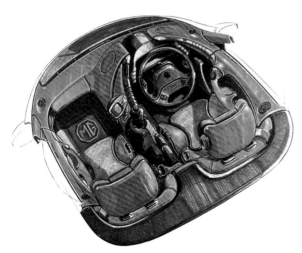

Gerry McGovern's presentation sketch (above) shows the definitive MGF style. Sketches of two stages in the evolution of the MGF interior show an avant-garde approach (left) and a rendering that is close to the final article (right).

These key MG features were cleverly married to details lifted from EX-E; the latter provided inspiration for the new rear lamps, the overall shape of the tail of the car and the distinctive sweeping curves of the door shut-lines. 'We wanted the car to be a clear statement which recognised the MG heritage, yet in a modern proportioned car with a cabin-forward style and raked windscreen,' explained Gerry McGovern.

Between September 1991 and February 1992, PR3 evolved towards its ultimate form and, as the designers decided to lop off an inch or two here and change proportions there, it would be fair to say that there was much wailing and gnashing of teeth by the engineers. The perfectionist McGovern lowered the rear 'deck' (making packaging of the folding hood more difficult), shortened the nose and insisted on retaining some features (such as those sweeping door shut-lines) that the production boys wanted to ditch. It was a hard road to follow but the journey was undoubtedly worthwhile.

With the collapse of Sterling sales, the US market was no longer important so pressure to make PR3 compliant with Federal legislation also disappeared. It was clear, however, that if the project were to have a serious future, it would need to be brought into the live product programme. During 1992, PR3 studies continued and gained an increased impetus in the wake of the RV8 launch. By this stage, the style of the car was already focused and if it was to proceed to fruition, there would need to be a Project Director to oversee and co-ordinate inputs from all the different disciplines. The man given that task was Nick Fell, who would bring PR3 to production, assisted by Brian Griffin as Chief Engineer; they had just two years to complete the job.

Identity parade: did the MG name still mean anything?

Before the designers, marketing men and engineers could commit themselves to a new MG sports car, they had to be certain that they appreciated what the customer expected of an MG. It would be no good producing their image of a brilliant sports car only to find that it fell wide of what buyers wanted. By the beginning of 1992, Graham Morris was overseeing the project to revitalise the MG name and Gerry McGovern recalls him asking if everyone was sure that they had not overlooked anything in their deliberations on the form an MG sports car should take.

Therefore McGovern, together with Tony Cummings of Rover Brand Management, set about organising an 'MG awareness' event, at which 450 people (mostly from within the company) were invited to pass comment on what MG meant to them. Recent prototypes (other than EX-E) were deliberately not shown – McGovern and his colleagues were not sure how appropriate some were – but a selection of old MG sports cars, including Old Number One, were put on display along with some sports car paraphernalia, while nostalgic archive films were shown in the background. The visitors were then asked to write down a list of the features they identified with the brand.

Some of the suggestions were impractical (wire wheels, bold bluff-fronted chrome grilles and fly-away mudguards) but some of the key elements were appropriate; the idea of the grille badge being mounted on a shield, the rounded headlamps and making a feature of the petrol filler cap. This research, which also highlighted the importance of the badge and the grille's form, was followed by a critique of

As the exterior shape of the definitive PR3 evolved, so did the interior. Here are two stages in the evolution of the full-size clay.

The final stage prior to sign-off of the design was the production of this fully finished GRP full-size model. One of the few details that would change prior to production would be to move the tail lights slightly further outboard – and to lose the 'MGD' name hinted at by the false number plate.

The MGF Design team at Canley. In the foreground are (from left) Rover Design Director Gordon Sked, Gerry McGovern and Studio Director Geoff Upex (who would become Rover Design Director when Sked left in late 1995).

McGovern's early clay for PR3 by some of the young designers in the studio. Asked for their honest opinions, all were totally supportive.

Throughout the final stages there remained pressure to cut corners but McGovern and Sked stuck to their guns and conceded little. There was a request, for example, to use lamp units which were common to other cars; McGovern was asked to consider sacrificing either the unique headlamps or rear lamps. He would not give way and there is little doubt that the purity of the design would have been compromised had he done otherwise.

Inside the car, McGovern was keen to give the interior something of the intimacy expected of an MG. This was achieved by adopting a symmetrical 'twin cockpit' theme, which offered some cost-saving benefits when it came to developing left- and right-hand-drive variants. The design team had been intrigued by the recent Ghia Focus sports car design study but although some themes inspired by this ultra-modern concept were explored, none was felt to be really suitable for an MG. Instead, what would become the definitive MGF interior drew quite strongly on the highly competent interior clay that had been presented by ADC at the outset.

The early styling models of the McGovern-era PR3 interior showed a smattering of chrome trim (something else that sprang from the 'MG awareness' exercise) but most was sacrificed either because it was felt to be 'over the top' or because it proved too expensive. Even so, another old MG tradition was followed: eight MG octagons were found inside the car. While not equalling Cecil Kimber at his most exuberant, these helped emphasise the fact that the car was much more than just a cabriolet version of a hot-hatch.

Making the project work:
the Mayflower deal

While the unbridled simple enthusiasm within Rover Group for making a new MG sports car was undeniable, the commercial arguments were not so clear-cut; what sounded exciting in engineering, marketing and design terms had to be balanced with commercial reality. With Rover now a part of British Aerospace, all projects had to be self-financing and require the minimum of investment.

With the removal of the US market from the equation, some painful truths had to be addressed with regard to the potential sales for a new MG. It was obvious that the PR3 programme would have to be tailored for lower production volumes and confined primarily to British, continental European and Far Eastern markets. Just as high volume

equates with large up-front investment, lower volume generally requires less initial investment. The catch, however, is that the lower-volume production methods make the unit cost higher; while it may be possible to increase the rate of production, this rarely reduces costs to a significant degree.

One of the biggest obstacles to getting a steel-bodied car into production is the tooling costs, particularly for the body; John Thornley had been horrified at a £2 million bill for the MGB tooling in 1960 but 30 years later the figure had multiplied 20-fold. With investment within Rover limited (there were other priorities) it seemed unlikely that the funding for a unique MG sports car body would be easy to justify, particularly if the projected sales volumes were between 15–30,000 per annum. It was clear that some creative lateral thinking was needed.

Several European manufacturers had already established partnerships with the design and manufacturing houses of Pininfarina, Bertone and Karmann whereby the two parties shared both investment and proceeds. Rover Group had no real track record in this arena but had formed a good working relationship with Mayflower Engineering, which had produced many of the body panels for the Land Rover Discovery. Mayflower's Motor Panels subsidiary had been intimately involved in the Phoenix programme and so was naturally keen to extend its association with PR3.

The motor industry had experienced a tough year in 1991. 'Sales and revenues were dropping and there was a need to take PR3 out of the capital programme in order to avoid it being dropped,' explained Brian Griffin. 'So the partnership idea started to be explored and the programme was allowed to slip back a year from 1994 to 1995.'

Rover Group entered discreet discussions with five potential partners but before long the list had been whittled down to Pininfarina and Mayflower; the cases for both were studied by Rover Group board members at the end of 1992. Pininfarina had many attractions, not least the possibility of brand association, but the downsides were its location (with the added expense and complication of transport) and the fact that it had played no part in the MGF design. After some tough negotiations with Mayflower, a deal was struck in which both parties agreed to invest substantial sums and to share the returns over at least six years of production.

Mayflower raised the necessary £35 million (£24.2 million for the PR3 project) through a rights issue in March 1993 and Pininfarina had a consolation prize of sorts in a contract to supply the folding hoods. Before long, Mayflower had recruited the first members of a team of 120 dedicated to PR3 engineering; among them was Tim Martin (from Leyland DAF), who would serve as Mayflower's counterpart to Rover Group's Nick Fell.

The process of turning Rover Group's design into

production reality involved Martin, Fell and others in distilling the body shape and internal structure while remaining mindful of many parameters, such as panel gaps, collision performance and a balance of tooling costs and low-volume production. Unlike many modern cars, the MGF does not have one-piece body sides because the cost of producing and pressing such large single panels (which take in the front and rear wings and sills) could not be justified. In the end, some 320 pressings were involved, all but 50 or so minor pieces being manufactured in-house by Mayflower.

Various small changes, driven by practical considerations as much as minor design rethinks, also took place at this stage. For example, the rear-lamp apertures were moved slightly outboard to give the car a wider stance (essential in view of its relatively high rear deck). By April 1993, however, the details had been largely resolved. As Tim Martin explained: '95 per cent of the work had already been done, but that last five per cent is still crucial to the whole development process.'

In a curious process of backward investment, Mayflower subcontracted some of the major body tooling to Rover Body & Pressings at the former Pressed Steel factory at Stratton St Margaret, near Swindon (source of the MGB bodyshells until 1980). Rover Body & Pressings further subcontracted some of the work to a Japanese company, so staff from Motor Panels ended up working in Japan with Rover Group Body & Pressings as the subcontractor, while at the same time reporting back to Rover Group in the UK.

After much blood, sweat and tears, the first PR3 bodyshells emerged from the new manufacturing facilities that Mayflower built at its factory at Coventry and were delivered to Gaydon and Longbridge for pilot-build programmes to start.

Engineering the details:
suspension and steering

The fact that the MGF uses Hydragas suspension is largely because the Metro/Rover 100 also used this technically interesting system; gas springing was not a design requirement. Even so, Dr Alex Moulton, inventor of Hydragas, was delighted at its adoption for an MG sports car, to which he considers it has brought special benefits. He told *Autocar*'s Steve Cropley: 'In a little roadster there is a higher than usual potential for the car to become unsettled on rough surfaces and the MG performs much better than the competition in that area, while continuing to handle and steer the way a small sports car should.' The benefits were confirmed by Nick Fell, who commented to *Autocar*: 'The brilliance of Hydragas is that it offers the low pitch rate of an interconnected system with the relatively high individual rates a sports car needs. We think this is the most successful Hydragas application yet.'

The front suspension (using a Metro subframe) worked fine but there were difficulties to overcome at the rear. There the same suspension set-up was all wrong: the built-in anti-dive properties caused the back end of the prototype to rise under braking and squat under power, added to which there was a destabilising problem due to a tendency for the suspension to 'toe-out' under braking.

Rover Group could not justify the cost of an all-new system and the subframes, which had cost £4.5 million to tool up and remained in production for the Metro, could not be changed drastically either. In the end, the chassis engineers adapted the subframe: they replaced the lower 'A' suspension arm with brand new bottom link, track control arm and brake reaction rod components (all anchored in different locations on the

Rover engineers acquired some secondhand Toyota MR2 sports cars and replaced the 1.6-litre Corolla engine with a 1.4-litre K-series. 'You could run down to Sainsburys in one and no-one would bat an eyelid,' claimed one engineer.

subframe) to provide optimal suspension geometry.

Although an unassisted steering set-up was considered desirable in the days of the MGA and MGB, the later MGC, MGB GT V8 and even the RV8 undoubtedly suffered from heavy steering. However, power-assisted steering was no longer the exclusive preserve of larger executive saloons and customers expected it in much more mundane cars.

It was obvious, therefore, that the MGF would have to offer power-assisted steering, even if only as an extra-cost option, but the mid-engined layout posed its own particular problems. While it was possible to feed a conventional hydraulic power-assisted steering system from the engine to a remote front suspension, this was very inefficient and potentially problem-prone. In Toyota's case, for the MR2 sports car, a nose-mounted electrically driven hydraulic pump had been used but this still introduced inefficiencies due to power requirements and weight.

For the MGF, therefore, Rover opted for a relatively new system known by its acronym of EPAS (electrical power-assisted steering) manufactured by the Japanese company NSK. Initially, the thought was that this system would be used solely at parking speeds, particularly for Japanese-specification models, but early tests showed that it functioned so well that it was swiftly developed to work all the time.

The EPAS system uses a much lighter mechanism weighing just 7kg (15.4lb), is totally independent of the engine (so can be sited in the best position) and only works when steering inputs dictate (unlike a conventional hydraulic system), so offers a claimed fuel saving of two to five per cent. At first EPAS was an option on the base model MGF and standard on the higher-performance version but eventually the take-up of EPAS was so great that it became a standard fitment within a year of the start of production.

Final development and testing: **bring on the 'mules'**

It is one thing to design a brilliant sports car on paper or in clay but quite another to make sure that all the bright ideas work and that the car will not only be buildable but will survive treatment by the most demanding owners and meet safety criteria. In the case of the PR3 programme, Brian Griffin and his team started early, for a project by some Rover-supported students unwittingly provided a useful reference point in the consideration of crash performance. They were given a Metro bodyshell and, when Rover got it back, this became the basis of the first rear impact test to explore the PR3 configuration.

By the spring of 1992 it was time to create the first PR3 'mules' (crude but effective prototypes that would allow clandestine testing of proposed underpinnings). The first simulator (SIM-1) had been built by ADC in 1991 using a Metro, but in March 1992 Rover Group built SIM-2, based on a Metro van, with the upper rear part of the bodywork cunningly converted into an opening hatch that concealed the mid-mounted 1.4-litre (85cu in) K-series engine and transmission. Dubbed the 'pizza van', this otherwise nondescript beige vehicle probably only drew attention because of its spoked alloy wheels, painted black to make them less obvious. SIM-3 followed shortly afterwards, so Rover soon had a small fleet of seemingly innocuous Metro vans running around the test tracks at Gaydon and the Motor Industry Research Association.

SIM-2, which survives in the Heritage Collection at Gaydon wearing enigmatic RTC (for Rover Test Centre!) decals, was the first of 15 Rover-built simulators, including four Toyota

For clandestine testing on public roads, what better than this mid-engined Metro van (one of several), known as the 'Pizza Van'? Note the tongue-in-cheek reference on the door to 'RTC – EXPRESS 24hr. DELIVERY'; RTC stands for Rover Test Centre. The 1.4-litre K-series engine is a neat fit in the specially fabricated engine bay.

MR2 sports cars cunningly converted to accept the K-series engine and transmission (and used for emissions testing) and four handbuilt PR3 prototypes. The Toyotas, bought privately, allowed testing to take place in everyday conditions on the open road without attracting unwanted attention. This was invaluable and had the added bonus that the 'prototypes' were relatively cheap to build.

When it came to the very first DO1 handbuilt prototypes, the cost and time involved made it necessary to ensure that the maximum use was obtained from each car built. Even allowing for this, the versatility and stamina of the prototypes was remarkable; Brian Griffin recalls that a single DO1 car was used for a 30mph (48kmh) rear impact, offset front impact, side impact, roof crush and *pavé* testing – although not necessarily in that order!

Next came 26 DO2 cars (very close to the final production specification) used for testing parameters that could not be resolved adequately with the earlier cars, including crash-performance and engine cooling. Testing continued with some of the cars wearing elaborate GRP disguises designed by Gerry McGovern, Alan Johnson and their modelling colleagues in Rover Group Design; these cars were finished either in NATO green or a weird-and-wonderful abstract black and white scheme designed to fool onlookers.

Dave Ovens, in conjunction with the trim and hardware shop at Canley, was responsible for the bizarre black graphics. Brian Griffin recalled: 'They cut out sheets of black vinyl on the trim boards at Canley and then applied the material to the cars.' The GRP disguises were effective but they did create both an aerodynamic and weight penalty and so for some testing a less dramatic disguise was called for. Other test cars appeared (sometimes at night or on closed test tracks) with less dramatic vinyl cladding designed to

allow final testing without revealing too much of the identity of the car.

This vinyl nose and tail covering (known as a 'bra') was fitted to one of the early DO2 cars. While it was being tested (by Rover Group Powertrain applications engineer Phil Gillam) at the famous Nardo circuit in Italy, a photographer managed to sneak a shot later published in a British car magazine.

After the DO2 cars came 34 D1 cars, which were closer to production specification and used a greater proportion of 'off-tools' components in production-ready form. Then there would be 64 QP (Quality Proving) cars (to test the production processes at Longbridge) and about 100 M (Method Build) cars, just prior to full production. The sequence is shown in the table below.

In November 1994, the same basic 'bra' disguise was used on a D1 car tested in the heat of the Arizona desert, where the extra insulation of the 'bra' probably only served to exaggerate the heat effects. The testing programme continued well after the launch at Geneva in March 1995, after which all disguises could be dispensed with. A Flame Red car was taken to Canada (for a Crest climatic shaker rig test) and this car made a guest appearance at a local MG club meeting.

Further south, other trips during February, April and July 1995 took in Nevada, Arizona and Death Valley in California. Phil Gillam explained: 'We were testing the air-conditioning system and to see how the engine and engine bay would behave in extremely high ambient temperatures – looking for things like heat soak – and we did find that some additional insulation would be needed if the car were to be sold into markets where such temperatures were possible.'

Cooling of an engine tucked tightly away behind the passenger compartment is obviously critical and the issue of

PR3: running prototype build stages

Code name	Description
PR3 ADC	Steel-bodied running prototype built by ADC.
SIM-1	Metro van body. Mid-engined running prototype built by ADC.
SIM-2 to SIM-4	Metro van pick-up body. Mid-engined running prototypes built by Rover.
Toyota MR2	Four test 'mules' fitted with K-series engines and used for emissions testing.
SIM-7	Hybrid crash-test mule. Metro front end and handbuilt PR3 rear. Used for US Federal 30mph (48kmh) rear impact test on 22 December 1992.
DO1	First running prototypes (SIM-8, 9 and 10) with handmade bodies, built at Rover's old Drews Lane plant. Some used for barrier impact tests.
DO2	Vehicle development phase after 'day zero' (board approval in November 1992). 'Soft-tool' bodies for engineering development.

Code name	Description
D1	First prototypes off tools. (July-August 1994). The two cars shown to the MG clubs and specialist press in February 1995 were D1 cars.
QP	First Quality Proving prototypes, made almost entirely from tooling and on the production line (autumn 1994 to spring 1995). The Geneva Show cars fell into this category.
QC	Quality Conformance. The second stage of proving production processes.
M	Method Build. Refinements to on-line production processes prior to volume production (commenced 3 July 1995).
AV	Advanced Volume. Just ahead of full production, addressing any problems identified during the previous stage. First production car (000251) completed on 24 July 1995 and now in the Heritage collection at Gaydon.

For testing of proper MGF prototypes, a special glass-fibre disguise pack (above) was developed in the studio during the summer of 1993, using clay moulded on to a GRP PR3 model.

The finished test mule (right), complete with disguise. This one has a striped pattern designed by engineer Dave Ovens, while others were painted NATO camouflage green.

airflow through the engine bay as well as over the front-mounted radiator was carefully studied in the wind tunnel. In the case of the radiator, a small 'bib' spoiler was found necessary to ensure that sufficient air was diverted on to the radiator matrix; an added benefit was additional downforce to resist aerodynamic lift at the front end. Gerry McGovern had envisaged engine bay air entering via the large oval side air intakes and exiting through narrow slots at the upper rear of the back panel, just below the edge of the boot lid. However, wind-tunnel smoke tests showed that there was insufficient suction to draw the air away from the cockpit properly, so the 'slot' (modelled on the rear of the EX-E prototype) became decorative. There was a side benefit, however, as it became a useful location for the high-level rear stop lamps, where fitted.

During the trip to Arizona in February 1995, some film was taken of an MGF being driven through the desert without any

disguises, for use in a launch promotion video. Similar film was also shot the previous month in the English Peak District, near Lady Bower Dam, on 11 and 12 January. 'We half expected photographs to suddenly appear in the press,' Mike Ferguson admitted, 'but fortunately no one caught us on those outings.'

A special drive session was also organised for Mark Blundell on Friday 13 January 1995. 'Nick Fell went out with him,' Ferguson recalled, 'and we got some very favourable feedback – and some useful advice to help us fine-tune the car.' By this stage, the MGF was very near to its definitive form, and this continual testing and fine-tuning was merely serving to ensure that the end-product was as near perfect as it reasonably could be. All that remained was to put the sales, marketing and servicing infrastructure in place and gear up for the launch. From now on, it was hoped, all would be plain sailing.

MGF testing continued in Arizona and Nevada (above) during the months after public launch.

An MGF in an anechoic chamber at Gaydon (the largest in Europe at the time) to check compliance with EEC noise requirements.

Bavarian invasion:
BMW on the scene

When British Aerospace (BAe) had taken on the Rover Group in 1988, for what many regarded as a rather special bargain-basement price, there were many who questioned the likely long-term status of this arrangement. Building highly sophisticated low-volume aircraft and large volumes of almost identical cars are in reality like chalk and cheese and frankly required different management and financing regimes. To give BAe its due, however, it recognised this disparity and allowed the Rover side of the business to function effectively under the guidance of its own management, leaning increasingly on its Honda partners, who had established an independent but complementary presence at Swindon, not far from Rover Group Body & Pressings.

Rover's continuing heavy losses prompted BAe to sell Rover Group in January 1994 – not to Honda, which had offered a £165 million cash injection by taking a 47.5 per cent stake in Rover, but to BMW for £800 million. Just three weeks later Honda, not surprisingly, terminated its partnership deal with Rover, though remaining a parts supplier.

For the PR3 programme, the end of the Honda-Rover relationship might almost be regarded as academic: although some parts naturally were drawn from the Honda-Rover parts bin, for the most part the new car had been engineered using non-Honda components. However, of greater concern to the champions of PR3 was the fact that BMW's own sports car, the new Z3, was waiting in the wings and might have been seen as a rival project and therefore a threat. It was clearly possible that the BMW people might not see the point in two totally independently designed and built sports cars chasing some of the same customers.

Inevitably there came a walk around the design studios by BMW's Chairman, Bernd Pischetsrieder, and Head of Research and Development, Wolfgang Reitzle. In the case of PR3, however, the visitors were in for something of a shock: Gordon Sked and his team had finished the styling model in a pearlescent 'flip' paint called Lipstick, a colour that showed variously pink or blue depending upon the light. 'When Bernd Pischetsrieder saw the MGF in this colour, he asked to review all the activities which had gone into the MGF project,' recalled Brian Griffin.

Frantic activity followed during the next few weeks and a great deal of material was pulled together in anticipation of Pischetsrieder's return, accompanied by BMW's Styling Director, Chris Bangle. In the meantime, the PR3 model had been resprayed metallic British Racing Green. Griffin remembers that Pischetsrieder took one look at the styling model and said: 'I don't have a problem!'

For production, Gordon Sked was keen to see a modern colour on offer – in particular a special one for the top VVC model – and so another pearlescent colour, Volcano, was settled upon. This striking orangey-bronze colour was swiftly dubbed Satsuma or Sarah (after the red-haired Duchess of York). However, Volcano would be quite a rare customer choice when the car eventually went on sale and within two years of the launch it would be dropped. The top-selling colours would be BRG and red, so perhaps the Germans were right on that score.

On the road to Geneva

By the time that PR3 had turned into MGF, the marketing men had had plenty of chance to comment on details of the design, but it was not until the year or so prior to the launch that they really had to put their efforts into high gear. There had been something of a dry run with the RV8 but that was a very different car to the MGF.

When it came to the name, many outsiders were surprised at the choice of MGF. There is a story that at least one speculative dealer in personalised registration numbers was surprised that Rover did not beat a path to his door when he bought up a batch of MGD numbers. To some extent the die had been cast with EX-E and Gerry McGovern's subsequent F-16 prototypes: whatever the reasoning, the final decision to go for MGF was taken in March 1992.

In July 1993, an MG Marque Values Day was attended by 30 people from right across the company, who were asked to define what MG meant in simple terms – distilling thoughts and discussion down to single words intended to capture the spirit of the brand. These key words and phrases would then be used as a tool in defining the parameters of the launch programme and ensuing advertising campaign. The five words felt to define MG were: desire, exhilaration, distinctiveness, 'Britishness' and value.

A year later, in June and July 1994, an MGF prototype was touring various venues in mainland Europe (particularly France, Germany and Italy) where it was displayed in customer clinics alongside vehicles considered as possible rivals. These included the Mazda MX-5, Toyota MR2, Peugeot 306 Cabriolet and the Volkswagen Golf GTI hatchback. 'There were relatively few sports cars actually on sale,' pointed out Mike Ferguson of

Rover Group's brand management team. 'We had looked at the market for hot hatches and cabrios as potential sources for our customers, hence the inclusion of the Peugeot and VW, both perceived as leaders in their respective sectors.'

According to Ferguson, the MGF (a DO2 car) was shown to the clinic visitors three times: firstly unbadged, then wearing MG badges and finally amongst the other cars chosen for display. 'At the end, people were asked to score all of the cars and they came down overwhelmingly in favour of the MGF, which they perceived as the most stylish car of the lot. People could identify it as an MG even without the badges and they liked both its practicality and the special little details such as the grille shape and headlamps, all perceived as being very British in style.'

When it came to sales and marketing of niche products, experience had shown that some Rover dealers handled these specialised models better than others, so Rover decided to limit the number of MG franchises to a core of 120 enthusiastic UK dealers. Overseas agencies were not necessarily handled in the same way. Three years later in Australia, for example, an interesting experiment was conducted with the imaginatively titled MG Garages, dedicated MG franchises that in some cases blended the showroom with a high-class restaurant.

At Rover's headquarters, a discreet MG Cars organisation was set up to handle the sales and marketing aspects of the MGF. From the moment of launch, Rover Group press office staff were always careful to ensure that press releases and publicity material were branded MG rather than Rover. This was felt to be particularly important in terms of establishing MG as a separate but complementary brand to Rover.

Just ahead of the official public unveiling, a special dealer conference was held at the Heritage Museum at Gaydon on 20-24 February. This was a truly international event with all markets (including Singapore, Japan and South America) represented.

At the Gaydon dealer launch the lower exhibition area was cunningly disguised with a false raised platform, which concealed display MGFs until the floor was opened up to give a dramatic unveiling, the two cars being raised on turntables to thunderous applause. That first get-together of all the dealers was a two-day event, with the first day devoted to presentations: by Nick Fell on engineering detail and Rod Ramsay on the sales and marketing approach. Some in-depth training sessions occupied the second day, so that the dealers could cope with public enquiries when the cars, which would not be available for some time, were announced

During this event, and many more, brand managers Greg Allport and Mike Ferguson were kept very busy ensuring that the right message came across. This all took place just a fortnight prior to the Geneva Show and the atmosphere was electric: not only were the people directly involved excited about the car but the motoring press was eagerly anticipating the unveiling of the first all-new MG sports car in nearly 33 years. Others noted wryly that the last time an all-British engineered design had emerged from the same stable had been the Austin and MG Montego of 1984; all subsequent cars had relied to a greater or lesser extent upon Honda platforms.

Shortly before the launch, Rover Group once more invited a group of selected enthusiasts, MG writers and club representatives to see the MGF in a special studio at the Heritage Museum at Gaydon, barely a mile from where the car had been developed. Needless to say, the reaction was very positive. There was perhaps a little uncertainty at the first sighting; the MGF, with its cab-forward stance and quite high tail, was undoubtedly a dramatic departure from MG tradition. There was no doubt that the car was a winner when Kevin Jones of Rover External Affairs drove one of the cars outside into the daylight; the natural light played effectively over the MGF's subtle curves and feature lines. Ever the inquisitive sort, I sought out the VIN plates of the two cars on show, and for the record their numbers were:

SPL2038M228D1V428 (Flame Red)
SPL2037M227D1V428 (metallic British Racing Green)

Steve Cox of MG Cars told us that of the 120 dealers approved, 110 would be 'up and running' at the time of launch. He added that it was hoped that by rationing the number of MG dealers, there would be less competition between them and better profits. 'There is also the need to encourage these dealers to become enthusiastic about dealing with second-hand Mazda MX-5s and even older MG sports cars,' Cox said.

There was never really any doubt about the actual launch venue. Mike Ferguson explained: 'We had a car on our hands which we knew would be a world-beater in every area – including security, handling and style – and so the launch had to be truly international; hence the decision to launch at Geneva rather than say Birmingham or Frankfurt.'

Two of those who had attended the preview (myself and *MG Enthusiast* contributor Andrew Roberts) took part in a special MG Car Club convoy of classic MG cars, driven from Abingdon to Geneva, where I was fortunate in meeting a well-placed member of the MG Car Club of Switzerland. Through him I managed to persuade the local

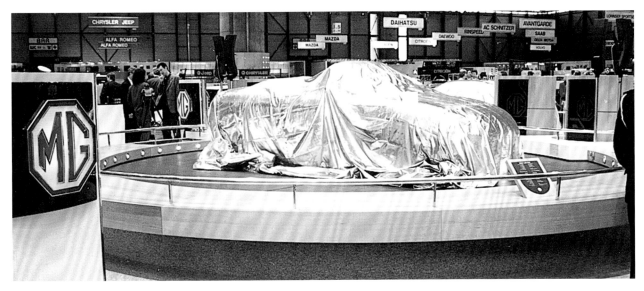

The MGF on the stand at Geneva on Press Day in March 1995, prior to its unveiling.

Gerry McGovern (right) discusses the MGF with the author and Julia Marshall of the MG Car Club.

authority to allow us to display our MGs in the public park immediately opposite the main entrance to the Palexpo exhibition hall, where the Salon de l'Auto was being held. It was a small gesture of solidarity for the MG marque and drew attention to the fact that there remained not only an enormous affection for MG but also an appreciation by enthusiasts of what Rover Group had done with the MGF.

Inside the exhibition hall on press day, John Towers took the stand again ahead of the unveiling of two MGFs concealed beneath gold sheets. Towers acknowledged the strong pressure there had been for a new MG: 'A couple of years ago, when we introduced the Rover 600, a journalist said to me that he wouldn't really regard Rover Group's recovery as complete until he saw a new MG sports car.' Accompanied by a Jazz ensemble named *The Fairer Sax*, the show cars were unveiled to a barrage of flashes from the many photographers, followed by loud and genuine applause. The MGF had arrived.

Both Gordon Sked and Gerry McGovern were on hand at Geneva to field questions from the press and explain their part in the story. 'At Geneva I felt that it was time to expose the designers to the public and so I got Gerry to come along to the launch,' Gordon Sked commented. 'Both Gerry and I had stood at the clay model wielding modelling knives; we were both closely hands-on with MGF during its development.'

Press reaction was very positive and so was that of the public. Most of the press complied with Rover's launch embargo but one UK publication broke ranks and published photographs slightly ahead of the launch. This was frustrating for those who had kept their promises: it was, after all, one of the biggest and best stories to come out of Rover for some time. All that remained was for the cars to be built...

MGF hits the road

As soon as PR3 had become part of the corporate programme, new areas of activity had begun; in tandem with the design and engineering development, the production and manufacturing engineering aspects began to get into gear.

Despite the undeniable importance of the famous Abingdon-on-Thames factory (closed in 1980) to MG history, some models have come from other plants over the years. In the BMC era most MG saloons were built at Cowley, while more recently the MG Metro, Maestro and Montego hailed from the various plants shared with their Austin siblings.

Rover Group had already established niche model

One car from the small fleet of MGFs used on the press launch in Warwickshire in 1995. 'The MGF is going to sell like lottery tickets on a roll-over week,' said *Autocar*.

manufacturing precedents by the time it came to producing the MGF; there had been the RV8, of course, built in a dedicated area at Cowley, and more recently the Rover 200 Coupé and Cabriolet and the Rover 400 Tourer. The latter three models were all built in Longbridge's CAB2 (Car Assembly Building No 2) in a special facility set up under the direction of Neil Jauncey, an engineer who transferred from Land Rover in July 1994 to oversee the necessary refit. So it seemed logical that MGF production be fed into the process, using broadly the same build teams.

Refitting the building while at the same time getting ready for production of a secret new car – particularly one as eagerly anticipated as a new MG sports car – was never going to be easy but somehow Jauncey and his colleagues managed to keep the appearance of the MGF a well-guarded secret. As the MGF moved gradually from handbuilt prototype into the line-built phase, staff were brought in to learn and at the same time help develop the build process.

At this point (known as Quality Proving or QP) Nick Fell and his engineering team were monitoring the results, checking for quality and working with their production colleagues to refine the operation. At the same time, suppliers and contractors were also ramping up towards full-scale production; for each successive batch of QP cars there would be progressively more and more parts made from the final tooling. This could be something of a double-edged sword; sometimes these parts would change subtly in the process, with a knock-on effect on other parts in terms of fit or finish.

An added complication was changes to parts at the eleventh hour: the hood fabric was upgraded from PVC to a superior 'flock' cloth and extra bracing was added to improve torsional stiffness.

The MGF assembly line at Longbridge

The MGF's build sequence starts in the Longbridge paint shop with the arrival of the basic unpainted bodyshell ('body-in-white') supplied by Mayflower. Priming and topcoats follow, using the latest environmentally friendly water-based paints. The painted shells are then stored in a 'buffer' area, which is capable of holding about half-a-day's paint-shop output (allowing for possible hiccups on the line). From there, they are transferred to the production line, where the fitting-out begins in earnest.

At the start of the line, plastic protective panels (embossed PR3) are fixed over the wings and doors and the build-order labels attached and checked before the appropriate wiring looms are wormed through the various grommets and pathways in the shell. Fuel tanks and the various fuel and brake lines are also installed at this stage, while the body is still relatively free of trim.

The build labels carry bar-codes that are scanned and send a signal via a modem to the various suppliers, which are then able to ensure that the parts are delivered literally 'just-in-time'. This saves storage space and also ensures that any problems (such as a faulty batch) can be dealt with immediately, possibly while the supplier is still geared up to produce more of the same components. 'In many cases the suppliers have as little as an hour and ten minutes to do this,' explained Rover's Vincent Hammersley, 'and you are never going to see more than about four hours' worth of material alongside the track.'

The next stage sees the cars mounted on the line – typically moving at about 19.5 metres (64 feet) per hour –

In early 1995, the first 'M-Build' car went down the line at Longbridge, an event recorded for Rover's in-house magazine Torque.

This pre-production Flame Red MGF was one of two cars shown to MG clubs and specialist MG press in a special preview behind locked doors at the Heritage Museum a few days prior to the official unveiling at Geneva. In the background are 'Old Number 1' and an MG TC.

Production line shot showing an MGF Abingdon, with beige hood.

where the doors are fitted out, including the drop-glasses. The interior carpets, trim and dashboard are installed, the necessary electrical connection work being done in tandem. In parallel, on a subsidiary line (known as 'engine dress') the pre-assembled engine and transmission units are fitted out with the various fixings and ancillary equipment necessary for the car. Another assembly line sees the build-up of the suspension sub-assemblies, including the installation of the Hydragas spheres.

This stage complete, the track rises up to allow what is unofficially (but graphically) known as 'engine stuff-up'. By this stage, the car is beginning to look more like the finished article and once the windscreen and hood are fitted each car passes through a test booth for 'rolling road' brake and emission checks. The final line section, known as 'finessing' ('rectification' no longer features in the modern car factory lexicon), includes various quality inspections, water leak tests and the fitting of various ancillaries such as the radio. Air bags are actually fitted outside the building for safety reasons and once the cars have passed final inspection for quality, they are driven out to the holding yard to await onward despatch.

The MGF **on the road**

For anyone used to traditional MG sports cars, the architecture of the MGF may have come as something of a shock. Just as the MGA provoked controversy when it broke with a long line of upright MG sports cars with separate wings, the MGF broke with the tradition of front engines and long bonnets. Of course, as we have seen, there had been ideas aimed at breaking the mould beforehand (most notably ADO21, the EX-E and F-16 concepts), but even so the MGF was bound to upset a few purists who preferred to look backwards rather than forwards.

The fact that the MGF was so well received by the majority of MG enthusiasts and sports car fans undoubtedly says a great deal for the efforts of all those involved – from its beginnings with Gerry McGovern's F-16, through the work done by RSP into the early iterations of PR3, to the production style with Gerry McGovern and a team of designers and modellers.

Some would argue that the RV8 softened the blow of the loss of a chrome-trimmed grille, although in truth that had passed away when the 'rubber-bumper' MGB first emerged back in 1974. This was still one of the few areas that drew criticism from the die-hard traditionalists when the MGF first appeared. However, their voices seem to have been in the minority for, despite the rash of customising kits offered by various entrepreneurs, a full chrome grille trim kit is noticeable by its absence (although

Part of the first shipment of 242 MGFs bound for Japan prior to loading on to the *MV Astro Coach* at Southampton on 22 October 1995.

Ghosted view reveals the MGF's compact layout and the neat way in which its engine is packaged. Either form of roof, hard-top (above) or soft-top (right), is neatly designed.

wheels backward, the resemblance to the MGB diminishes rapidly, although the simplicity of the body sides (in particular the smoothly rolled-under sills) is in tune with MG tradition.

The doors, with their sweeping rear shut-lines, are based more on the EX-E, while the side engine air intakes are entirely novel for an MG. These subtly rounded intakes, lifted more or less from MGA's PR3 styling clay, eschew the hard edges and straight lines that would have jarred with the friendly MG image. A neat touch is the petrol filler cap, with its racing-inspired collar complete with mock Allen key bolt heads. The relatively high rear deck is neatly blended in to the overall body lines to such an extent that the car looks lower than it really is; it is only from certain angles, or against a rival sports car, that the MGF could be said to look slightly 'chubby'.

At the rear, unique lights are unlike those of any MG production sports car (Gerry McGovern cites the EX-E as a starting point for their inspiration) while air intakes and exits are neat, simple and unadorned. The deep rear bumper incorporates twin slots that allow engine and underbody airflows to exit and conceals the transversely mounted rear silencer with two separate outlet pipes. The engine cover, situated just behind the passenger cockpit, is hardly noticeable and largely concealed by the hood. Low maintenance requirements mean that the owner needs to access the engine only for minor checks and most of these can be done from within the luggage compartment.

Neatly linking the front and rear of the car, and providing a degree of smooth continuity that is pleasing to the eye, is a subtle 'chord line'. This runs from just behind the headlamp, just below the windscreen and through to the top of the tail, giving the styling a slight but noticeable degree of 'tension' and ensuring that the car is a homogeneous whole rather than a mishmash of shapes. The windscreen surround on 'pre-2000' cars is finished in gloss black, which Gerry McGovern maintained looked better against the black hood or optional gloss-black hardtop; it is interesting to note that with the 2000 Model Year face-lift (see Chapter 8), the surround became finished in body colour.

Under the front bonnet, with its neatly contoured lines (with just a hint of MGB curves), the forward compartment houses the spare wheel and various components such as the brake servo. The space has been left fairly open to discourage storage, as it is crucial for impact performance, and any heavy loads carried up front would in any case affect the balance of the whole car.

The interior follows a 'twin cockpit' theme, with neatly symmetrical lines and a curved cowl over the Rover 200-

admittedly a chrome mesh grille kit has proved to be a popular option).

The MGF has a neat and simple 'face' that clearly echoes that of the MGB. Most noticeable are the rounded headlamp 'eyes' (with just a hint of the recessed 'pockets' of the MGB) and the twin grille openings (on either side of the central grille 'rib') that mirror the similar clean openings of the 'rubber-bumper' MGB. Taking its cue directly from the MGB is the small moulded plinth just above the central MG badge, which is mounted, like that of the MGB, on a shield background.

Whereas the faired-in bumpers of the last MGBs were clearly an afterthought, forced by legislation, those of the MGF are properly integrated and flow smoothly into the adjacent body panels. The shut-lines also carry faint echoes of those of the MGB, although in the case of the MGF the panel marriage is a happier one. From the front

Cockpit is snug and well-finished, even if not quite as exciting as some expected. Overall proportions (left) cleverly conceal the fact that the MGF is mid-engined.

derived instrument pack, finished specially for the MGF with cream faces (changed to silver for the 2000 Model Year cars, the changes for which are described in Chapter 8). A bold MG badge is moulded into the top surface of the facia and is clearly visible through the windscreen, but in general the use of MG octagons within the interior is reasonably restrained.

At launch, the choice of fabrics was limited but included black/green and a quite vivid red; in the course of time, the range of options has grown to take in leather, walnut dashboard trim and various enhancement kits. As befitted a car in its price range, the MGF interior was simple, unfussy and practical but there were mutterings of discontent about some aspects (most notably the unremitting grey of the plastics) that led to early work on upgrades.

Whereas the basic Mazda MX-5 made do with unpretentious but ugly steel wheels, from the start all MGF models had attractive 15in (381mm) alloy wheels that equalled in visual appeal most of the aftermarket wheels of a similar specification. The stance of the MGF is very dependent on a correct ride height, however, and production problems in ensuring that the Hydragas suspension was set and maintained at the right values were to prove a constant source of frustration for Gerry McGovern in the period after launch.

In engineering terms, the MGF bodyshell is extremely rigid for a car of its type; Rover engineers claim that it equals the torsional rigidity of a typical family three-door hatchback, which has a stressed roof that the MGF so clearly lacks. The mid-engined configuration helps with this, as do the bolted-in subframes, and the combination of a rigid body and well-mounted suspension plays a major part in the MGF's excellent ride quality – clearly the best in its class.

Press reaction to the MGF

By the autumn of 1995, when the first full-production MGFs reached their owners, Rover Group had given the world's motoring press ample chance to try the car. A press launch was held in the Midlands, with groups of journalists entertained at the Coombe Abbey Hotel and then let loose in cars for a drive around the Warwickshire countryside, taking in lunch at the Heritage Museum.

The reaction of the press at such events (particularly motoring correspondents and journalists prepared to accept a fairly 'lightweight' introduction to a new car as the basis of a report) is usually pretty warm and favourable but then that is undoubtedly one of the reasons why press launches are held in this way. For a more in-depth appraisal, however, the leading motoring magazines – particularly British market leaders *Autocar* and *Car* – subject the model to more thorough testing.

Some magazines also run an example of a significant new car on their long-term test fleets, with regular running reports on how the car has lived up to everyday use. The reputation of a car can be easily made or broken dependent upon how it fares in such conditions, so MG Cars was obviously anxious to see how its new baby was rated.

The MGF team, in particular the chassis engineers and the stylists, always realised that they would run the risk of some adverse reaction from those in the press who wanted a more 'extreme' motor car. In the real world, however, it would be no good making a car that swung into tail-out oversteer at the slightest provocation, or provided such minimal comforts that the driver and passenger would look forward to a journey's end rather than arriving feeling fresh and ready for more.

The tail has echoes of the earlier MG EX-E concept design. The colour of this car is the relatively rare Volcano.

The *Autocar* road test of 20 September 1995 was one of the first and the outcome was eagerly awaited by Rover employees and MG enthusiasts alike. *Autocar* particularly liked the style of the MGF, its strong brakes, good grip and build quality, but was less enamoured of the cabin design.

The test was of a standard 1.8i and the performance obtained by the magazine included 0-60mph (0-96kmh) in 8.7sec, a top speed of 123mph (197kmh) and 30-50mph (48-80kmh) in third gear in 5.6sec – all highly respectable if not class-leading figures, earning a four-star rating. 'There is, if anything, not quite enough drama in its progress meaning the MG feels slower than it is. An MX-5, slower on paper, feels faster on the road,' the testers said.

In the handling stakes, *Autocar* acknowledged that even if the MGF did not offer quite the same level of entertainment as the Mazda, it was supremely effective as a rapid, comfortable and fuss-free drive. 'It will corner easily at speeds which would have the Mazda skittering nervously. Its body control is top drawer and even at its limit it remains absolutely faithful in its responses. No other car with an engine behind the seats has ever felt this safe to drive fast.'

'The MGF is going to sell like lottery tickets on a roll-over week,' *Autocar* concluded, adding that Rover had 'created what is, in all probability, the world's most complete and affordable open two-seater'. On the down side, *Autocar* felt: 'The only people who will feel left out are those who had hoped for a genuinely thrilling driving experience. For all its talents, it is the one service the MGF manifestly fails to provide. Many see this as the first priority of an open two-seater sportscar and some will rule the MG out on those grounds alone. And while they would be missing out on a truly great new car, we, enthusiasts all, understand how they feel.'

The MGF's rivals

The success of the Mazda MX-5 did not only attract the attention of the Rover Group, for sales figures regularly in excess of 50,000 per annum are not to be sniffed at. So at the same time that Project Phoenix was under way, other teams of engineers, designers and marketing men were sharpening pencils for their own responses to the little newcomer from Japan.

In Italy, Fiat decided to go for the front-engined front-wheel-drive route (rather like Phoenix PR1) with its pretty retro-styled Barchetta (pictured left), launched on to the world stage at Geneva at the same time as the MGF. The Barchetta relied heavily on the floorpan and general engineering of the mainstream Fiat Punto but, being Italian, these mainstream cars were hardly humdrum. The Fiat Barchetta might not have been as pure a sports car as the MGF but it undeniably oozed Italian brio; undoubtedly MG Cars should be grateful that the product planners and accountants in Turin did not sanction a right-hand-drive version of the Barchetta for the British and Japanese markets.

Of rather greater significance, however, were the plans being hatched in Munich by BMW, yet to become involved with Rover. BMW wanted to strengthen its presence in the USA and decided to build a new factory there to free itself from high German labour costs and the vagaries of the Dollar-Deutsche Mark exchange rate.

Construction of a $400 million 1.2 million sq ft (111,484sq m) factory at Spartanburg, South Carolina began in September 1995. BMW's bold plan was to build a sports car based on the 3 Series and aimed at the Mazda MX-5, with (in typical BMW fashion) numerous engine and equipment options to tempt buyers into higher-priced

MGF road test results

Model	Autocar	Autocar	Car
	MGF1.8i	MGF VVC	MGF 1.8i
Publication date	20.9.1995	8.4.1998	October 1995
Acceleration (seconds)			
0-30mph (0-48kmh)	2.8	2.7	3.0
0-40mph (0-64kmh)	4.3	4.0	–
0-50mph (0-80kmh)	6.2	5.8	–
0-60mph (0-96kmh)	8.7	7.6	9.1
0-70mph (0-112kmh)	11.5	10.3	–
0-80mph (0-128kmh)	15.4	13.4	–
0-90mph (0-144kmh)	20.3	16.1	–
0-100mph (0-160kmh)	27.0	23.5	30.4
30-70mph (48-112kmh) through gears	8.7	7.6	–
30-50mph (48-80kmh) in fourth	7.4	6.5	7.8
50-70mph (80-112kmh) in top	12.1	11.0	–
Maximum speed			
Mph	123	126	120
Kmh	197	202	193
Fuel, overall consumption			
Mpg, Imperial (US)	26.4 (22.0)	28.3 (23.6)	28.4 (23.7)
Litres/100km	10.70	9.98	9.95

Car magazine declared the MGF VVC 'white hot' in its May 1996 issue, rating the car higher than the BMW Z3 and Alfa Romeo Spider.

Nose is filled with spare wheel, battery and various ancillaries.

purchases. Naturally, selling the vast majority of Spartanburg's output in the USA would also help the balance of payments nicely. By the latter half of 1995, the factory was ready to ship the first examples of the new BMW Z3 sports car.

In the meantime, of course, there had been exciting developments back in Europe. Naturally, there was concern in the PR3 camp when news of BMW's acquisition of Rover became known: it could well have spelled an untimely end for the British sports car project. Fortunately, however, the two cars had been conceived in different ways and with subtly different objectives.

The Z3 (pictured above) was a more traditional front-engined rear-wheel-drive sports car aimed primarily at US sales, whereas the MGF was a more modern European sports car interpretation not intended for sale in the USA. Thus the two would only cross swords marginally (the MGF VVC being a possible rival for the BMW Z3 1.9) and then only in relatively few markets. In fact, both BMW and MG Cars people claim that the two cars rarely appear on the same short-list: it seems that you are either the sort of person who wants an MG or someone who wants a BMW.

It is instructive to compare production outputs of the MGF and BMW Z3. At around the same time that the 30,000th MGF left Longbridge (destined for Germany) in late 1998, the 100,000th BMW Z3 (destined for the UK) rolled off the production lines in Spartanburg, just over two years after production had begun. Obviously, in sales terms at least, the Z3 punches in a league higher than its British cousin.

Of course, had BMW entered the game earlier and bought Rover in, say, 1991 then the MGF might not have happened. But then the Z3 might not have become a BMW.

MGF in competition

Motor sport has always lain at the heart of the MG story, with many successes firmly embedded in the annals of history. MG sports cars of every type have proved very successful in a variety of events – from small trials to big-league affairs such as the winter Monte Carlo Rally or the rigours of the Le Mans 24-hour race. Also, in more recent times, both the MG Metro Turbo and the exciting mid-engined MG Metro 6R4 acquitted themselves admirably and did much to keep the MG name alive when it could so easily have been allowed to wither on the vine. So it was perhaps inevitable that MG Cars should look at continuing this tradition.

Warren Hughes in the Team Firstair MGF – with Chelsea Football Club livery – won the 1999 MGF Cup.

Tentative thoughts about entering the MGF in some form of motor sport began to take shape even before the car was announced in March 1995. However, it was clear that without a massive budget it would be unlikely that a factory MGF could compete in the upper echelons of rallying or racing. In any case, there were probably other cars in the Rover stable better suited to such arenas and the glory days of open sports cars thundering through special rally stages or round La Sarthe were well and truly past.

However, Rover already had good experience in one-make championships, starting with the Metro and ranging through to the Rover 200 coupé series. Also, as Mazda had already had some moderate success with race series for its MX-5 sports car, there seemed to be a good case for repeating the experiment with the MGF. There was also the prospect of tying in to established club-racing series, a facet of motor sport with a strong MG tradition.

For the first two years, however, Rover's UK motor sport arm, Roversport, was fully committed to the Rover 200 championship, supported by other minor series. In any case the marketing men could fairly argue that while they could easily sell every MGF they could make, there was less of a need to take the new car to the track. In other markets, however, the situation was less clear-cut and with the enthusiastic encouragement of the local Rover importers and dealers, MG Cars began to plan two specific championships: one in Japan and the other in France.

Development work began just six months after the launch of the MGF, with a white development car being wheeled into the motor sport section at Rover Group's Gaydon design headquarters so the process of turning it into a racing car could begin. Naturally there was a great deal of hardware that the engineers could tap into; not only from inside the company, through experience with the other championships but also through working with trusted outside specialists and suppliers.

Wynne Mitchell was one of the team involved in building a race car from that white car and Mitchell relied on his old friend and ally Tony Pond (veteran of many British Leyland and Rover championships) to assist with the practical testing. The input of a driver of Pond's calibre was obviously a crucial part of this development process; engineers may be reasonably competent drivers but an excellent driver with a good grasp of practical engineering is worth his or her weight in gold.

Pond explained that his experience with the competition development of the MGF goes back to the first Japanese specification car. 'Rover Japan wanted a very cost-effective championship and we really started with a blank sheet of paper and an MGF! Even at that stage, the prospect looked very exciting on paper and we were able to enthuse our Japanese friends of the potential.' The first part of the exercise was to sit down with the chassis engineers and explore their pavé testing results. 'We then set about making the improvements we needed,' added Pond.

The theoretical attractions swiftly translated to reality: 'As soon as I started driving the car, I found it to be great fun. It worked very well on the circuit and it also worked well on stages, because of course the car had to cope with both disciplines to take in the French series too. The car was so well balanced, you could quickly grow horns as a result of driving it; at the same time, I was testing the Rover 200 and I suddenly realised that God never wanted the front wheels of a car to be driven!'

Once the basic specification had been determined, Tony Pond, Wynne Mitchell and colleagues Alan Reed and

Japanese-specification competition MGF made its first appearance at a test session for invited competitors and journalists at Castle Combe on 21 February 1996.

Initial MGF competition development

Date	Details
16 June 1995	Meeting to discuss development of an MGF competition car for Rover Japan
9 September 1995	First car available, standard run and assessment
14 November 1995	Initial discussion with tenderers
23 November 1995	Initial feedback
8 December 1995	Roversport issues a job specification
13-21 December 1995	Tenderers present their proposals to Roversport
22 December 1995	Letter of intent to successful tenderer
January 1996	Award of contract to Janspeed
22 January 1996	Cars made available by Rover
1 February 1996	Initial kit of components issued by Rover
21 February 1996	Test session at Castle Combe for Japanese guests
24 February 1996	First ten cars available
24 February 1996	Compliance and function testing begins
16 March 1996	Last batch of cars to be made available to Rover Group
18 March 1996	Compliance and function testing ends
19 March 1996	Last date for rectification
20 March 1996	Cars to dockside
22 March 1996	25 cars leave for Japan

Roy Ford took the prototype to South Africa for a four-week tour of that country's race circuits, where they were greeted with great enthusiasm by the local MG Car Club enthusiasts. 'We had completed 860 miles [1,384km] in the UK,' Wynne Mitchell remembered, 'of which 700 miles [1,127km] – some 90½ hours – were spent running on a rolling road in a climate chamber, fine-tuning the cooling system and so forth.' The trip to South Africa was intended to explore the initial specification and after 2,431 miles (3,767km) on four different circuits, the team was eventually able to conclude that it had got things just about right.

The circuits used were in the area round Johannesburg and included Kyalami, Midvaal ('A tight circuit – very hard on the car,' according to Mitchell.), Goldfields and Gerotek. The latter is a former military base near Pretoria that boasts a high-speed oval; some 600 miles (965km) were run there alone. Mitchell is understandably proud of the reliability and overall performance of the car: 'We got 14.2mpg [11.8 US mpg, 19.9 litres/100km] overall and used virtually no oil – and this was testing in high ambient temperatures, typically 26-30°C [79-86°F], much of it on the high veldt under the strong sun, with Tony at the wheel.' A small logistical problem that Roy Ford fortunately managed to overcome was the lack of a good supply of 95 octane unleaded petrol in South Africa, where it had only just been introduced, and even then the rating was 91 octane.

Tony Pond explained that part of the justification for going to South Africa was simple value for money. 'Kyalami, where we got up to 110mph [177kmh] on a lap (about a second slower than their Group N cars) only cost us about £1,000 a day and Goldfields and Midvaal were an incredible £20 a day,' he said. 'The owner of the Midvaal circuit, a multi-millionaire, even asked us if he could buy a car like

Roversport

Speaking to me in October 1997, Wynne Mitchell explained the origins of the department within Rover that was responsible for the MGF's competition development. 'Roversport was set up about seven years ago, for the 216GTi and Metro GTi championships, and basically most of the original development work was carried out by Tony Pond Racing UK Ltd at its premises at Malmesbury, Wiltshire. We used the Gaydon test track as our test facility. Then, when Tony Pond Racing Ltd was wound

up, Steve Carter, who was at Gaydon, said that he would lend us some manpower to enable us to build a car and it all started from that really... but there was no area identifiable as being Roversport. In those days, there was an attitude within certain quarters within Rover that motor sport stank.'

When BMW came on the scene, there was soon a fundamental rethink on how the marque should be handled. It was decided that the Rover image would be of luxury and a more relaxed type of motoring, so it was no longer appropriate

for Rover, as a marque, to compete in motor sport. Consequently the racing championship for the Rover R3 (200), which Mitchell's team had been developing for 1997, was shelved in November 1996. 'But, of course, MG and Mini are not the same as Rover; they are obviously sporty marques,' commented Mitchell. 'And so, after sitting down and thinking about motor sport, the decision was reached that there is no reason why MG should not continue to be seen as a sporty, competitive vehicle.'

BMW's inherent interest in all

aspects of motor sport resulted in the relaxation of the anti-motor sport policy and Mitchell's team was allocated an area at the Gaydon Test Centre within the prototype build section. This proved rather awkward: if a supplier came in for discussions, everything had to be screened off. So now Roversport is the sole occupant of a building that is completely separate from the main design centre. 'Not that we want to keep people out,' said Mitchell. 'We welcome people's interest because I think that their enthusiasm, if it is spread ours as a pace car; he was even talking about buying a set of 25. The locals were really impressed at how the car just kept going and it was certainly durable: we did 2,000 miles [3,219km] on a single set of discs, for example.'

For the Japanese series, the specification was not too exotic: 'The Japanese specification, which we developed, was a very controlled car and I always wanted to move development on a step,' commented Pond. 'The opportunity, of course, came subsequently with the UK-specification MGF Cup car, adding bigger horsepower, bigger brakes and building a proper racing car. And it has just been great fun; the package is very balanced.'

Pond believes that consistency is one of the watchwords for the MGF. 'The car always does the same thing: be it wet or dry; you get a touch of understeer when you turn in, followed in the middle of the corner by a neutral phase. And you can provoke some oversteer if you want to by jabbing the throttle, making it lean a bit further. I drive round and round the test tracks and frankly I don't want to get out of the car at the end! Some tests I run are 100 miles [160km] long but I don't get to the end thinking: 'I don't want to do that again'. Not only was the car extremely good from the start, it simply kept getting even better.'

The first Japanese specification cars were unveiled on 21 February 1996 at England's Castle Combe circuit, where Rover Japan's Osam Morikawa received the first of 25 cars set aside for the 1996 championship. Gerry McGovern was on hand at Castle Combe to explain the part that his department had played in designing the logo and graphics for the series. 'Peter Stevens actually designed a racing hardtop for the MGF, with my input,' McGovern told me. 'Peter had this idea to fit the roll cage in such a way that it protruded outside the hardtop itself, which was very interesting but perhaps a bit too 'off-the-wall' for the MGF.' Racing began in July 1996 at Tsukuba, the first of four venues that year, and Rover Japan reported very high interest from the outset, with 47 competitors applying for cars.

Whereas the Japanese cars were right-hand-drive single-seaters, for the French Trophy series the set-up was left-hand-drive two-seaters, with the bias towards road racing rather than circuit competition. The cars were sold ready to race, complete with a full roll cage, bucket seats, harnesses, a hardtop, fire extinguisher and cut-offs for fuel and electrics. Inside, the carpets were removed but the electrically operated windows and the standard console, to which an oil-temperature gauge was added, were retained. The French series began in 1996, with initial plans for nine races, three tarmac rallies and a couple of hillclimbs. One of the early cars was driven by Phillippe Chevalier, who went on to win the 1996 championship. English ex-pat Mark Mansfield bought this car and drove it with some success during the 1998 round. 'The car required a great deal of work and I finished up by getting the car and engine rebuilt in England just in time for the first race of the season,' Mansfield remembered. 'It was very much a 'gentleman' drivers' series with, for the most part, a pleasant atmosphere among the drivers.'

The car, while not especially powerful, was a great pleasure to drive and was relatively quick. However, once the back end broke free it could prove to be a handful. The other French drivers described it as a bon école (good school) for learning to race.

The Hydragas suspension was useful for the multi-discipline race series, allowing the ride height to be adjusted easily to suit the conditions of a smooth circuit or a much bumpier road rally.

---

throughout the company, is good for morale, good for the workforce and it is good for us too.'

Mitchell explained the composition of the team: 'I am contracted to Tony Pond Racing but I am based in Gaydon. Roy Ford is a Rover employee who has joined Roversport and he is the Rover man there. We also have two Rover mechanics who were based at Gaydon and have transferred over to work with us. So there are four of us who are the full force within that department.' To help with the MGF project, Don

Kettleborough was appointed as the Project Manager with administrative responsibility both within the company and externally. 'To make sure that while we have our heads down, doing the development work, the overall project is progressing along the right lines,' commented Mitchell. 'We have fortnightly meetings with all those involved to ensure that we are meeting targets and to resolve any problems. That effectively constitutes the re-establishment of the old Roversport management committee but

under a new title now.'

Mitchell's association with Tony Pond is a long-standing one, going back to 1977 when Pond was contracted to BL and Mitchell worked for Chrysler UK. 'We borrowed Tony to come and help sort out what turned out to be the Sunbeam-Lotus and then he came and drove for us the following year. That was when I really started working with Tony... This was followed in due course by the 6R4, the Metro, Rover 216GTi, Tomcat and some 800 test miles in the R3. We understand each other.'

The 1998 championship was won by 29-year-old Fabien Vericel, a driver with a fair amount of rally experience. After an enjoyable time racing his MGF, Mansfield sold it on to Roy Ford, former MG Competitions Manager, who restored it to its original condition. The MGF Trophy continued in 1999, with venues including Le Mans, Circuit de Ledenon, Val des Viennes, Circuit de Nogaro and the Circuit de Nevers at Magny-Cours.

The MGF Trophy cars continue to race in 2000 competing in circuit races with other GT de serie (standard production two-seater) cars. Several of the drivers have been racing the MGF since the Trophy began 1996.

MG racing comes home at last: **the MGF Cup**

Right from the start, there was an understandable desire on the part of both the Rover people and the British motor sport contingent for a UK-based race series for the MGF. There was a latent desire to do something along these lines but at the outset the priority was to respond to Rover Japan's interest. However, when an early competition specification car was shown at the Autosport Show at the beginning of 1996, the stand was swamped with enquiries about the prospects for a UK series.

Wynne Mitchell pointed out that with the MGF Cup, the company was aiming firmly at professional drivers, who are supported by sponsorship, have a proper team backing and can boast previous experience in motor sport. 'The decision was made to make the vehicle more exciting, because we are in competition with some other one-make championships in the UK – and we have to appeal to drivers who might

otherwise have gone elsewhere.' This naturally necessitated an attractive combination of light weight and greater power.

For the latter, Mitchell explained: 'We chose the 195PS [197bhp] version of the Rover 1.8-litre [110cu in] K-series engine, with a close-ratio gearbox.' More power, of course, meant that the chassis had to be much tauter, without the comfort-driven compromises of the road car. 'That entailed, for instance, substituting spherical metal bearings for rubber bushes in the suspension; obviously refinement is of less importance on the track than on the road. We generally sharpened the car up – using 16in [406mm] wheels and stick tyres as opposed to the 15in [381mm] wheels and semi-racing tyres previously used – so the grip has gone up as well and the loads carried into the chassis have correspondingly risen.'

Making the suspension stiffer puts more stress and strain on the bodyshell. 'We have had to take measures to reduce the possibilities of deflection and distortion in the subframes and body which you would expect to have as a consequence of these higher loads. The brakes have also been uprated to cope with the fact that the car is considerably quicker – not so much in terms of maximum speed but because it can accelerate faster on the straight and this results in the need to kill more speed at the corners.'

The natural preference was to use as many in-house sourced parts as was feasible but the MG Competitions team was not hamstrung by this policy. 'We have chosen the best components for each task,' Mitchell emphasised. 'In the case of the brakes, for example, we went to AP Racing, which is a company that services and designs and develops braking components for vehicles worldwide. We have quite a long association with AP; they were involved with the Rover Turbo Cup cars from the very beginning. They

Competition version of the MGF, complete with hard-top, on the Rover Sport stand at the Autosport Show in January 1996.

Team Spirit

Within any organisation it is healthy to foster a sense of teamwork and close co-operation. One way to do that is to provide tacit support for activities, by staff in their own time, that not only add value to the business but provide a bit of fun into the bargain. That was the philosophy behind Team Spirit, a motor sport team formed by a group of Rover engineers and fitters back in 1989. That was some time before MG's renaissance but just in time to pick up the good vibes when that project got under way.

Tom Conway, a current member of Team Spirit, recalled how it all started: 'We had just launched the new Rover 200 Series and there was a lot of optimism about the future. Various people at Longbridge and Gaydon (including fitters and technicians) got together and asked the management if they could have a car to work on in their own time. The response was favourable: they were given a Rover 827 Vitesse.' The team had no shortage of enthusiasm or car-building talent but readily acknowledged that it had relatively little serious competition skill. So Gaydon engineer Don Kettleborough was recruited, bringing with him several years of experience in rallies and races.

During 1990, the team went forest rallying in the Rover and Don achieved an impressive fourth in class in the Welsh Clubman's Championship. At the end of 1990 Rover Group formed Roversport, a new motor sport division that would run two one-make series in 1991: one was a race series for the Rover 216GTi, while the second used the Metro GTi in a mixture of races and rallies. Team Spirit built a car for this championship, known as the Metro GTi Challenge. Don came second overall in 1991 and won in 1992 and 1993. In 1994, the team switched to the National Saloon Car Cup, Don winning the up to 1,400cc (85cu in) class.

In 1995, Team Spirit entered the *Motoring News* rally championship and Don and co-driver Pete Chapman finished second in class and 15th overall. However, the feeling was that the Metro was nearing the end of its development; it was time for a new challenge.

During 1995 the team, led by Don Kettleborough, decided to build and develop an MGF for racing in the 1996 season. Don was a member of the MGF project team and could see the new car's potential: it was mid-engined, handled well and used the latest 1.8-litre (110cu in) K-series engine. An ex-engineering QP test car was saved from the scrap heap and race preparation began. Meanwhile, discussions with the MG Car Club led to the MGF being allowed to compete in the Club's 1996 Anglia Phoenix Challenge race series. A small section of the team continued to use the Metro in rally events throughout 1996.

The car made its motor sport debut as seen in the photograph on 16 March 1996 at Silverstone – the first competition appearance of an MGF. Don proceeded to win the race, giving the MGF a maiden victory. From this very encouraging start, the Team Spirit MGF proceeded to run an extremely good season, being in the top five in all events, the only slight mishap being a fuel problem at Mallory. The team ended up first in its class and third overall in 1996. Similar success followed in 1997, with second place overall and another class win, but for 1998 the team turned its attention to the new MGF Cup. 'We had to build a new car,' Conway explained, 'so we were building the new car over the winter of 1997-8. In the meantime, the 'rally' part of the team decided to abandon the Metro and build an MGF too: they got hold of a shell, seam-welded it, put in a roll cage and assembled it in the workshop alongside the MGF Cup car.'

Preliminary test day for the Cup was 17 March 1998 and, according to Conway, it was a bit daunting to be lined up alongside the true professionals. However, Team Spirit was perhaps 'professional' in a different sense and the competence of both the driver and the build team was very evident. 'Don was generally qualifying in the low twenties and finishing several places higher, and he had the distinction of starting and finishing every race. In terms of damage, too, we did very well; we only had to replace one bumper and one windscreen all season.' Another competitor changed no less than 19 bumpers in the 13-race series! 'We proved what an amateur team could do,' Conway maintained.

At the end of 1998 the car went back to Edwards of Stratford (the enthusiastic Midlands MG dealer that had supported Team Spirit) and Mark Hazell drove it in 1999. Meanwhile, Team Spirit's Rob Stone and Martin Prestage took the rally MGF into the 1998 National Macadam Safety Devices Tarmac Rally Championship. They achieved second in class B10 (for two-wheel-drive cars up to 2 litres against Escorts, Astras and Sunbeams, some with as much as 250 horsepower.

Another Team Spirit member, Graham Askew, used the original MGF (now known as Old Number Five) in the MGCC Moss International Speed Championship. He won his class in 1998 and 1999 and set times fast enough to beat a class of V8 Ferraris on one occasion.

In 1999, Don Kettleborough returned to the Anglia Phoenix Championship, driving Old Number Five, and had some battles-royal with Roy McCarthy's demon MGA. 'Don won his class and the championship overall, which we believe is the first championship win for an MGF outside the various one-make championships,' Conway said. Meanwhile the rally team came second in class and 11th overall in the NMSD championship, which included the first International rally class win for the MGF at the Elckerlyck Rally Sprint in Belgium.

completed a data sheet for the MGF Cup cars and this provided a specification they considered suitable for the task.' Special Mintex brake pads were chosen for both front and rear and there is a special bias adjuster fitted that the driver can use to fine-tune the brakes during a race.

Outside suppliers were invaluable but where appropriate the team did its own thing. 'The brakes were a very specialised area, whereas we have designed many other things ourselves in-house. The spherical bearings were designed by us and are being made specially, and the up-rated subframes have been produced by taking a standard subframe and reinforcing it in areas where we have seen problems in extreme usage or from the experience of pavé testing advised to us by the chassis development team at Rover. We work very closely with such people, saying to them: 'This is what we intend doing. Have you got any concerns?' On the basis of their response, we act accordingly. So we do work with the mainstream engineering people when we uprate a car.'

In the past, such two-way communication between MG Development and the Competitions Department had often proved mutually beneficial, with MG road cars benefiting from lessons learnt on the track. Mitchell is optimistic that this can still hold true: 'Obviously, MG is here to stay and, who knows, we could easily see an uprated version of the MGF in years to come.' He hopes that, as the company always has done in the past, the designers would come to them and ask: 'Have you had any problems with this?' or 'What did you do to that?' or 'What do you think we should do to this?' Mitchell added: 'Rover engineering has assessed what we consider to be a suitable road specification model, based upon the trophy car, with lowered suspension.'

Of course, what is suitable for blasting round a competition circuit may not be practical for everyday road use. 'Whilst assessing this for durability they have to look at more mundane but important considerations like jacking – always the bane of our lives when it comes to lowering a car,' Mitchell pointed out. 'If you cannot get a jack under a car to hang a wheel with a flat tyre you obviously have a problem.'

Much of the testing was done on one car: the white MGF used for developing the French and Japanese race series. 'That remarkable car was used for all the test work, all the endurance work and after that was used for press demonstrations and things of that sort,' Mitchell commented. By the time that the MGF Cup was announced, the white car had amassed over 6,000 very hard miles since it started its time with MG Competitions in September 1995. 'We used it as the basis of the MGF Cup car, at least until such time as we got far enough down the road to finalise the specification,' explained Mitchell, 'when we built a proper replica to form our pukka development car.' This new car was then used for endurance running over the winter prior to the start of the series proper.

Whereas Janspeed had been used as a contractor to supply turnkey cars for both the French and Japanese Trophy cars, MG decided to adopt a different approach for the MGF Cup. 'It was decided that we would maintain the tradition that we used on the Rover 216 GTI, the Metro Challenge and also the Tomcat (Rover Turbo Cup),' explained Wynne Mitchell. 'We would supply the customer with a suitably prepared rolling shell, which had been seam welded and with a certain minimum amount of trim and components on it which will allow it to come off the end of the track at Longbridge, from where it will be shipped to Cowley. From Cowley, it would be supplied to the customer in kit form, complete with a big load of bits – including

The MGF Abingdon Trophy

The MGF Abingdon Trophy was announced alongside the MGF Cup, to be administered by the MG Car Club, and aimed at newcomers, perhaps as a first step on the ladder into serious motor sport. Unlike the MGF Cup, cars competing in the MGF Abingdon Trophy remain largely standard, with only certain mandatory regulation safety features such as a roll cage (bolted in to facilitate quick removal), four-point seat belts, fire extinguisher and electrical master switch. A

special hardtop, which (unlike the standard version) will fit over the roll cage, was available as an optional extra.

In addition to the obvious pre-requisite of ownership or access to an MGF, the would-be competitor had to prove that his or her ability reached a minimum standard – a sensible requirement which should enhance safety on the circuit. Before the season got under way for the first time, the MG Car Club offered a special session, organised in conjunction with the Ian Taylor Motor Racing School, at the

Thruxton race circuit. At this special track day and get-together new drivers were able to take the necessary Association of Racing Drivers' School test and obtain an RAC MSA competition licence.

Partly because the Abingdon Trophy is aimed at the competitor using his or her own road-going MGF, there are two separate categories: for the standard MGF 1.8i and the VVC model. The requisite safety-related parts were available to registered competitors at a subsidised price through Rover's own

Motor Sports Parts outlet and even the neophyte racer should not find it difficult to have all these ancillaries installed.

Recognising that many of the cars taking part will also be expected to transport their drivers home after the event, a fair amount of effort went into ensuring that the hood can be erected with the roll cage in place. Thus the hardtop, whilst a desirable optional extra, was not mandatory when the car was being used off the track!

For the opening series, there

engine, gearbox, suspension components, brakes and things of that sort.' MGF body manufacturer Mayflower carried out the seam welding, enhanced the damper mountings and installed location brackets to facilitate installation of the roll cage.

From there, the customer would be free to either build the car himself or go to his favourite race preparation company. Mitchell explained that they had considered appointing a reputable company to build some of the cars but had decided against it. The reason was that the price 'waved about' when trying to attract competitors would be for the component parts and the kit, 'whereas if the car was sold built-up it would be seen as a different price category altogether'.

To bring the weight of the car down, anything extraneous has been removed; gone is most of the standard interior trim and although silhouettes of the original door trims and centre console remain, they are thin shells formed of carbon-fibre reinforced resin. In place of the radio is a neat panel with the regulation isolator switches while, within the cowl in front of the chunky competition steering wheel, a functional liquid crystal display substitutes for the normal instruments.

According to Mitchell, a lot of interest came from those involved in the Rover Turbo Cup, which was going to be in its fifth year in 1998, while the Rover 216 would be in its eighth year in 1999. Even so, interest also came from many other quarters: 'Lots of people, although they establish a rapport with a car, with the people supplying the bits, with the tuning firm and with the organisers, end up wanting a change,' explained Mitchell. 'So we could easily be seeing some people coming over from other championships.'

Interest from potential competitors is one thing but of course without ground-level support from the sales and marketing people, a factory-backed motor sports endeavour

would be very unlikely to take flight. Wynne Mitchell gratefully acknowledges the support that he and his colleagues received from the MG Cars brand management team and particularly Guy Pigounakis (MG's Brand Manager for the UK), who is part of the Rover management structure. 'He can see value in us doing a championship of this sort, contributing not only to increasing sales but of course also to reducing the age of the average MGF owner,' commented Mitchell. 'When the MGF was announced, many of the customers who were attracted were those who remembered MGs from years ago. We now want to extend the appeal to those who maybe have never really heard of MG before but who want to own a car because it is a good looking sporty one, which goes, rides and handles well. This activity, Guy feels, will help to channel their interest and buying power into MG dealerships.'

Mark Mansfield pilots his MGF at the July 1998 Rallye de Rouergue.

would be 12 events in total, split between six qualifying races and six speed events, the latter comprising three sprints and three hill climbs. According to Peter Browning, who administers the trophy series on behalf of the MG Car Club, one event from each category could have been dropped, leaving ten events required to count towards a placing in the series. Prizes were allocated at the end of the season not only for the outright winners but also for the youngest driver, for lady drivers and novice competitors, thus reinforcing

the friendly atmosphere of the series.

MG Cars supported the full season for 1998 and 1999 and the two-pronged theme of speed events and racing was maintained. There were almost 30 entrants for 1999, of which two thirds went for the speed events as an economical route into motor sport. Full grids of MGFs were not always possible in the 12-round championship (staged as far apart as Finlake in Devon and Harewood in Yorkshire) but by far the largest presence was with 20

cars at Silverstone. Winner of the Speed Championship in 1999 was newcomer Paul Kershore, while Malcolm Gammons made a valiant but ultimately unsuccessful bid to wrest the overall championship from 1998 winner John Dignan, who retained the cup. The MGF Abingdon Trophy was planned to continue in 2000 and beyond; would-be competitors were encouraged to contact Peter Browning at the MG Car Club office to join the mailing list and keep abreast of developments.

After all the initial development, the MGF Cup was announced on Motor Sport Day at the October 1997 London Motor Show. In fact MG Cars declared two separate championships: the MGF Cup and the MGF Abingdon Trophy. The latter was a lower-key championship to be administered by the MG Car Club and was aimed at the more impecunious motor sport enthusiast who, it was suggested, could drive his or her car to the event and, with luck, drive it home again afterwards.

The MGF Cup itself was announced as a 12-round, high-profile UK race championship, to be administered by the British Racing Drivers' Club and scheduled to take place during 1998 alongside major British Formula 3 events. There would be additional supporting races at the British Grand Prix and the Silverstone rounds of the Fédération Internationale de l'Automobile's GT and F3000 series. The total prize fund for the MGF Cup in its first year was over £90,000 and included a new MGF VVC as the prize for the overall champion. The number of competitors was limited to 30 to ensure the highest calibre of competition: the typical driver would be expected to have at the very least an RAC Motor Sports Association national 'B' competition licence or equivalent.

Whilst it was expected that most of the grid would be drawn from the ranks of the well-funded professionals, there would be room for the determined privateer. Wynne Mitchell remembered that during the Tomcat (Rover Turbo Coupé) championship there was one car that was always extremely well presented and was entirely built and maintained by the driver and his two friends. He commented: 'It all goes to show that at the other end of the spectrum from the full-blown professionals, if you have the diligence, time and expertise, you could build, run and maintain a very good car yourself.'

A month after the initial announcement, Chris Belton of Roversport reported that there had already been over 120 expressions of interest and by early December, when 380 people attended a special conference at Gaydon, there had been 500 serious enquiries from potential competitors and teams. At this presentation, MG Cars personnel stood alongside their motor sport colleagues to emphasise that the championship would be truly marketing led and would consequently receive a high level of support from the company. Following various announcements about the sporting and technical regulations, Chris Belton pointed out that, despite the high level of interest, the limit of 30 cars was

MGF Cup competition specification

Body
Type	Two-door two-seater steel monocoque, seam-welded and strengthened for increased torsional and bend stiffness and fitted with full integral roll cage
Chassis	Integral with body

Engine
Type	Four-cylinder all-alloy twin ohc K-series with through-bolt construction. Sealed unit, developed for racing with steel rods, crankshaft and forged pistons. Dry sump lubrication system
Capacity	1,796cc (110cu in)
Bore and stroke	80.0x89.3mm (3.15x3.52in)
Compression ratio	11.0:1
Maximum power	192bhp (190PS) at 7,250rpm (standard car 121bhp [120PS] at 5,500rpm)
Maximum torque	195Nm (143lb ft) at 6,000 rpm
Output per litre	107bhp (105PS)
Power-to-weight ratio	198bhp (195PS) per tonne

Transmission
Type	Close-ratio five-speed sealed unit with straight-cut gears and Quaiffe limited slip differential. AP Racing clutch

Suspension
Type	All-independent with Hydragas springs
Front	Hydragas with external damper and 3-setting anti-roll bar
Rear	Hydragas with external damper and 3-setting anti-roll bar
Brakes	AP Racing discs front and rear with driver-adjustable bias. Mintex controlled pads
Wheels	16in (406mm) alloy
Tyres	Dunlop Sport
Dry	210/605-R16 A8D 894
Wet	210/605-R16 A22W 404 compound (CR9000 pattern)

Dimensions
Length	3,910mm (153.94in)
Width	1,630mm (64.17in)
Height	1,200mm (47.2in) approx
Wheelbase	2,380mm (93.70in)
Track, front	1,400mm (55.12in)
Track, rear	1,410mm (55.51in)
Weight	970kg (2,138lb) (standard car 1,060kg/2,337lb)
Fuel capacity	55.0 litres (12.1 Imperial gallons, 14.53 US gallons)
Price	£24,000 (£200 deposit)

likely to stay although a rethink remained a slight possibility.

The racing was highly charged and exciting from the outset, with an interesting fairly cosmopolitan driver mix, including the vivacious Suzy Hart-Banks. Several drivers were in contention for the top slot but the eventual winner of the championship was James Rhodes of Team Firstair, although Alastair Lyall and Nick Kelly were both snapping at his heels. The series got off to a good start on 5 April 1998 at Silverstone, where former single-seater driver James Rhodes came from 11th place on the grid to drive his way to the winner's podium. Second place was taken by Brian Heerey with Suzy Hart-Banks third, just over five seconds behind the leader.

During 1999, the MGF Cup received sponsorship support from *Evo* magazine, a new publication aimed at performance car enthusiasts. Guy Pigounakis, MG's UK Brand Manager, stated: '*Evo* is a perfect partner for us; the readership profile is right in the middle of MGF territory'. Leading contenders in the championship included 18-year-old Katherine Legge (known to her friends as Penelope Pitstop) and the husband and wife team of Judit Forro-Hunter (from Hungary) and Jamie Hunter. At the head of the pack though was undoubtedly ex-Formula 3 racer Warren Hughes, driving for Team Firstair in a car supplied by Epsom Motor Group.

Hughes was off to a good start with a win in the opening round at Silverstone on Sunday 28 March 1999. The 12 venues involved a further three visits to the Northamptonshire circuit, including a 'double-header' during the MG Car Club weekend on 5 June and the final round of the series on 9 October. By about midway through the championship, it was already obvious that Warren Hughes's position was almost unassailable but even so there were some strong performances from other drivers – notably Jamie

Hunter, who came second behind Hughes at Silverstone on 10 July, during the British Grand Prix weekend. Hunter was leader for most of the race at a rain-soaked Brands Hatch in September (he was narrowly beaten by Kelly) but went on to triumph by winning the final race, in which Hughes – by now confirmed as championship winner – came third. Clearly Hunter would be one of the talents to watch in 2000.

Hughes told *Safety Fast!* magazine: 'It has been a fantastic season. We achieved what we set out to do, which was to dominate the series and it has been very useful for me. We have had some terrific publicity...' Among his goals for 2000 is a drive in the celebrated Vingt-Quatre Heures du Mans.

For 2000, the MGF Cup continued (still with 12 rounds) starting at Thruxton on 25-26 March with plans, as usual, to end up at Silverstone on 7-8-October. This time the Cup formed part of the BRDC Power Tour package that also included British GT2 and GT3 racing, National Saloons and Formula 3, while a particular highlight was the visit to Belgium's famous Spa circuit in September.

At the time of writing, it is too early to say what 2001 will bring; there is a lot of support for continuing the MGF Cup, although it was originally budgeted for three seasons with support from MG Cars. When it was in the running, Alchemy Partners announced that it would be initiating a 'vigorous motorsports activity' for MG, including a possible return to Le Mans with a Lotus-engineered car. Under Phoenix, MG will also see an increased motorsport activity, possibly with input from Lola and – cheekily taking a cue from Alchemy – a Le Mans entry is also not out of the question. Whatever the future of the factory-backed MGF Cup, however, there is no doubt that the MGF has acquitted itself well in motor sports terms; surely Cecil Kimber would have been proud?

Spot the skirmish in the background as Daniel Mason powers on ahead of the pack.

Back to Bonneville

As the MGF race series in Japan and France began to get under way, rekindling the sporting heritage of the MG marque, it was perhaps inevitable that the thoughts of someone, somewhere would turn to the idea of record-breaking. MG's background in this rarefied arena is virtually unrivalled.

Quietly demolishing expectations (as demonstrated at Le Mans, Sebring and elsewhere) had always been part of the MG make-up and so the idea of building a 200mph (321kmh) MG to take to North America's Bonneville Salt Flats had an obvious appeal. There was also the added factor

Californian Terry Kilbourne pilots the 1.4-litre turbocharged EXF to over 217mph on the Bonneville Salt Flats in August 1997.

that it was nearing the 40th anniversary of the debut of EX181, when Stirling Moss had first taken the diminutive streamliner to 245.64mph (395.31kmh). In an article about EX181, which appeared in the October 1997 issue of *MG World* magazine, I even speculated on the idea of a new MGF-based record breaker. When I wrote it, I had no idea of the exciting plans taking shape at Gaydon.

Chief Engineer and key member of the team who developed the car was Wynne Mitchell, who also had the MGF competition cars under his belt, not to mention a key role some 13 years earlier in the MG Metro 6R4 programme. 'Now, with the passage of time, we are not quite sure how it came about,' Mitchell claimed. 'It was something which was discussed at a much higher level than us and it was again with the benefit of some BMW influence on policy.' According to Mitchell, there was no great belief within BMW in one-make championships at the time; they were acceptable as a bit of extravagant corporate self-indulgence but it was felt that they were not a sensible commercial prospect.

'But it was eventually recognised that we should be doing something which showed the world that MG was better than its competitors,' Mitchell added. It did not take long for this thought process to filter down to reflecting on the record-breaking exploits of George Eyston and 'Goldie' Gardner. Mitchell explained that there was 'a long-standing association between MG and the Bonneville Salt Flats' and that somebody had said: 'Why don't we take an MG to Bonneville again?'

Probably the greatest advocate of this idea was Nick Stephenson, by this stage Rover's Director of Engineering and quite a 'petrol head' in his own right; despite his mild-mannered Clark Kent exterior, Stephenson enjoys nothing

more than fiddling with his 7-litre Chevrolet Corvette drag racer. Crucial support also came from Rover Group's Sales and Marketing Director, Tom Purves, a powerful former Rolls-Royce and BMW figure. Purves, who now heads BMW North America, happened to be a knowledgeable MG enthusiast of old and is a man with a keen eye for a 'unique marketing opportunity'.

However, the venture was not given official status, being described by company spokesmen as a spare-time activity by the relevant Rover personnel. Of course, if the exercise proved successful, then the company could happily ride on the coat-tails of the good publicity; if the venture did not succeed, it would have been a glorious bit of fun for all involved.

Gerry McGovern emphasised that the idea of the speed car was to project the image of the MGF: 'Whether it was done as a spare-time activity or as a proper exercise is pretty irrelevant. The idea was to take a stock car and maintain its identity, carrying over as many components as possible, while aiming at a vehicle that would ultimately beat the existing MG speed record. We knew that we wouldn't do that in the first shot but we had to start somewhere...'

The next thing that Wynne Mitchell and his colleagues heard was an announcement by Dr Dave Kewley, Rover Group's Director of Vehicle Validation. Kewley told them: 'We are going to do this chaps – we are going to have to do it – and the date is the 16th of August and I expect you to be there!' The importance of the date was that it was when the Southern California Timing Association's Speedweek took place and so the car could be timed properly. Of course, before this could happen, a number of rather fundamental things had to be put into place. Apart from the car itself, there were also other less tangible aspects such as planning

Mock-up of EX255 made its first appearance at a special briefing at Gaydon in May 1998, in company with EX181.

the necessary resources, transport, support and engineering logistics, and the little matter of locating a driver qualified to drive at the Bonneville Salt Flats. Eventually, all these would fall into place but at the outset, in the latter part of 1996, it seemed an almost impossible task.

Clearly, the word 'impossible' has been torn from Wynne Mitchell's dictionary, for he immediately began to sketch out the bare bones of what would be required. It was clear that the marketing people wanted a car that, in visual terms at least, bore a strong resemblance to the road-going MGF; so a diminutive tear-drop streamliner like EX181 was not an option. This immediately posed quite a problem, for a fundamental factor in achieving extremely high speeds is the degree to which the car can slice through the air. It is obvious that a car presenting a larger cross-sectional area would require much more power than a pure streamliner.

Ultimately EX181 had achieved 254.91mph (410.23kmh) from a supercharged 1,489cc (91cu in) engine (running on an exotic blend of 85 per cent methanol laced with nitrobenzene, acetone and sulphuric ether) and had taken an official class record based on the engine capacity. It was clear that a similar class record was not feasible with an MGF-sized car. Effectively, the team had to choose between trying to break the record for the fastest MG ever (by adopting a powerful larger engine far removed from that of the standard car) or trying to squeeze the maximum from the Rover K-series and thereby demonstrating the ability not just of the car but also of Rover's mainstream engine.

One option briefly considered was to shoehorn a Hart grand prix racing engine into an MGF shell and aim to shatter Phil Hill's 1959 MG record. However, this idea was swiftly discarded as being the wrong way to go – even though the basic idea still appealed and might form a starting point for a future effort. There was also the thought that as Speedweek was essentially an event for amateurs, a heavy-hitting approach by Rover might backfire.

'At first, the idea was to break the Stirling Moss and Phil Hill records, for which we were looking at a potential 300mph (483kmh),' Mitchell confirmed. 'For that, we would have needed something like 800–1,000bhp and we were looking at the sort of engines that would give us that. But common sense prevailed and, because of the short space of time, we decided that we would go with something which looked as much as possible like an MGF and using a K-series engine. Once we had settled on that, we set ourselves a target of 200mph (321kmh) – the objective being to be able to show that we had created the world's fastest MGF.'

It did not take long for the engineers, aerodynamicists and designers to begin their complementary tasks of putting flesh on the bones of what would become known as the MG EXF. This designation blended the old experimental register code and the new MG model name and, at the same time, neatly picked up the experimental baton from the EX-E concept car of 1985. David Woodhouse, a young designer in Gerry McGovern's team, was charged with the task of establishing the form of the car and he was keen to ensure that the car symbolised that slightly eccentric but pioneering British sense of adventure typified by George Eyston.

Starting point for shaping EX255 was wind-tunnel modelling and testing at MIRA, using an MGF base car.

Pre-war record-breaking with George Eyston

In 1930, record-breaking enthusiast Captain George Eyston was toying with the idea of establishing a speed record for a small car, the idea being to try to achieve 100mph (160kmh) – the so-called magic 'ton' – from a 750cc (46cu in) Class H car. There were various options open to him but through an old college friend, who happened to be an MG dealer, Eyston was introduced to Cecil Kimber and so a long association with the marque began. Kimber and his men were already working on a chassis design for a new MG Midget and this soon became the basis of the first MG record-breaker, known by its MG experimental number of EX120.

The basic chassis design was beefed up considerably and a special 743cc (45cu in) engine was mounted in it, initially unsupercharged but later adapted to run a Powerplus supercharger. For its first serious outing, with a view to aiming at the 100mph (160kmh) record before the end of 1930, EX120 was sent to the Montlhéry racetrack (just south of Paris) on Boxing Day. On the day before New Year's Eve, Eyston frustratingly failed to crack the 100mph (160kmh) mark in EX120, which was running on ethylene glycol racing fuel.

In the meantime, Sir Malcolm Campbell had begun to aim at the same target but using a car developed by deadly rivals Austin. Spurred on by Campbell's efforts, EX120 returned to Montlhéry in February 1931 and after ten tough days Eyston finally achieved his goal. More runs followed during 1931 until in September the car caught fire with Eyston at the wheel; the big man somehow extricated himself from the burning car and threw himself onto the track. Thanks to a Citroën 'Good Samaritan', who was using the track at the same time, Eyston was taken to hospital where he recovered successfully from his injuries. EX120 was less lucky and the remains were unceremoniously scrapped.

The seed had been sown, however, and so another

record car – EX127 (dubbed the Magic Midget) – was planned. This time a completely unique purpose-designed chassis was created, with input by MG draughtsman Jack Daniels and MG Competition's Reg Jackson; the target was now 120mph (193kmh) – two miles (3.2km) per minute. EX127 was ready while Eyston was still recovering from his injuries and so when EX127 ran for the first time in October, Eyston's friend and associate Ernest Eldridge was at the wheel. Eldridge

managed 110mph (177kmh) at Montlhéry but 120mph (193kmh) eluded him because of a burst radiator.

In December Eyston – now sporting a special asbestos fireproof suit – managed to achieve 114.77mph (184.70kmh) on an icy surface at Paris. Shortly after this, it was announced that record attempts would henceforth have to be established on the basis of the average of two runs in opposite directions. This understandably more or less ruled out the use of racetracks, which were

disinclined to close their circuits for the sole use of record breakers like Eyston. The result was that Eyston took EX127 to the long sandy beach at Pendine in South Wales and set up camp there early in the New Year of 1932.

On 8 February, both Eyston and EX127 were ready and set off to try to achieve 120mph (193kmh). On one run, Eyston was timed at 122mph (196kmh) but was frustrated to find that the official timekeeper's equipment had run out of ink.

Further runs failed to reach the necessary speeds and so for the time being Eyston remained unlucky. The following December, however, he was back at his favourite Montlhéry and this time achieved 120.56mph (194.02kmh). Further records were broken thereafter, sometimes with diminutive mechanic Bert Denly taking the place of Eyston (it has been suggested that MG deliberately reworked EX127 so that only the popular Denly would fit!).

Woodhouse's sketches often feature photocopied pictures applied to the background to reinforce the theme. In the case of EXF, his sketch included a picture of John Le Mesurier, the archetypal British 'gent' from so many 1950s and 1960s films and immortalised as the hapless but decent Sergeant Wilson in the classic BBC TV series Dad's Army. The first step, however, was for aerodynamicist Geoff Howell to work out how best to reduce the MGF's coefficient of aerodynamic drag to the minimum.

'We started off by doing some preliminary wind-tunnel work with an MGF bodyshell, which soon made it obvious that it would be necessary to extend the tail by 400mm (15.75in) and cut the screen down,' explained Mitchell. 'Having decided on some of the fundamental things, we then involved Gerry McGovern and Dave Woodhouse to mock-up the shape, in clay, which we needed to meet the aerodynamicist's requirements.' In fact, according to McGovern: 'We produced the master model in a 'skunk studio'; I got Dave Woodhouse to do his sketch, we got an MGF in, stripped it all down and built the back end out by 400mm (15.75in) with clay.' The clay, therefore, was laid straight on to the MGF shell – shades of the RSP Adder prototype.

Initially, McGovern was not too enamoured with the result: he telephoned Geoff Howell and told him in no uncertain terms that he didn't like the look of it. McGovern added: '...so he came over, we took the mock-up into the wind-tunnel and we worked on it there and then.' This was done in a remarkably short space of time and, using the resulting patterns, the car was built entirely at Gaydon but, according to Mitchell, the process was not a simple one. 'We employed people who were, frankly, not used to this type of work,' he admitted, 'and it was very difficult for them, taking

them some time to fully understand what we wanted. It was a long painful learning curve for all of us...'

Building a one-off car can be a cathartic experience, of course, for while everything still has to be fit for the purpose, there are no production, parts-sourcing or homologation headaches for the engineers to worry about. The canopy, for example, was blow-moulded by a glider canopy specialist, while the turbocharger plumbed into the engine was the type specified for the Ford Escort RS Cosworth, with the intercooler coming from an Aston Martin DB7. The chassis retained the standard Hydragas suspension – shorn of anti-roll bars as cornering ability was not high on the list of priorities.

Understandably, expertise in high-speed runs on the salt flats was not in great supply in the UK, so Mitchell and his Gaydon colleagues were very dependent on help from the USA. 'We, overseeing the engineering side of it, were in difficulty in as much as we did not really know what a Bonneville car was like,' commented Mitchell. 'We knew about race and rally cars but not a speed car: this meant that occasionally there were problems of communications – us trying to understand what they were getting at and them not understanding what our problems were!'

Work on the project required absolute dedication and there were several times when noses were well and truly to the grindstone. 'Some of the lads worked all through the night on two occasions,' Mitchell recalled. 'And, in fact, because we were inside Gaydon, they were sent home in the morning because they had violated all the union rules and they were not allowed to come in until a certain number of hours later. If anybody walked into the workshop, he was given a job, whether it was carrying, lifting, holding or painting – so we are indebted to lots of people who helped us.'

Whereas EXF (renamed EX253) had made do with a four-cylinder K-series engine, EX255 used a 4.8-litre Rover V8. This is the second of the original supercharged engines, producing over 940bhp on unleaded fuel.

Having begun to determine the basic layout and the choice of engine, other problems emerged: 'Initially, our own powertrain people could not allocate test bed space for the engine development, so we enlisted the help of Janspeed Engineering, working with the Rover Powertrain people to jointly develop the engine. We started off with an 1,800cc (110cu in) engine but during development it was considered that, probably, the 1,400cc (85cu in) version was the better way to go and that certainly proved to be the case. Between Rover Powertrain and Janspeed, the two of them developed the engine to give 328 horsepower (323PS) and over 330Nm (243lb ft) of torque.'

Don Kettleborough, also on the engineering side, noted: 'It soon became obvious that there would not be a torque problem with the EXF; there was a massive amount of torque. From a standing start, even on tarmac, the acceleration was pretty gradual and even though there was plenty of power there, it was not particularly severe on the transmission.' The choice of a 1.4-litre (85cu in) engine rather than the 1.8-litre (110cu in) unit and the fact that the normal head rather than the VVC version was chosen, may be a surprise to some. However, Don Kettleborough explained that not only did the 1.4 (85 cu in) engine allow the EXF to mimic the EX181 capacity class, it also possessed a stronger block than the 1.8 (110cu in) unit – obviously a critical factor with the high outputs and engine speeds. Similarly, the complexity of the VVC's variable valve cylinder head would have offered no advantage at such rarefied power outputs.

One of the EXF team's principal allies in the USA was Terry Kilbourne, a technician at a Land Rover dealer in California's Simi Valley, near Los Angeles. Kilbourne was already something of a seasoned veteran at the Salt Flats, with a licence to drive at over 200mph (321kmh) at Bonneville – a speed he had already beaten by 26mph (41kmh). 'He is a member of the Southern California Timing Association and, when he is not competing, he is one of the scrutineers,' Mitchell explained. 'He knows his way around the club, knows the pros and cons – all of which helped lift that part of the learning curve from our shoulders.'

Kilbourne's help was invaluable from the driving, engineering and organisational point of view: 'He came over to Gaydon for a day and pointed us in lots of directions of which we were unaware,' said Mitchell. When it comes to the bureaucracy of rules and regulations, the SCTA is no exception and here Kilbourne's knowledge was invaluable to the team. For example, five-stud wheel fixings seemed to be preferred and the rule book specified that if four-stud fixings were used, they would each have to be of at least half an inch (12.7mm) diameter; those of the MGF were 0.47in (12mm). There was also concern about 3¾in (95mm) pitch circle diameter fixings, so they used the Maestro van hub, which has a 4¼in (108mm) PCD, with 0.55in (14mm) studs.

The wheels, too, posed problems of their own as speed-record wheels are not exactly off-the-shelf items. 'Because we could not get an alloy wheel manufacturer to certify a wheel for this application,' Mitchell explained, 'we used the Rover 800 space-saver spare wheel, which is a steel wheel with a 4½in (114mm) rim.' The tyres were a Goodyear Bonneville type specially imported from the USA.

The inertia at the very high rotational speeds also gave rise to problems with the driveshaft boots splitting. 'There was concern because of the very high wheel speeds – quite astronomical compared with a standard car – which led to worries about these boots,' commented Mitchell. 'The driveshafts were basically to standard specification but

Rover's Neil Thomas points out the intricacies of EX255's layout to Andy Green, the pilot in waiting.

carefully balanced with additional banding around the joints to stop them blowing out but even so they did start to fail. That is something we had to address for future runs.'

To ensure that they were on the right track, Mitchell turned to his old friend and colleague Tony Pond – the two having worked together many times and most recently on development of the MGF Cup cars. 'We ran EXF at Gaydon late on a Sunday night,' related Mitchell. 'It was pitch dark and I asked Tony to come up and drive the car, at which point it had never turned a wheel. We towed it around the emissions circuit for three laps, to 'bed in' the brakes, before we went up the braking straight. We had to park a car at the bottom end of the straight, with its headlights lighting the way. Tony ran the car up and down about three times and he was able to say 'yes, the gear change is alright; the brake pedal isn't too heavy; the steering wheel is okay' – just to give us some feel for the car.

According to Mitchell, Pond probably did not exceed about 100mph (160kmh), 'but bear in mind that this was in the dark. I knew that Tony would give me... a balanced opinion on things we did not have the opportunity of trying beforehand. For example, we had a pedal box on EXF with separate twin master cylinders (specially made by Alan Reed) which we had not been able to try, so it was critically important to see if the brakes were too heavy or just right.'

Assessment of the custom braking system was important for Mitchell: 'It was a unique set-up, with no servo on it, a special throttle linkage which Alan had made (because we had to pull all the pedals back as the roll cage had to go past the driver's feet) and so the gearchange was difficult to get at. And we were able to establish with Tony's help that it was still acceptable. Finally, of course, I was confident that Tony would not shunt it; he went

a lot quicker than we thought he would go – the boys chased him back in the road car and said he was easily doing over 100mph (160kmh) as they could not keep up with him.'

When it came to ensuring that Kilbourne could be squeezed into the EXF, Mitchell and his colleagues took no chances. 'He had dimensioned a pin-man drawing I had made, with sizes from his backside to the top of his helmet and his overall height and so forth. And we had tried to fit the corresponding space into the car but even so it really was necessary for him to actually sit in the car and say 'yes, I can see' and 'yes, I have got enough head clearance'. He had a massive helmet, thick racing overalls, gauntlets and huge boots that came up his legs. He had chains or straps from his gloves to his waist, from his chin to his waist, so the constraints on him were very different to those we would normally be used to for a driver. We had to ensure that he could reach and see everything and all this had to be done inside a day.'

Preparations of this sort continued right until the eleventh hour and in fact the final work took place on the drive of Kilbourne's house in Simi Valley. 'We even had to wait for some bits which were impounded in customs until four o'clock of the afternoon we left,' Mitchell remembered. 'We finished the car at 5.30pm and left at 6.10pm to drive 640 miles (1,030km) through the night to Utah to set up for Bonneville – and the following morning we had to go straight out on to the site for scrutineering. It was hectic to say the least!'

Base camp was near Wendover, scene of so many previous MG record-breaking adventures. Mitchell described Wendover as 'a pretty small state-line town with basically a single road straight through it, with hotels along each side; it is essentially a gambling town on the border with Nevada.'

Pre-war record-breaking with 'Goldie' Gardner

Following George Eyston's exploits with EX120 and EX127, attention moved to a newer and larger car. EX135, which would become known as the Magic Magnette, was loosely based on the outstanding new MG K3 Magnette. In 1934, Cecil Kimber sold EX127 (apparently much to the disgust of Eyston) to German MG distributor and race driver Bobby Kohlrausch, who pushed the 750cc (46cu in) car to over 130mph (209kmh)

in May 1935 and to over 140mph (225kmh) in October of the same year.

At first, EX135 raced with a choice of two bodies – a 'track' body for record runs and a 'road racing' body for events such as the 1934 Manin Beg race. In October, Eyston used the new car to take a number of records at Montlhéry but a Nuffield crack-down on MG racing in 1935 put paid to further efforts later that year. It seems that various actions by Kimber, notably instructing that EX135 be fitted with non-Powerplus

superchargers (despite the fact that Eyston had a commercial interest in that company), only served to contribute to Eyston's disaffection

By the following year, however, there was a new champion of MG record breaking in the form of Captain 'Goldie' Gardner. He had acquired a special single-seater MG Magnette from Ronnie Horton and in August took the car to a Brooklands race meeting, where he managed to attract the interest of Cecil Kimber. Somehow Kimber managed in

turn to sweet-talk Lord Nuffield into sanctioning a limited return to MG record breaking and so in October Gardner ran the ex-Horton car at Frankfurt, breaking his own flying mile and kilometre records.

The following February saw the Eyston EX135 advertised for sale at London's Bellevue Garage for £425 and Gardner promptly bought it and returned it to Abingdon for further development. At Frankfurt, Gardner had been watched by Auto Union's Eberan von Eberhorst, who

Of course, the MG team was not there to gamble but to play on the salt. Their hotel was a combined casino/hotel and there was a lot of noisy gambling in the area where they sat for meals. 'They don't really like motor sport people there,' commented Mitchell, 'because we get up in the morning and go out on the salt all day long when, of course, we cannot be inside gambling!'

At Bonneville, the salt is just outside the town; to get there the team had to drive on the main road towards Utah and then branch off onto a concrete road which was straight for about two miles (3.2km). At the end of that, there was a 3½-mile (5.6km) drive across the salt to the pit area. The salt flats are not for the fair-skinned or faint-hearted, Mitchell explained: 'The place is incredibly hot. There is no shade and the reflection from the surface is such that you even get sunburnt up your nostrils! I did not think that it was quite as hot as I had expected but you certainly could not stand the heat for very long.' Dave Kewley is less delicate in his illustration of the power of the sun: 'If you wear shorts, Bonneville is the best place to get your patented dry-roasted nuts!'

Fortunately, the MG team had brought along a pair of air-conditioned Winnebago motorhomes and these were very welcome bolt-holes during the inevitable long periods between runs. 'There were two courses and, because it was a new car, we had to qualify for both the short and the long course,' elucidated Mitchell, 'meaning that we had to exceed 175mph (282kmh) over the short course – and that is timed between the second and the third mile. Now on the first run, we only achieved 168mph (270kmh), which was quite disappointing but we were suspicious that the turbo intercooler system wasn't working efficiently'. Evidence for this came from the fact that the

17-gallon (20.4-US gallon, 77-litre) water tank was comparatively cold and yet it was impossible to keep a hand on the turbocharger intercooler, as it was so hot.

'We suspected that the pump was not working and after we had changed it, we did 183mph (294kmh) on our second run which was satisfactory for qualifying. We then qualified for the long course, achieving 195mph (313kmh) on the first run but we were still not happy that the turbo system, which was obviously vital to achieving the necessary power output, was working properly.' After a short amount of head-scratching and lateral thinking, it was realised that the larger capacity air pump on one of the Winnebagos might be sufficient and in the event this proved to be the right answer.

A clue that the Winnebago pump might prove beneficial came as a result of another improvisation that had already taken place. 'We had taken over with us a cradle with a battery on it and a water pump and some hoses,' explained Mitchell, 'because the intention had been to keep the liquids cool between runs. We intended to drain the system after every run, to cool it and only refill it at the last minute. The cradle on wheels was intended to do that but we found that its performance was not really up to the task. So in Los Angeles the lads went out and bought a Winnebago pump as we knew that its capacity was far in excess of the pump fitted in the car. The actual Winnebago we were using had an identical pump fitted to it, so we were pretty confident that it would be better – and it was!'

'The Winnebago pump improved the cooling through the turbo intercooler and in addition we super-cooled the fuel and water by buying dry ice. We could not apply the dry ice directly, as it would simply evaporate, so the lads came up with a scheme where they kept the dry ice in plastic bags.

had helpfully suggested that what Gardner needed was a specially designed aerodynamic body. So during 1937 EX135 was used as the basis of a new car complete with a Reid Railton-designed body. Railton had designed John Cobb's striking Land Speed Record car and so it was no surprise that the 'new EX135' was hardly less breathtaking in appearance.

The new car was so thoroughly changed from the old EX135 that perhaps it should in fairness have been given a new number, even

though much of the bodywork was done away from Abingdon. To the general public it was the 'Gardner MG Record Car' but even so MG people continued to refer to it as EX135 and so the association continued.

A year after his discussion with von Eberhorst, Gardner was back at Frankfurt and broke the 300kmh (186mph) barrier for both the flying mile and flying kilometre Class G records; needless to say, the Germans were impressed by the efforts of the gallant Englishman and his 'little' car.

In May 1939 Gardner was back in Germany again and this time broke the 200mph (322kmh) barrier in both 1,100 and 1,500cc (67 and 92cu in) categories – by the simple expedient of reboring the engine in situ after one record and then going out to take the other two days later. Needless to say, Gardner would have liked to take EX135 to even greater heights later that year but the outbreak of war in September meant that there were other more pressing matters to contend with than record breaking.

We got the fuel down to about 1°C (34°F) and the water down to 3-4°C (37-39°F) – it took over three hours to cool the thing down – and filled this lot, virtually on the starting line, and we just blasted up to 217mph (349kmh).'

The cooling system of a state-of-the-art speed car like EXF is quite unlike that of a conventional car. 'The cooling system for the engine runs through another cooler positioned approximately where the passenger would be (in a normal MGF) and also circulating through that was water from a 25-gallon (30-US gallon, 114-litre) water tank at the front. There were no radiators in the car at all,' Mitchell divulged. 'We had two pumps pumping water from that water tank but we had just one of them pumping from a 17-gallon (20.4-US gallon, 77-litre) water tank alongside the driver to the intercooler, which was positioned above the gearbox, between the turbo and the intake manifold.'

Part of the benefit of having a large water tank is the superior aerodynamic flow – no need for cooling vents – but also the significant ballast effect. 'You cannot have aerodynamic aids on the car to increase stability because they will also increase drag,' Mitchell elucidated, 'so you have to have as smooth a car as you possibly can. And the way in which you make it stable is to allow it to be heavy but with

the weight in the right place.' The car weighed 1,430kg (3,153lb) without the driver. In addition to the 25 gallons (30 US gallons, 114 litres) of water in the front, there was also an oil tank (the engine had a dry sump lubrication system) and a 30-litre (6.6-Imperial, 7.9-US gallon) fuel tank. The 17-gallon (20.4-US gallon, 77-litre) water tank for the turbo was alongside the driver and there was a fuel cooler in the boot area. 'So altogether, the EXF ended up very much heavier than the standard car,' commented Mitchell, 'but nevertheless it still suffered from wheel-spin until fourth gear!'

Mitchell explains that getting off the line was quite tricky: 'On the very first 168mph (270kmh) short course run, to quote Terry Kilbourne, 'we used up a lot of real estate'. In other words, he was on the rev-limiter in first, second and third. Subsequently, therefore, on his advice, the car was pushed off the line up to 30-40mph (48-64kmh) to save him spinning the wheels but nevertheless, until he was in fourth gear, we did not have the grip needed.'

In order to get the car up to speed, therefore, it was necessary to give it some help and this was done by nudging it with another vehicle. One of Terry Kilbourne's team of three (all speed event competitors in their own right) had fitted a board on the front of his vehicle and so this was used to push against the parachute housing at the back of EXF. 'It had not been clear to us at first why this was being done,' Mitchell confessed. 'Because some of these cars are doing 200-300mph (322-483kmh), they are so high-geared that they have great difficulty in getting off the line. So instead of slipping the clutch, they are assisted up to 40mph (64kmh).'

On the long course, the car was timed from three miles (4.8km) on to the run and then the terminal velocity was measured at 130 feet (39.6m) after the end of the five miles (8km). 'I think we did something like 215mph (346kmh) between the fourth and fifth mile (sixth and eighth kilometre) mark, with a terminal velocity of 217.4mph (349.8kmh). At that point, the engine was doing about 7,600rpm – it was absolutely screaming.'

The result was impressive but even so the perfectionist in Wynne Mitchell was not satisfied: 'We could probably have squeezed a little more speed out of it, because we have larger rear tyres, which we had fitted originally. But when we did not achieve the 175mph (281kmh) required on the short-course run, we had changed the gearing simply by changing the tyres and the attitude of the car because we were afraid that we were lacking power. But in the end, as I said, it proved to be the inefficient turbo-cooler that had been the root of the problem.'

In the end, though, the EXF team achieved what it had set out to do – to run the fastest speed in an MGF-derived car, have some fun and set the scene for a possible return.

EX255 and Bonneville 1998

Wynne Mitchell admitted that the weather smiled on them – something that certainly cannot be guaranteed: 'It is very much a lottery at Bonneville: it rained while we were there and so for one day we were not allowed to run at all. We had to escape off site because it floods. It rained in the afternoon and we had to flee the salt. We were not allowed on it the following day and in fact we could not go back until halfway through the day after that. Even then, only the long course was usable and we still had not qualified. The car queued for five and a quarter hours in the sun, waiting its turn. On the day we achieved 217mph (349kmh), the salt had dried out quite well and there was a slight cross/tail wind, so conditions were good.'

It had been a promising toe in the water for MG's new record-breaking exploits and even before the August 1997 run, plans were being sketched out for a return in 1998; Terry Kilbourne's 217mph (349kmh) ride helped firm them up. The next time, however, Nick Stephenson was determined that MG would be back in a big way, with the goal of breaking that elusive 300mph (483kmh) barrier. As Stephenson said at the time: 'Project EXF is the culmination of a passion within the company to see MG return to Bonneville – a 'back-to-the-future' adventure. It is terrific to see the pent-up enthusiasm within our talented design and engineering team resulting in an achievement so true to the spirit of MG. It is fitting that they should be rewarded with the knowledge that they have produced the fastest production MG ever. My colleagues on the Rover Group board gave the project their blessing in June and we are delighted to see the team exceed their target of 200mph (322kmh) in such a short period of time. They cannot wait to return to the salt next year with their sights firmly set on the records of Stirling Moss and Phil Hill.'

Hardly had the EXF team returned home when the boffins at Gaydon were already sketching out their plans for a return in 1998. Wynne Mitchell recalled that the debate was whether they should go for a proper streamliner with the existing engine or continue with something that looked more like a standard MGF. The dilemma was that the latter would require a lot more power, which might rule out using the K-series engine. The preferred course was for the car to look as much as possible like an MGF and to use the K-series engine derivative. 'I think that we, as engineers, recognised that you could get more mileage out of convincing the general public that this is certainly an MGF-based car,' commented Mitchell.

While shattering records obviously had its attractions, there was the nagging thought that trying to go all-out for new records might produce the wrong reaction among the regulars at Bonneville. 'The class for 1,500cc (91cu in) cars is about 105mph (169kmh),' explained Mitchell, 'and we would have totally eaten this but we thought no, that would not be fair on those people who came there as amateurs.' The official event is in September, when the FIA attends and monitors the fuel and runs have to be in two directions within an hour of each other (like the Land Speed Record). The MG team preferred to go in the 'fun' week and see how quickly the car could go.

In designing a second generation MG speed car, Mitchell and his colleagues were able to learn a lot from their visit in 1997. 'Dave Woodhouse came out and looked over all the other Speedweek competitors,' said Mitchell. 'I am sure that

Confident of success, MG Cars prepared postcards to celebrate what they hoped would be 'the fastest MG ever'.

MG EX255 Bonneville 1998
"The fastest MG ever" Driver: Andy Green

he would very much like us to do a streamliner, with which he could allow his imagination to run riot, but we had to balance enthusiasm for such an idea with commercial logic.' By December, the options were short-listed and Don Kettleborough made a presentation at Christmas; the objective by now was to crack the magic 300mph (483kmh) barrier by going back to Bonneville in style. 'Now that the next car was an official project, everyone began voicing an opinion!', Mitchell pointed out.

A press conference was called at the Heritage Museum in May 1998. There Nick Stephenson and Dave Kewley set out their objectives and revealed a mock-up of the car – not yet a running prototype. Alongside the new car – christened EX255 – were EXF, now retrospectively named EX253 (EX254 was the MGF Super Sports show car) and EX181, brought in from the nearby museum display and looking remarkably diminutive alongside the relatively massive MGF-based cars.

Beside the two engineers was the third figure of Andy Green, who had risen to fame as the successful pilot of Thrust SSC, which had broken both the Land Speed Record and the sound barrier at the Black Rock Desert in Nevada the previous year. Andy Green explained that he had first heard about the MG record car at the Guild of Motoring

MG EXF (EX253) **specification**

Body type	Steel and carbon-fibre reinforced epoxy panels based on MGF monocoque. Full tonneau with forward-hinged canopy and 'bubble' over driver. Paint finish Brooklands Green. Chrome Moly safety cage. Six-point seat belts with leg and arm restraints. Seat moulded to fit Terry Kilbourne
Chassis	Front body structure to rear bulkhead standard MGF
Engine	All-aluminium alloy Rover K-series four-cylinder fitted with Garret AiResearch T2 turbocharger and Aston Martin DB7 water/air intercooler. Omega racing pistons
Cooling System	No radiator; recirculating 110-litre (24.2-Imperial, 29.1-US gallon) tank with specially designed heat-exchanger
Capacity	1433cc (87.4cu in)
Maximum power	328bhp (324PS) at 7,000rpm
Maximum torque	336Nm (247lb ft)
Output per litre	229bhp (226PS)
Power-to-weight ratio	229bhp (226PS)/tonne
Transmission	Modified Rover 220 Turbo race specification transmission and clutch

Suspension	
Front	Double wishbone, based on MGF. Non-interconnected Hydragas units
Rear	Double wishbone, derived from MGF. Anti-roll bars deleted
Brakes	Custom-made twin-servo braking system
Wheels	15in (381mm) 4½J steel wheels (space-saver from Rover 800) with flush-fitting disc covers
Tyres	Goodyear 15in (381mm) diameter slick tyres: front 5in (127mm) wide, rear 4.5in (114mm) wide

Dimensions	
Length	4,310mm (169.7in)
Width	1,625mm (64.0in)
Height	1,200mm (47.2in)
Wheelbase	2,380mm (93.7in)
Front track	1,390mm (54.7in)
Rear track	1,400mm (55.1in)
Weight	1,430kg (3,153lb) without driver

Coefficient of drag	
Cd	0.24
Frontal Area	1.53sq m
CdA	0.37sq m

Performance	
Maximum speed	Achieved 217.40mph (349.87kmh) on 20 August 1997

Post-war record-breaking

After the Second World War, EX135 was taken out of mothballs and rebuilt with the surviving 750cc (46cu in) engine. Record-breaking in Germany was, for the time being at least, neither practical nor politically feasible and so Gardner turned his attention to Belgium and the Jabbeke highway. At the end of October 1946, EX135 took the 750cc (46cu in) Class H record for the flying mile at over 150mph (241kmh) at Jabbeke. During 1946 and the following year, EX135 continued to run with an

MG engine but, due to Nuffield indifference to record breaking, without direct MG input.

Disagreements led to the car running with a Jaguar engine in 1948 as the 'Gardner Record Car' but, thanks largely to the ministrations of John Thornley, Gardner and his car were running an MG engine again the following year. The ostensibly six-cylinder engine ran as a three-cylinder 500cc (31cu in) unit with a special Syd Enever-designed crankshaft in 1949 and in July 1950 one of the remaining three pistons was removed to make a two-

cylinder 330cc (20cu in) engine, with which Gardner took Class I and J records respectively.

In 1950 and 1951, EX135 also ran with either an XPAG MG TD Midget-type four-cylinder engine or a Wolseley 6/80-based six but an accident at Bonneville in August 1952 precipitated the 67-year-old Gardner's retirement from the record breaking arena. Even though Gardner and his car would no longer provide front-page copy for the *Salt Lake Tribune* or the news pages of *Motor Sport*, it would not be long before MG's old friend

George Eyston was back in the record-breaking hot seat. With the support and encouragement of Eyston, and financial backing from Wakefield Castrol, Syd Enever and his chassis engineer Terry Mitchell were soon beavering away at EX179. This was an all-new record breaker based on a spare chassis from Enever's EX175 sports car proposal (a replacement for the T-series).

EX135 was undoubtedly still a good starting point and so EX179 not surprisingly looked quite similar. Fitted with an XPEG engine, the new EX179

Writers' dinner in October 1997 and had expressed interest in getting involved as adviser. 'As we worked with Andy, who is a fine engineer as well as an experienced high-speed driver, it soon became obvious that he would be the best candidate to drive EX255,' Stephenson declared.

When the decision was made to go for the outright record – coincidentally requiring a speed of at least 255mph (410kmh) – it was clear that the K-series engine could not be expected to deliver the 900 horsepower required. However, this time, there were no thoughts of buying in an exotic racing engine; rather the team began to look at building on the sound basis of the latest development of the classic ex-Buick Rover V8 engine. This had the added advantage that it had seen service in both the MGB GT V8 and the MG RV8. Even so, the task of extracting almost five times the output of a production Land Rover Discovery V8, and putting that power through the wheels, would not be an easy one. 'We have a very strong cross-bolted engine block, bored out to 4.8 litres (293cu in),' Nick Stephenson explained, 'and we had some very carefully prepared components, such as crankshafts, to handle the high internal stresses involved.'

As soon as EX255 was at Wendover, the MG Competitions team completed work on it. New side exhaust outlet was a consequence of the change from supercharger to turbochargers.

It was obvious that forced induction would be needed but the question was what to use – supercharger or turbocharger? 'Speaking very honestly, we intentionally said 'pressure charging' because we are looking at both options,' Stephenson confessed at Gaydon. 'We have test bed work going on at present and we haven't decided yet which to go for, although twin superchargers seems most likely.'

For the transmission, the team went for a modified Hewland type NMT six-speed sequential transaxle, installed upside down with a 'step-up' overdrive gear between the engine and gearbox to achieve the required gear ratio and to lower the engine within the car into the bargain. Taking the power too was a 5½in (140mm) triple-plate sintered AP Racing clutch. 'The reason we went for this particular gearbox was simply to handle the torque,' explained Dave Kewley. 'The fact that it was sequential was almost incidental, although it does give the driver less to worry about.' Nick Stephenson added that as the installation used a transaxle configuration, '90 per cent of our in-house production gearboxes wouldn't have been suitable for the purpose in any case'.

EX255 was finished in a particularly striking modern interpretation of the traditional MG 'EX green'. This colour, from paint specialists PPG, was called Andes Green and the pun was not lost on the driver-to-be, who confessed during his talk at Gaydon that his first sight of the new car had been when he pulled the covers off a few minutes earlier. The body design of EX255 was a clear development of EXF/EX253, with a similar 400mm (15.75in) tail extension, although because the engine chosen was now a longitudinally mounted Rover V8, there was also an extra 250mm (9.84in) let into the wheelbase. The engine and transaxle assembly was carried in a specially fabricated

---

visited Bonneville in August 1954, where it was driven by Eyston and Ken Miles to achieve some endurance records. Thereafter it went on to serve as an important part of MG's record-breaking exploits for the next five years, including taking no fewer than 16 class records in August 1956, in the hands of Ken Miles and Johnny Lockett.

By the following year, however, the art of MG record breaking had been shifted into an all-new ball game with the creation of EX181, known as the 'roaring raindrop' on account of its drop-tank

inspired tear-drop shape. A large number of model studies were made for this project (ranging from the clever to the seemingly absurd) but in the end it was the simplest shape that won through, developed almost entirely by Terry Mitchell under the supervision of Syd Enever. Engine power was provided by a prototype MGA Twin Cam unit, the production car being still a year from official launch.

In August 1957 EX181, finished in metallic silver blue, was shipped out to Bonneville where it was tested by top

American driver Phil Hill. He was intended to be the 'warm-up man' and so, despite some very promising runs, was not allowed to set any official records in EX181 – at least not for the time being. A week after Hill's first successful test runs, Stirling Moss flew in and prepared to shatter a few records with the almost sure-fire certainty that MG efforts seemed to guarantee.

Despite problems with the fickle weather, Moss was eventually rewarded with a two-way average of 254.64mph (409.80kmh) on 23 August,

breaking five international Class F records in the process. The week beforehand, EX179 had also taken more records using a 948cc (58cu in) A-series Morris Minor engine.

EX181 was stripped down and rebuilt for 1959 (refinished in the more familiar metallic green) and in October returned to Bonneville for what would prove to be its final visit. This time, Phil Hill was behind the wheel and he was rewarded with a top two-way speed of 254.91mph (410.23kmh), which still stands as the fastest official speed for an MG.

tubular steel support structure fixed into the monocoque, along with a strong cage around the driver.

However, right from the earliest stage, the EX255 team was always sailing close to the wind. The car shown in May was a mock-up, as the real car was still in the early stages of construction, and the promised shake-down tests in front of the press never materialised because there was simply no time to spare. Then in July, barely two weeks before the car was due to be despatched to the USA, it was decided that the superchargers, upon which the engineers had pinned their hopes, were not up to the task in the extreme conditions in which they were expected to operate. Superchargers had been preferred for various reasons – not all of them engineering-led – but now there was no option but to bite the bullet and switch to turbochargers.

Needless to say, changing the method of pressure-charging is easier to say than to do. As the car had been tightly packed around the supercharged V8 unit, changing to turbochargers meant a great deal of re-routing of other equipment, much of it done on the ground at Wendover. Visible changes included the exhaust outlets, which now emerged through a plate on the side just aft of the nearside air intake vent. Having abandoned superchargers, the engine itself was set up at Janspeed and found to be giving a reliable 942bhp (929PS) on the standard unleaded Fina pump petrol.

At Wendover, Nick Stephenson, Dave Kewley and the team set up camp in a former Second World War bomber hanger but it was clear from the outset that this adventure was to be no sinecure. The late change of plan meant that there was a great deal of catching up to do, as the car had not even turned a wheel in anger before being shipped

across the Atlantic. Among the small group of people invited to witness the intense activity at firsthand was Andrew Roberts. He recorded in *MG Enthusiast* that the Monday of Speedweek was a crunch day for the team: 'Every member of the team was working flat out and Andy Green was quietly applying Letraset to the instrument panel, oblivious to the constant throng of visitors to the hangar.'

By late afternoon on the same day, preparation had advanced sufficiently for the first firing up of the engine. At just after five o'clock, the mighty V8 burst into life and the rasping engine note reverberated around the hangar as though the ghost of a long-forgotten B17 had returned to haunt the airfield. However, there was no time to pause for such reflection, for shake-down testing was programmed for 2pm the following day and there were plans for a photo-call the following evening when, hopefully, the light would be at its best.

The team, already tired and struggling to meet the impossible deadline, worked right through the night but by daybreak it was obvious that things were not going to plan. Problems with a clutch seal – buried, with the engine and transmission, deep within the heart of the densely packed body – meant that the car would not be able to run without an estimated 32 hours of further work. This truly looked as though it would be the straw to break the camel's back. By Tuesday evening, Nick Stephenson announced that it looked as though the hard work had been in vain; he knew that he could not expect his men to work through another night.

Wednesday was declared a day of rest but, although they were downhearted, the men were not broken. It transpired that the hangar being used by the team had fairly recently

Ken Moss and the Blind Speed Record

With the cancellation of mainstream MG record-breaking efforts, it seemed likely that both EXF and the EX255 would spend the rest of their days in the Heritage Museum. However, in 1999, the original MGF record car received a new lease of life for a rather unusual purpose. Ken Moss was a policeman on duty one Saturday in November 1992 when a terrible accident very nearly cost him his life; doctors gave him a five per cent chance of survival.

Despite this, Moss managed to make a remarkable recovery but the injuries cost him both eyes.

Ken Moss is not the sort of person to give up without a fight and he was determined to prove to the world that, with the right aid and encouragement, disabled people can do many things others assume to be impossible; driving a car is just one example. However, Moss was not content with driving a car – he wanted to set a speed record for an unaccompanied blind driver.

Established in 1915, St Dunstan's is a special charity catering for the needs of blind ex-service men and women and Moss's ambition was exactly the sort of independence of spirit that it was intended to foster. With the help of Neil Swan (Head of Fund Raising and Legacies at St Dunstan's), it was a short step – apparently following a discussion in a pub – to recruiting the aid of Tony Pond and, through him, the MG competitions team and Wynne Mitchell. In addition, Swan was able to secure the

crucially important help of Dr Graham Rood and Paul Kellett, scientists at the Defence Evaluation and Research Agency (DERA) at Farnborough, Kent, who could provide the special technology that Moss would need to provide his 'eyes and ears'.

While the MG team adapted the EXF to its new task, the DERA scientists developed a special guidance system (using a clever combination of aural and tactile aids) to assist Moss on his ride at DERA's Boscombe Down test facility. DERA produced the gyro,

computer system and specially adapted Tornado GR7 helmet; bleeps relayed through the helmet would tell Moss if he began to veer off course, while a tactile indicator fitted to his neck provided guidance, through a pulsating sensation, on when to change gear at optimum revs.

Moss's close ally and tutor was the indomitable Tony Pond, who simply summed up his pupil thus: 'The last time he drove a car by himself he had nearly died: in my view, the guy is a hero.' Prior to the unaccompanied run, Moss

(with Pond as a passenger) drove the BMW Alpina chase car, in which he promptly broke the accompanied blind driver record at 154mph (247kmh). During the afternoon of Saturday 16 October 1999, however, it was the turn of the MG EXF and soon after one o'clock Moss took the car up to 131mph (210kmh), his run being filmed by BBC Television for its popular *Tomorrow's World* programme.

'I have demonstrated that given the right support, disabled people are just as

capable as able-bodied people,' Moss said afterwards, adding that he wanted to 'raise awareness and funds for St Dunstan's, who provided my rehabilitation and training and helped me to 'live' again.' The record cannot be categorised as 'official' (for that a driver needs a competition licence, not available to blind people) but that is surely a technicality; nobody could deny the incredible courage needed to drive a car at such speeds without the ability to see anything at all.

Resplendent in special Andes Green paint, EX255 glistens in early evening sunlight on the eerie Bonneville landscape.

been used for filming Con Air and among the various effects left behind by the film crew was a sink complete with fittings. Team member Dave Paget found that one of the washers attached to the sink was potentially suitable for machining to suit as a repair for EX255. Andrew Roberts recorded the outcome in *MG Enthusiast*: 'So, in the true tradition of motor sport mechanics the world over, a machining shop was found in Wendover and the one-time plumbing accessory was given a much more dramatic lease of life. Installed, it was to prove the perfect seal.'

The Thursday proved wet, with dramatic thunderstorms, and so the MG team worked on EX255 afresh while welcoming occasional visits from curious Speedweek competitors, prevented from venturing on to the now moist salt. The following day saw better weather once more and EX255 was made ready to roll out of the hangar. The engine was fired up but almost immediately a small oil leak manifested itself – perhaps another ghost but this time from MG's own past. To prevent the risk of engine damage, it was reluctantly decided to call time and abandon hope of a shakedown run. As the cameras clicked, EX255 was rolled out on to the salt in the evening for one last time but sadly the hoped-for run on the salt never materialised.

Nick Stephenson announced in the wake of the decision to postpone the attempt: 'We are confident that this car is a winner but time was not on our side... We will re-schedule our record attempt for the near future.' Echoing the sentiment were Nick Vandervell, Corporate Affairs Manager for Fina Plc (the project's main sponsor) and Andy Green. Vandervell stated: 'It would have been great to exceed the record at the 50th Speedweek festivities in Bonneville... I am sure they will succeed.' Andy Green pronounced: 'Our team have produced a formidable machine that is easily capable of achieving our

aims. This is a great car and I am excited at continuing my association with the team and the prospect of driving the fastest MG ever.'

For a while, there seemed to be a faint hope of returning later the same year, although there was no certainty that Andy Green could afford the additional holiday time away from his 'day job' of flying RAF Tornados. At the end of September, MG Cars issued a press release entitled 'MG Team Plan Return to Bonneville', with positive words from Fina's Nick Vandervell stating: 'The team has our enthusiastic support for next year's record attempt at the 51st Bonneville Speedweek.' It was clear, therefore, that the decision had been made to work towards a return in August 1999.

However, changes in the way that BMW ran the Rover Group operation dominated all the company's affairs from October 1998 through into the early part of 1999. In the New Year, further surprises came as first Rover Group Chairman Walter Hasselkus left, followed by Bernd Pischetsrieder and Wolfgang Reitzle. By March, there were new faces in charge of both BMW in Munich and Rover in Warwick.

Seen in the context of the major battle at the head of the company, it is easy to understand how the small matter of MG record breaking slipped off the list of priorities entirely. When Tom Purves accepted a senior position at BMW North America in March 1999 and Nick Stephenson left the company altogether just a month later, it seemed that – for the time being at least – thoughts of shattering that 1959 record would have to wait for another day. By May 2000, however, Nick Stephenson was back at Rover Group, and one of his early tasks was to review all MG projects shelved by BMW. With regard to record breaking, all Stephenson will say for now – with a big grin on his face – is 'watch this space!'.

The team behind EX255 pose proudly behind their charge – sadly a new record was not within their grasp.

MG EX255 **specification**

Body type	Steel and carbon-fibre reinforced epoxy panels based on MGF monocoque. Underfloor area modified with three-stage step diffuser to improve aerodynamics. Full tonneau with forward- hinged canopy and 'bubble' over driver. Paint finish PPG Andes Green. Chrome Moly safety cage. Six-point seat belts with leg and arm restraints. Sheet aluminium alloy seat moulded to fit Andy Green
Chassis	Front body structure to rear bulkhead standard MGF. Rear extended with specially fabricated spaceframe of 2in (50mm) diameter mild-steel seamless tubing
Engine	All-aluminium alloy Rover V8 fitted initially with twin superchargers, changed at 11th hour to turbochargers. Engine block reinforced and cross-bolted. Crankshaft machined from solid steel billet with 2.1in (53mm) big-end journals and 2.25in (57mm) diameter main bearings. Cylinder heads specially engineered with large valves and improved porting. Inlet valves 1.9in (48mm) diameter, exhausts 1.6in (40mm) diameter. Omega forged pistons, with forged H-section steel connecting rods. Dry sump lubrication with twin scavenge pumps. Laminova-type oil cooler plumbed into water system and/or air blast cooler under rear of car. Sequential fuel injection system with self-learning fuelling strategy
Cooling system	No radiator; recirculating 150-litre (33.0-Imperial gallon, 39.6-US gallon) tank with specially designed heat-exchanger
Capacity	4,800cc (293cu in)
Bore and stroke	94.0mmx86.4mm (3.70inx3.40in)
Maximum power	900bhp (887PS) at 8,000rpm with 16psi (1.1bar) boost (942bhp (929PS) in final form)
Maximum torque	800Nm (590lb ft)
Output per litre	187bhp (184PS)
Power-to-weight ratio	642bhp (633PS)/tonne
Transmission	Modified Hewland type NMT six-speed sequential transaxle installed upside down with a step-up gear between engine and gearbox to achieve overall gear ratio and to lower the engine within the car. Triple-plate sintered AP racing clutch, 5.5in (140mm) diameter

Suspension

Front	Double wishbone, based on MGF. Non-interconnected Hydragas units. Front subframe solidly mounted using MGF Cup suspension mounts
Rear	Double wishbone, derived from MGF but raised in body to reduce aerodynamic drag. Geometry and travel modified to improve anti-squat, give clearance to underbody and accommodate narrower rear track
Brakes	Four-wheel ventilated cast-iron discs as MGF Cup car. Disc diameter increased from 260mm (10.24in) to 310mm (12.20in). No servo. Uprated competition calipers with high temperature pads rated to 800°C (1,472°F). Additional retardation provided by twin braking parachute system stored in 400mm (73.70in) diameter tubes; 12ft (3.66m) diameter high speed, 15ft (4.57m) diameter low speed chutes
Wheels	Mooneyes steel wheels with flush-fitting disc covers. Front wheels 4.5Jx16in (406mm); rear 7Jx18in (457mm)
Tyres	Mickey Thompson tyres rated to 375mph (603kmh). Front 24.5x7.5x16in (622x190x406mm); rear 26.5x9x18in (673x229x457mm)

Dimensions

Length	4,560mm (179.53in)
Width	1,630mm (64.17in)
Height	1,170mm (46.06in)
Wheelbase	2,630mm (103.54in) (250mm (9.84in) greater than standard MGF)
Front track	1,400mm (55.12in) (as standard MGF)
Rear track	1,250mm (49.21in) (reduced from standard 1,400mm (55.12in))
Weight	1,400kg (3,086lb) without driver
Fuel capacity	30 litres (6.6 Imperial, 7.9 US gallons), supplied by sponsor Fina

Coefficient of drag

Cd	0.180-0.195 dependent upon additional aerodynamic aids employed
Frontal area	1.48sq m (15.93sq ft)
CdA	0.266-0.289 (sq m), 2.867-3.106 (sq ft)

Performance

Maximum speed	Theoretically c300mph (c483kmh)
Fire safety	Two carbon-fibre AFFF 4000R fire extinguisher systems: front bay and cockpit, and engine bay

Towards the future

Even at the time of launch, the designers were already giving some thought as to how the MGF could be developed, albeit some way down the road. For obvious reasons, relatively little happened in this regard until the car was in full production but once the MGF was running down the line at Longbridge, it was possible for the engineering and design teams to give some thought to the future.

At the time of the first test drives, in September 1995, one of the engineering team confided to me that already there had been discussions about marrying the CVT transmission of the Rover Metro Automatic to the MGF engine. Also being

The MGF Super Sports in its third incarnation, as revealed at the 1999 Frankfurt Motor Show.

considered was what was then referred to as a '1997½' interior face-lift – it was acknowledged already that perhaps the interior could have been a little more special. In fact the CVT idea had been part of the PR3 concept from the very beginning, for Nick Stephenson's May 1991 report to the Rover Executive Committee had stated: 'CVT will be offered just for Japan where automatics are very important.'

So far the CVT transmission had been offered only with smaller K-series engines and there were naturally some concerns from the engineers that mating it to a higher performance engine in a sports car application could be fraught with problems. Although engine cooling in the MGF was efficient, the confined engine bay and lower natural airflow did mean that a hard-worked CVT transmission could overheat. In addition, the all-important Japanese market demanded air conditioning and if this were to be married to an automatic in a hot climate, the potential problems were all too obvious.

Before long, a CVT test 'mule' was running and, as it was felt that the 'elastic band' feeling inherent in an infinitely variable transmission would be unsuited to a sports car, the combined engine/transmission management system was mapped carefully to allow a series of artificial ratio 'steps'. These mimicked a conventional automatic transmission and allowed the driver some degree of control over the engine revs. The latest Formula 1 racing cars used highly developed transmission systems with up-and-down selection controlled by 'paddles' and obviously anything that appeared to echo this concept could be a sales advantage.

First in the road-going automotive world to adopt this approach was Porsche with its Tiptronic transmission and it was not long before stories began to appear in the motoring press and on MG enthusiasts' internet bulletin boards of Tiptronic-type MGF developments. I spoke to an MG Cars insider at the time and he told me that he had driven the test 'mule' and that it promised a 'very exciting ride'. Priorities elsewhere – and the fact that, for the time being at least, Rover could build almost as many MGFs as it could sell – meant that the MGF automatic would have to wait for another day.

As production built up, minor changes took place (an improved fixing here, a seal change there, revisions to the hood and so on) but there were never any plans for a major redesign. Gerry McGovern explained that the design was felt to be sufficiently pure to last for at least seven years. Inevitably, however, there were minor trim and colour changes. Soon after the launch, I happened to be discussing the MGF with Mike Ferguson and expressed surprise at the omission of some paint colours – in particular silver, which I felt sure would be a popular choice.

Ferguson grinned and admitted that in considering the final choice, it was he who had dropped silver. There were felt to be only so many colours that should be offered at first and in any case it was predicted, accurately, that the biggest take-ups would be with Red or British Racing Green. During the years of MGF production, colours came and went: Volcano was an early casualty, because of the relatively low take-up, while additions included a metallic silver, a new 'Anthracite' metallic graphite grey and the short-lived Morello Plum, which replaced the like-it-or-loathe it pearlescent purple Amaranth.

There were new alloy wheel accessory designs and other trim options, including various interior leather trim combinations and colours. Gerry McGovern was particularly keen to respond to the clearly expressed customer demand for more ways of personalising the MGF (demonstrated by the healthy business of independent trim specialists like Mike Satur) by creating in-house alternatives. Soon there were special trim options – some factory applied, some fitted by the dealer or customer – such as walnut console trims and

A sketch of Northamptonshire MG dealer Stephen Palmer's 'Cheetah' conversion, a retrimmed and upgraded MGF with a turbocharged VVC engine. Sales were never that good: £25,000-£30,000 could have bought a Porsche Boxster instead.

chrome packs to add a dash of extra sparkle to the car.

McGovern does not mind saying that he is no great fan of some of the customised MGFs on the road; in his view they destroy the visual balance of the car, making it look 'tough and aggressive' in a way that he and his colleagues never intended. Naturally he respects the rights of owners to do what they wish with their own cars but, in common with others at MG Cars, he is nervous of the effects on the MGF's reputation from poor quality products over which BMW/Rover has no control.

Partly in response to this, McGovern and his design colleagues sat down and began to plan (in conjunction with their engineering counterparts, who had some exciting ideas of their own) a more sporting version of the MGF. The first iteration of this drew considerably from McGovern's personal transport, a dark green MGF with lowered suspension and Minilite-style wheels.

MGF **Abingdon**

In September 1997 (on the second anniversary of the MGF actually going on sale) a Limited Edition was announced for the German market. According to MG Cars, this was 'not a regular limited edition but a modern rendition of classic MG sports cars of the past' and it was anticipated that it would be sold out 'before production commences for the 1998 spring season'. MGF sales were growing in Germany and so this special was launched at that country's Frankfurt Show. The engine was the standard 1.8i, and EPAS (electronic power-assisted steering) and anti-lock brakes were fitted as standard.

'The new Limited Edition epitomises the genuine British sports car, with luxury throughout its interior and exterior executions, exemplified by its Brooklands Green paintwork and leather upholstery. The spirit of MG is further encapsulated in the chrome detailing and the application of leather, cues of luxury MGs of the past,' MG Cars crooned. 'On the exterior, Brooklands Green paint is carefully co-ordinated with a beige hood and new-style 16-inch alloy wheels are fitted with 215/40ZR tyres. Chromed door handles and chromed grille and side air intakes complete the detailing.'

Inside the car were leather seats and a special walnut facia and console trim pack. It was 'specially developed for this limited edition and comprises a combined set of features currently not available on MGF, even as factory fitted options; 'walnut' leather seats, head restraints, steering wheel, gear lever and handbrake gaiters; a black leather handbrake grip with chromed release button, a wood/alloy gear knob shaped to reflect the characteristic fuel filler that personifies the MGF and wood grain finishers around the console and facia vents. The interior detail is completed with a chromed ashtray.'

The exclusivity did not rest with the German market for long, however, for shortly afterwards a very similar home-market equivalent (the MGF Abingdon) was introduced. The name, intended to be evocative of MG history and tradition, was chosen by Steve Cox of MG Cars; he also happens to be a Director of the MG Car Club and an avowed MG enthusiast of many years standing. However, whereas the German version was intended to be a 1.8i version alone, for the Abingdon there would be 350 1.8i and 150 VVC versions.

The Abingdon limited edition responded to the demand for a new version of the MGF but McGovern and his team had even bigger fish to fry; they began to consider a special concept car based on the MGF and using some of the components for the MGF Cup race series. At first they might not have intended to show it to the general public but before long they were sufficiently enthused that work focused on an unveiling at Geneva, on the third anniversary of the MGF's launch.

Why the MGF is not sold in the USA

We saw earlier the reason for the PR3 project winning over the PR5 proposal, and how the withdrawal of Rover from the Sterling sales operation put paid to any idea of selling an MG sports car in the USA for the time being. The MGF was developed in the knowledge that it would be aimed at other markets – particularly the UK and Japan, followed closely by mainland Europe – and so production was planned with a certain volume in mind.

The USA has some of the lowest new car prices in the world, matched only by Japan. For the MGF to have competed, it would have had to have been built in much larger volumes to lower the unit costs. With a higher volume rival already established in the form of the Mazda MX-5/Miata (and within a year of the MGF's launch, the BMW Z3 too), an over-priced MGF would have had a tough time.

The question was often asked during BMW's ownership – and indeed doubtless will continue to be asked until the end of MGF production – as to whether the MGF could be exported to the USA and arises again with a new owner in charge. There are, sadly, sound reasons why this is most unlikely to happen.

Firstly, it is important to appreciate the history of MG sales in the USA and the manner in which British Leyland extricated itself from that market. When the death sentence was passed on the MGB, the US dealers who depended upon the MG for a large part of their business were understandably more than a little peeved, to the extent that they threatened to sue. Some rapid manoeuvring by Jaguar Rover Triumph Inc at Leonia, New Jersey, led to promises of MGB deliveries well into the 1981 Model Year and generous deals on spare parts for those with MG franchises.

Within a couple of years of the MGB's demise, the TR7 followed suit and so those dealers were left selling Jaguars (the Rover SD1 came and went in the US market with barely anybody noticing). As late as 1984, Jaguar Cars Inc (as JRT had become) was still promoting the fact that Jaguar

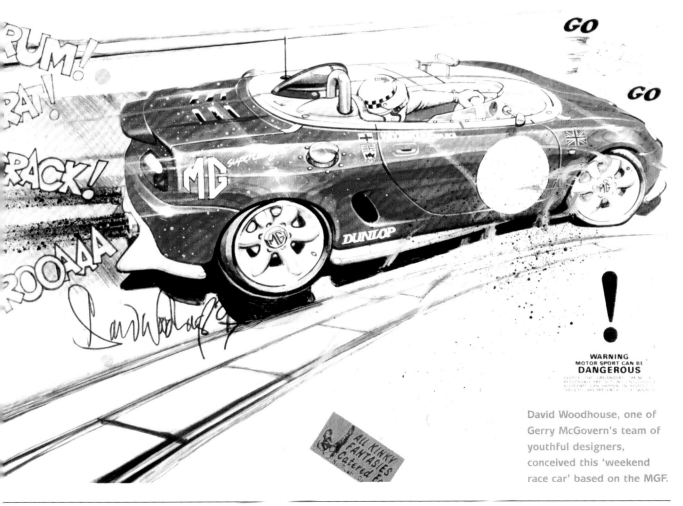

David Woodhouse, one of
Gerry McGovern's team of
youthful designers,
conceived this 'weekend
race car' based on the MGF.

dealers were able to offer factory-backed servicing for MG and Triumph sports cars. In October of that year, Jaguar Cars was finally split from BL and privatised. Naturally Jaguar Cars Inc in the USA went with the parent company.

When Austin Rover decided to return to the US market, it eschewed the old JRT dealer network and decided to set up a partnership with Norman Braman, based in Miami. Partly because of some potential unresolved issues with the old JRT dealers in the notoriously litigious USA, Austin Rover

fabricated the new Sterling name to avoid using its portfolio of existing marques. In 1989 Jaguar fell into the arms of the Ford Motor Company and, of course, Jaguar Cars Inc and the remaining dealers were still part of the package.

By 1990 Rover Group was thinking of bringing MG back to the USA but was aware that some of those former MG dealers might mount a legal action to gain either the right to sell the cars or, more likely, to seek a settlement in lieu. The situation was complicated by the fact that Ford had a

controlling interest in Mazda – maker of a potential rival to a new MG sports car – and therefore Ford could conceivably have given tacit support to such dealers. When I asked a former highly placed manager from JRT Inc for his views on the subject, he was quite sure that there could be a case to answer. 'Some of the dealer franchises, depending upon the lawyer they found, could probably stand up and stake a claim. Frankly, if I had formerly been a successful MG dealer and a new car came in, I would be tempted to stand up

and say I want to be counted.'

So, the MGF is not, and will not be, sold in the USA. Yes, it could be re-engineered, any legal battles fought and the sales and marketing effort mounted but, at the end of the day, it would require a lot of money to be spent on a car which is already more than halfway through its life.

Let us not mourn the non-appearance in US showrooms of the MGF but instead hope that when the 'MGG' (or whatever it is called) arrives, MG's new owners will be committed to US sales.

The MGF **Super Sports**

What became known as the Super Sports (the name being a homage of sorts to the very different 1924 MG of the same name) began life as a series of sketches by one of Gerry McGovern's designers, Dave Woodhouse. McGovern and Woodhouse (designer of the distinctive one-off Land Rover based 'taxis' used in the futuristic Sylvester Stallone film *Judge Dredd*) were keen to inject some of the sporting character of the 1950s motor sport scene into MG. Another source of inspiration was James Dean's Porsche Spyder and his car's name (Li'l Bastard) appeared on the tail of the Super Sports styling model.

Rover was keen to see a fully-finished concept car rather than just a styling clay and so Mayflower Vehicle Systems was invited to participate in the exercise to create a 'running' prototype. The challenge was quite a tough one: the brief was to take Woodhouse's concept and turn it into a rolling prototype within 11 weeks. Meanwhile Chris Lee, Product Development Director for MG and Mini at Rover Group, oversaw the operation from the Rover Group end.

In less than a week from agreeing to do the job, Mayflower had the logistics in place, an overall Project Manager had been appointed and there were senior managers in charge of key functions: programme management, supplier management, engineering design and manufacturing engineering. The clay model was delivered to Coventry by covered lorry from Rover's Gaydon studio and meanwhile a donor vehicle was stripped in readiness.

During this first week, Mayflower worked in conjunction with three different Rover Group departments (Sports Car Engineering, Design and MG Competitions) to firm up the final specification. At this stage, for example, it was decided to use aluminium alloy for the new body. This entailed additional work in the creation of an entirely new body and the associated production of a number of special 'soft' tools, which offered the possibility of producing a very limited number of replicas.

Tooling methods actually varied, dependent upon the nature of the part; in some cases it was possible to simply use the standard MGF tooling, adapted to press alloy in place of the usual steel. In the case of the boot lid, however, a special clinching method had to be developed to secure the boot lid outer to the corresponding inner pressing. When it came to the bonnet, Mayflower found that while, in theory, the original tooling could have been used, Dave Woodhouse's styling changes had made it necessary to produce new tooling, as for the wings.

At the outset, it was necessary to measure the surface shape of the styling model precisely. To do this Mayflower used photogrammetry, a process involving a pair of cameras that captured more than 500,000 points in three dimensions for each new panel. Once this information had been processed into a computer database and corrected for errors ('surfacing'), it could be used directly to cut the rubber press tools and panel-beating formers by the use of numerical control cutter path programming. The formers were made from Eppowood, Urial and Lab 900, all special materials designed expressly for this type of work.

As the Geneva Show date approached, so the pace of work at Mayflower began to heat up. The aluminium required for the bodywork could not be sourced from within the UK in time and so a delivery was shipped in especially from Switzerland; rather ironic in view of the intended venue for the public unveiling. The resulting pressed panels were then attached using special Permabond structural adhesive and Henrob self-piercing rivets. This combination not only ensured that the body was exceptionally stiff but also the adhesive provided insulation between the steel and aluminium alloy panels, thereby reducing the risk of galvanic corrosion.

Other one-off parts included unique road wheels and carbon-fibre composite moulded panels, including the front and rear bumpers and the rigid tonneau over the passenger compartment. Trimming of the interior (in dazzling white Connolly hide) was carried out by a local company, while a special yellow-tinted Perspex spyder-style windscreen was moulded and fitted to the finished body. When it came to painting the car (in a special rich shade of red called Diana) Mayflower made sure that there was room in its 'E-coat' paint facility to provide the same degree of paint preparation and protection as a standard MGF.

The finished article was completed in exactly ten weeks and four working days from Day One. Dennis Evans, Sales and Marketing Director of Mayflower Vehicle Systems, was proud of the part his company had played in turning the MGF Super Sports from a styling model into a real car. 'Mayflower played an instrumental part in returning MG sports cars to the market in 1995 and we are committed to supporting Rover Group's ambitions for the MG brand into the next century... Rover Group and Mayflower people worked side by side to produce this vehicle and the finished car is a source of great pride to both companies.'

At Geneva, there was an air of expectation around the MG Cars display on press day; indeed for those of us who arrived the day before, the sight of specially erected hoardings and uniformed security guards only added to the sense of drama. On press day itself, the MGF Super Sports lay concealed by the customary dust-sheet, while not far away, MG collector Peter Green's fabulous K3 Magnette also hid from the gaze of onlookers under its protective sheet. There was no officially organised unveiling – BMW Chairman

David Woodhouse at the wheel of his creation at Donington Park (above), accompanied by a 1933 MG Magnette K3 at Starkey's Bridge. Rear view, photographed at an earlier stage, shows the 'Little Bastard' name (inspired by James Dean's Porsche 550 Spyder) and gold wheels – two details that were to be changed.

The MGF Super Sports took pride of place on the Rover stand at the 1998 Geneva Show, with its designer, David Woodhouse (right), and MGF designer Gerry McGovern in attendance.

Super Sports interior is an orgy of white, polished alloy and chrome.

Bernd Pischetsrieder just swept on to the stand unannounced and whipped the covers off.

Naturally, several senior members of the Rover Board were on hand to explain the purpose of the Super Sports, among them Rover Group's Design Director Geoff Upex: 'Basically we just thought that this was the way that MG should be perceived at the limit. It is very much about putting a bit of racing pedigree back into MGF. In fact turning the car into a spyder like this is the classic thing to do.' In answer to the inevitable question about a production version of the car, all Upex would say at this stage was: 'Everybody always says, when they do a car like this, that they are just gauging reaction. Yes, we are doing that to a certain extent. I am sure that there are bits and pieces on the car which will appear on the production vehicle but whether it will ever happen exactly like this is a very moot point. It is more to do with the spirit of this car. I think that is the important thing about it.'

Dave Woodhouse explained the source of his inspiration: 'We started off by looking at the older cars and their more ornate appearance. You can get sick of so many modern cars, which are just utterly stripped out and provide no interest in the way they are finished. When it came to a source of inspiration, it was very much the classic sports cars of the 1950s, especially the Mille Miglia and Le Mans cars of that time, which were genuinely road-usable. There was always a sense of occasion about those cars; you could drive them on the streets and then take them straight on to the race track.' Woodhouse acknowledges that there was a wide variety of such cars at that time, quite apart from MGs, and that inspiration came from a number of sources.

Gerry McGovern was typically forthright in his summation of the Super Sports: 'I would describe it as an MGF that has been working out in the gym for three hours a day, every day – maybe having popped a few steroids as well! It shows the extreme potential of MG in terms of how you can grow it and for it to still work. It is still believable and yet it has grown considerably.' McGovern also confirmed that a more feasible version had been looked at. 'The car would work very well even with the standard screen on it – we have looked at that. This is the extreme version, with the little screen and full panelled tonneau. Put a standard screen and hood on it and it still looks good...'

When it came to details (such as the flared wings and round front indicators, lifted straight off a Mini), it was obvious that, if Rover chose, these could be adopted on a face-lifted standard MGF. With a nod to still-secret work on developing the MGF and with a gentle side-swipe at the customisers, McGovern added: 'One of the things we are doing is to develop refinements and changes for what we call our 1999½ model year programme and we will look at this very carefully in terms of what we incorporate into that programme. There is a whole bag of goodies there that potentially we could develop, as accessories or whatever, but the most important thing is the fact that these features have been designed by the designers who know about MG and are qualified to actually design things; not somebody in his back yard doing his own thing.'

Dave Woodhouse explained the many differences between the standard MGF and the Super Sports: 'The only basically standard panels are the doors and the boot lid itself. Everything else is modified to a lesser or greater extent. The wings are hugely different – you are talking of an extra 40mm (1.57in) width each side at the back end and about 20-30mm (0.79-1.18in) at the front each side. So they've 'blown' locally around the wheelarches and there is a much more pronounced Coke-bottle shape.'

The exercise also allowed the designers to 'correct' one or two of the features that had disappointed Gerry McGovern and Gordon Sked when the MGF first appeared. Back in 1995 they said that the 'chord line' (running the length of the car at the upper portion of the wings and doors) had lost a little of its sharpness in the transition from clay to finished article – a fairly common occurrence. For the Super Sports, there was no repeat of this. 'In fact this has been an opportunity to tighten some of those areas up,' Woodhouse said. 'You will notice that the main feature line through the wings now actually tightens through the centreline over the wheelarch.'

When it came to the power unit, Rover's Director of Engineering, Nick Stephenson, expressed enthusiasm for the supercharger route in getting more from the MGF. 'Clearly we are always looking for possibilities to increase power output of the K-series and indeed the MG is the prime test bed for that,' Stephenson told me. Having said that, he was quick to deny that there had been a definite 'green light' for a supercharged MG: 'We are not declaring that we are

definitely going to produce a supercharged engine... but once again we are interested to see what the response to such a power unit is... The K-series is a very strong engine and could withstand, I believe, more horsepower and the MG would be a perfect chassis to take it.'

Stephenson admitted that the supercharger was only one of a number of potential methods of shunting the MGF into a new performance league: 'Obviously pressure-charging is one way forward, or alternatively a completely different engine. In terms of pressure-charging, clearly you can go either for turbocharging, as we did on the 1.4-litre (85cu in) engine we took to Bonneville in EXF, or supercharging as with the MGF Super Sports. These two projects have kept us abreast of the capabilities of K-series in both forms. The other route obviously would be to put something more substantial in the car, in other words a bigger engine.'

Naturally, in 1998, Stephenson would not be drawn on this engine. However, the options – already pretty much of an open secret – were: the 2- or 2.5-litre (121 or 152cu in) Rover KV6 (then only used in the 800 but intended for the 75) or the all-new NG (New Generation) engine that was being developed jointly by Rover and BMW. This unit would be built at a brand new £400 million factory, then under construction at Hams Hall near Birmingham, which was due to come on stream during 2000 and was planned to produce up to half a million 1.6- to 2-litre (97 to 121cu in) engines per annum.

Once again, it could be imagined that MG could be a test-bed for the Rover range, perhaps with the new BMW/Rover 2-litre (121cu in) engine (in standard or supercharged guise) finding its way into the MGF soon after production, scheduled for 2000, begins. 'I would certainly like to think that ultimately the MGF will have sufficient life that we could put the NG4 in,' commented Stephenson in 1998. 'Obviously that engine goes up to 2 litres (121cu in) and has some very interesting high-output variants and I think that could be a very exciting power unit for the MG – but we are talking long-term for that. However, I think that the life of the present car could well be sufficient to allow us to contemplate that.' With BMW's subsequent disposal of Rover in spring 2000, however, all such plans were put back in the melting pot.

Back at Longbridge, meanwhile, there were musical chairs with the production facilities. The move was prompted by discontinuation of the Rover niche products that had shared the MGF lines and rebuilding work in advance of the new Mini, due for production in 2001. On 29 July 1998 the last MGF (number 46957 in Tahiti Blue) went down the line at CAB2 and, during the ensuing two weeks, the whole MGF facility was transferred to CAB1, where production (in batches of 12) was interspersed with Minis.

The special 75th
Anniversary MGF of 1999
was painted Mulberry Red
or Black for the UK market,
but elsewhere it was
available in silver.

Interior carries a numbered
badge on the moulding
between the seats to show
the car's position in the
production sequence of
2000 examples.

The MGF 75th Anniversary Limited Edition

MG Cars decided that 1999 would be a convenient occasion to mark the 75th anniversary of the MG marque – ignoring the fact that the MG badge had been seen 76 years previously. However, 1924 was regarded as the date that the first identifiable 'MG' appeared and was also when the MG name and logo were first registered, so during 1999 a number of new advertisements began to appear, featuring '© MG Cars 1924'. In celebration, MG introduced a new limited edition, available in a choice of silver (outside the UK, where it was already the third most popular colour), black (with Grenadine Red hood) or Mulberry Red (a deep pearlescent maroon). To be built in a limited number of 2,000 for all markets (with 500 for the UK), the MGF 75th Anniversary LE was offered in both 1.8i and 1.8i VVC versions.

Needless to say, there were many other one-off goodies unique to the LE model, including 16in (406mm) eight-spoke Minilite wheels and Goodyear Eagle F1 215/55-16 low-profile tyres. The interior was specially trimmed in Grenadine Red leather on the seats, doors, handbrake, gear-lever gaiter and steering wheel, while wood trim and some chrome-plated fittings gave it a slight retro look. Special badges were fitted: one on each of the wings and a uniquely numbered one applied inside the cockpit between the seat backrests.

Second coming for the Super Sports: Geneva 1999

The bright red Super Sports concept car at Geneva in 1998 drew a lot of attention and sparked much debate – not all of it positive. However, there was no doubt that some of the features – its high-performance engine, boldly flared bodywork and aggressively re-worked nose – could find a welcome home in a new top-of-the-range MGF aimed at those who criticised the existing models as too soft. The extent of this criticism was illustrated by the success of the brilliant Lotus Elise, a small and very light mid-engined sports car that used the MGF engine and yet offered a purer sports car thrill for the enthusiast driver.

There was never any question of the Elise being as competent an all-round everyday car as the MGF but it was certainly more athletic and minimalist and yet at the same time extremely high tech, with its novel hydro-formed alloy chassis and traditional Lotus composite bodywork. The fact that the Lotus used the K-series engine to such useful effect only served to rub salt into MG's wounds. For a long time, the Elise was only available with a Lotus-tweaked version of the standard 1.8-litre (110cu in) K-series but eventually it could also be had with the VVC version; in one fell swoop, any pretences to superiority that the MGF VVC might have maintained were swept away.

The ongoing success of the MGF Cup showed that the MGF chassis had bags of reserve and could easily handle more power – the race cars coped with a 192bhp (190PS) version of the engine. Indeed Rover Group drew on the talents of its old friend and consultant Tony Pond to assist with honing the chassis of the Super Sports to ensure that at least the prototype could drive as well as it looked.

So at the 1999 Geneva Show a second version of the Super Sports appeared – this time in road-going guise, with conventional trim and windscreen, but retaining some of the less wacky features of the car shown the previous year. Finished in glossy black, the new car looked stunning but did not photograph well. The project was overseen by Julian Quincey, one of Gerry McGovern's acolytes on the original MGF team, although in fairness most of the hard work had already been done the previous year by Dave Woodhouse (who had by then left Rover Group to work at GM).

Geoff Upex explained the purpose behind the second showing of what was still described as nothing more than a concept. 'Last year we showed the 'extreme' version of the Super Sports – it wasn't completely feasible but was really more of a styling 'statement of intent'. This car is much more feasible as a road car; it has the same 200PS (202bhp) supercharged engine but the windscreen and interior are more conventional. It retains the 'blown' wheelarches of the earlier car, so there is still a very tough look to it. If the standard MGF could be said to be feminine in appearance, the wider form and track makes the Super Sports beefier. I guess you could compare the process to that of the Porsche 911, taking the standard car and tweaking it to make it more muscular.'

Whereas the all-white interior of the 1998 Super Sports had been completely over the top, that of the 1999 iteration was far more realistic. It sported a fairly conventional looking (albeit 'jazzed up') MGF interior with leather-trimmed sports Recaro seats, Grenadine leather trim (borrowed from the concurrent MGF 75th Anniversary LE), drilled alloy pedals, alloy driver's heel-mat, brushed aluminium trim and Super Sports door kick-plates. Outside, the chrome script Super Sports and Union Jack badges were carried over from the earlier car.

I suggested to Upex that the fact that MG was able to show a view of its own future – sharing its international

The second version of the MGF Super Sports, revealed at Geneva in 1999, was a much more practical proposition for road use.

Right: Great view of a Super Sports, at the Goodwood launch of revisions for the 2000 model year.

limelight with the much more significant Rover 75 – surely boded well for that future. 'We would be crazy to do anything else with the MG brand other than exploit it sensibly,' Upex assured me.

Dave Saddington, Studio Director for MG and Mini, had been responsible for overseeing the revised Super Sports. 'We are getting closer to a feasible car,' he confirmed, echoing Geoff Upex's comments, 'but in developmental terms we still haven't committed to production just yet.' Comparing the Super Sports with a standard MGF, Saddington explained that the main differences were 'the substantial increase in width driven by the chassis development. The larger wheels and tyres front and rear, together with the bigger front and rear bumpers, also contribute to amplify the mid-engined muscularity.'

I asked Nick Stephenson why, with the Super Sports 'Mark II', MG was playing the concept car card twice in succession.

'We are keen to hear reactions to the car,' he said 'but we also have to consider this against the backdrop of the whole set of Rover Group priorities... There are some very important discussions going on at present surrounding our small and medium cars. Clearly issues like that are extremely critical but within all that busyness, we have to consider whether we still have time for the Super Sports as a sensible business proposition.'

I expressed my concern that history had so often shown that MG could slip down the list of priorities. It could always be argued that there were much more important things to do than develop the MG sports cars; the result could be stagnation and decay – the MGB being a case in point. Stephenson acknowledged this but countered: 'Clearly you must have business reality as a backdrop to your whole operation but having said that I can guarantee that we are not going to allow MG to go off the boil. The

MGF Super Sports lineage includes the 1945-49 MG TC and 1962-80 MGB – both seminal classics.

reintroduction of the brand so far has been enormously successful, so why would we now take a step backwards? So even if the Super Sports were to remain a concept car, it is still a very clear demonstration that we are very serious about MG's future.'

Chris Lee, Product Development Director for MG and Mini and therefore Dave Saddington's engineering counterpart, explained the significance of the lumping together of the MG and Mini brands: 'Originally, my patch was called 'small and sports cars' and I think that what this arrangement really represented was putting together the two niche brands and making the best use of our time and manpower. It doesn't imply that we are going to put the two together on the same technology platform or anything like that – it is more for operational convenience and efficiency.'

Lee emphasised that the Super Sports 'Mark II' was not just a mock-up but was a fully-functional working prototype: 'We've driven it in anger ourselves and it uses the 1.8-litre (110cu in) K-series base engine supercharged to give a stated 200PS (202bhp) although in reality we got a bit more than that. The gearbox is basically the PG-1 unit out of the standard car but suitably upgraded to cope with the higher output.' On the other hand, Lee stressed, the sequential gearbox was 'something for the near future'.

The suspension of the MGF Super Sports was understandably derived from that of the MGF Cup cars, with a ride height lowered by some 30mm (1.18in) from standard, special valves in the Hydragas units and racing-style brakes, marrying AP Racing calipers with 295mm (11.61in) discs. The wheels were seam-welded KN alloy 17in (432mm) three-piece units, shod with 225/45-17 Goodyear Eagle F1 tyres.

At the time of the 1999 Geneva Show, it was an open secret that Toyota was working on its own MGF rival, shown as the MR-S prototype and later in the year as the new MR2. Chris Lee and his colleagues were fully aware of the challenge from this and other quarters and the need to ensure that the MGF was not left behind. 'The new Toyota is going to be a natural competitor; the whole sector that MG sits in at the moment is moving on and up,' Lee commented. Naturally this brought the question of whether the Super Sports would sit separately above the MGF range, or become more integrated with it. 'That is the $64,000 question at the moment,' he confessed. 'Do we leave Super Sports as a range-topper or do we take the technology out of this car and put it into the base car, with this supercharged version at the top? There is a lot more work for us to do before we can really answer that question.'

Changes at the top: **BMW strengthens its grip**

When BMW acquired Rover Group in 1994, the intention was to build up the British company and reduce its dependence on its erstwhile partner Honda in terms of platform sharing and engineering. Rover Group's Nick Stephenson described BMW's approach to Rover as being 'integration with independence' – a reasonably hands-off approach to design, engineering and marketing except where economies of scale were obvious. Hence Rover Group retained a considerable degree of autonomy in handling its own affairs; there remained a Rover Group board, reporting to John Towers as Chairman, who in turn reported to BMW Chairman Bernd Pischetsrieder in Munich.

While this process was fine in theory, there were some signs of discontent even at this early stage. Gordon Sked (Rover Design Director during the run-up to the MGF launch) stayed through the very early stages of BMW involvement but departed in late 1995. 'We stayed pretty independent while I was there,' he commented, 'although I have to say there is almost an implicit feeling of inferiority when you work for a company that has been taken over by another; that is just inevitable.' The resignation of John Towers followed in spring 1996. His place was taken by Dr Walter Hasselkus, an affable Anglophile from BMW, whose most recent job had been running the BMW motorcycle business and who had run BMW Great Britain for a time in the late 1970s. Closer integration of basic engineering and purchasing functions soon got under way, although perhaps not to quite the extent that some thought would (or indeed should) have been the case. One shining example of the close co-operation between the German and British engineering teams was the development of the all-new NG engine range referred to earlier. BMW acknowledged that the engineers who had designed the K-series had done a fine job and there was a desire to tap into that valuable resource in the development of a new engine that would meet part of BMW's and Rover's needs for the beginning of the new Millennium.

At the very top of the BMW organisation there were two very powerful and quite different characters – the Chairman, Bernd Pischetsrieder, and his effective number two, Design and Research Director Wolfgang Reitzle. A very focused man, Reitzle is rightly credited with much that was good about the direction that BMW had taken in engineering its own product lines. Not a man to suffer fools, Reitzle's approach to business was always straight and to the point; although he found a lot to respect within Rover Group, there was also much that worried him. He was not totally convinced of Pischetsrieder's 'hands off'

approach to Rover and is said to have favoured downgrading Rover's engineering responsibility for replacing the Honda-related 200 and 400 series in favour of platform-sharing with another manufacturer – often thought to be either Ford (with the Focus) or Volkswagen (with the Golf). Efforts at Rover Group would then have been put into developing the profitable Land Rover marque (the main reason for BMW's initial interest in Rover) and exploiting the still under-utilised MG and Mini brands.

During 1998, rumours began to abound of trouble within BMW/Rover. High interest and exchange rates badly affected the cost of building cars in Britain for export to Europe and there was effectively a 'double whammy' in that foreign cars also became cheaper to sell in the UK. News began to leak out that Rover's much-vaunted recovery plan under Walter Hasselkus was not going to achieve the turn-round in fortunes as early as planned and there were even dark rumours that BMW might post a loss – something it had not done for over 20 years.

Things were probably not helped by the decision to drop the Rover 100 – admittedly dated but still providing a substantial part of Rover's income. Dropping it without a direct replacement was bound to put a hole in the profits. In the early design stages of the 1995 Rover 200, there had been thoughts of badging it as a new 'Rover 100', as a slightly larger replacement for the old Metro-based model. Instead Rover management decided to move up out of the 'supermini' sector and make the new car more of a premium-priced product. The consequence was that while the new 200 was much admired, its Achilles heel was that it was smaller inside than the previous-generation Rover 200 – the company had not laid an egg like that since it replaced the ADO16 1100/1300 range with the Allegro.

One bright spot was sure to be the launch of the first all-new 'BMW era' Rover: the important Rover 75 replaced both the 600 and 800 series and benefited from research that BMW had carried out into front-wheel drive before it acquired Rover. All eyes, therefore, were on the Rover stand at the British International Motor Show at the NEC in October 1998, when the new 75 made its debut. Originally the 75 was due to appear at the 1999 Geneva Show (and all development was geared to that date) but, at the eleventh hour, BMW – at the BMW Chairman's insistence but against the Rover Group board's advice – decided to show the new Rover at the same time as Jaguar was unveiling its new S-type. BMW had long been keen on such showmanship; it unveiled two Mini concepts at the same Geneva show that arch-rival Mercedes-Benz revealed the ground-breaking A-class.

The 75 was unveiled by Dr Hasselkus and its virtues were displayed by an enthusiastic Nick Stephenson: 'This is the car we had to build,' he told the onlookers. Many observers, myself included, were very favourably impressed by the appearance of the new Rover; quite a few of us thought that the Rover 75 was in many ways a more creditable effort than the equally important small Jaguar.

However, much of the good seemed to be undone in the late afternoon at the BMW press conference. Just when Rover needed a good news story, the BMW Chairman decided to ram home the message of the high Pound, Britain's non-membership of the Exchange Rate Mechanism (aimed at harmonising currencies within the European Union) and the 'inefficiency' of Rover's factories – what Pischetsrieder called the 'productivity gap'. Alongside Pischetsrieder and Hasselkus on the platform was a gleaming Rover 75 but press interest was focussed on the Chairman's woes – the new Rover seemed almost an afterthought.

Despite this, the Rover 75 went on to win many justified accolades in early reports – although production did not get under way until the spring of 1999. The official story was that the delays were necessary until BMW expressed itself 'fully satisfied' with the quality of production vehicles, although, as we have seen, the reality was that the original programme had been geared to production in the summer after a March 1999 launch.

Meanwhile, however, the first big bombshell was dropped: on 2 December 1998 Walter Hasselkus announced that he had asked the BMW supervisory board to accept his resignation – not only from his chairmanship of the Rover Group board but also from the BMW AG board itself. He was succeeded as Rover Chairman by 56-year-old Professor Werner Sämann, who was the manager of BMW's Engines and Chassis Division and had been appointed to the board of BMW AG on 1 December. Professor Sämann was an unknown quantity at Rover other than through his connection with the Hams Hall engine project.

More major changes followed with the resignations on 5 February 1999 of BMW Chairman Bernd Pischetsrieder and his effective number two, Design and Research Director Wolfgang Reitzle. It seemed that various members of the BMW board (including the union representatives) were unhappy at handing power to Reitzle, whose preferred options for both BMW and Rover were perceived – rightly or wrongly – as ruthless; it was feared Reitzle would undo many of the investment plans that Pischetsrieder had masterminded. With British car enthusiasts Pischetsrieder and Hasselkus gone, Rover's guardian angels had flown the coop and as a consequence there were understandably some nervous people in the Midlands.

Professor Joachim Milberg, until the previous day BMW's board member responsible for engineering and production, emerged from the rubble as BMW's new top man and radical changes at Rover soon followed. The Rover Group board was dismantled gradually: on 16 March, Sales and Marketing Director Tom Purves was appointed Chairman of BMW (US) Holdings, and Communications Director Bernard Carey became a BMW government adviser in London. Nick Stephenson, Rover's Design and Engineering Director, and Paul Kirk, Manufacturing Director, tendered their resignations on 13 April. 'With the successful integration of Rover Group functions into BMW and the transfer of strategic decision making for Rover to the BMW Board, both have decided to pursue their careers outside the group,' the official statement recorded bluntly. There were similar rationalisations at other levels within Rover and it became apparent that the hitherto jealously guarded Rover independence would be no more; many Rover people took early retirement or voluntary redundancy. Just before the London Motor Show in October 1999, the Rover Group name was set aside and the British operations became a subsidiary of BMW Group UK.

In the meantime, however, there had been some welcome activity at the MG Cars camp. We saw earlier how a second version of the MGF Super Sports had been built for the March 1999 Geneva Show and had been accompanied by the MGF 75th Anniversary edition; just four months later, an even more important step in the MGF story broke cover.

The MGF **Steptronic**

As we saw earlier, the idea of marrying an automatic transmission to the MGF was at the back of the project team's minds from the beginning but for the time being it was not the main priority. Early quality problems with the MGF (particularly overheating engines) kept the engineering team busy for the first two years but by 1997 it was possible to contemplate introducing a new member of the MGF family about 18 months hence, to coincide with the 2000 Model Year changes described below.

John Houldcroft oversaw the development of the new application, in his role as engineer in charge of development of all Rover automatic transmission applications. The unit itself was developed in conjunction with Belgian company ZF Getriebe NV Sint-Truiden, one of Europe's leading CVT specialists, which already supplied its VT1 gearbox for the Rover 216. Understandably, according to Houldcroft, the Rover CVT had followed an evolutionary path: 'We started with the 1.4-litre (85cu in) K-series in the Rover 100 and moved up to the 1.6-litre (97 cu in) engine in the 200 range; this was really the next step.'

Houldcroft explained that advances in electronics had helped: 'In the past four to five years, there have been many developments in the application of electronics to

The Platinum Silver of this MGF Steptronic has a suitably 'high-tech' look that matches the state-of-the-art transmission technology under the skin.

transmissions in general and the CVT was no different in that respect. We were able to use electronic control in several areas, including the artificial step ratios in Steptronic.' The latter idea, which ensures that the Steptronic avoids as far as possible the peculiar 'slurring' sensation inherent in most CVT applications, was first demonstrated as a concept. 'We developed the concept as a demonstration of what CVT could do and used it to gauge the level of interest in the company,' Houldcroft said. 'Then around the end of 1997 we were able to say that we had something worthwhile and it was soon agreed that the MGF would be the ideal platform in which to launch it.'

Some markets might resist the idea of a sports car with automatic transmission but Houldcroft believes that the choice of actuation methods – a combination of conventional central lever and steering wheel-mounted buttons – should be sufficient to tempt most drivers.

'Japan, for example, is a key market for us with MGF and with the level of congestion in Tokyo, their level of take-up of automatic transmissions is high in any case,' he added.

The Japanese market would prove particularly challenging, for the high ambient temperatures in summer mean that air conditioning is almost essential for cars sold there. Naturally, just like the CVT transmission, air conditioning leads to higher engine temperatures; an air-conditioned Steptronic could prove quite a challenge to keep cool in all conditions. 'We have a special oil cooler on the Steptronic,' Houldcroft explained. 'In terms of the basic functionality of the transmission, with a wet clutch plate system, the temperature control of the oil is absolutely critical. A lot of effort has gone into the system so that we can keep the oil at a safe working temperature.'

The press got its first chance to drive the MGF Steptronic at its launch in July 1999 in Sussex and I shared the driving of a

Steering wheel gear-shift controls in the MGF Steptronic resemble silver golf balls and fall easily to hand. Silver-faced dials were common to all 2000 model year MGFs. The transmission lever can be used in conventional automatic 'P-R-N-D' mode or, by moving it to the left, as an 'up-down' shift control that echoes the functions of the steering wheel buttons.

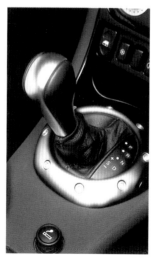

silver specimen with friend and fellow writer Andrew Roberts. We approached the car with similar levels of misgivings but by the end of a day spent driving the car we were both pleasantly surprised. Andrew, who drives an MGF 1.8 on an everyday basis, was convinced that the Steptronic would be quicker across country than the manual in all but the most extreme situations and that the driver would arrive at his destination more relaxed than if he had been stirring the gearbox.

I found myself playing with the steering wheel buttons, which both operate in the same manner rather than the up and down paddles of F1 cars. ('We had tried those earlier,' admitted John Houldcroft, 'but in the end it was decided to go for the production version, if for no other reason than to avoid the potential confusion when the wheel is on full lock – something you do not get to the same degree in an F1 car.') Andrew Roberts, on the other hand, concentrated on using the floor shift and found the simple up-down shift of the lever easier to use – or indeed to leave in auto mode. If nothing else, this suggests that Rover was right to offer the choice.

At the end of the day, I concluded that I would rather put the extra cost of the Steptronic (as a separate model in its own right) towards a VVC but I could quite understand a decision to buy one. Naturally, both Rover Group and the wider motoring world looked forward to the definitive *Autocar* road test, which duly appeared in the 8 September 1999 issue. *Autocar* found that, in absolute terms, the Steptronic performance was some way behind the manual; it achieved 0-60mph (0-96kmh) in 10.4sec (versus 8.7sec for the manual MGF tested in 1995) and a top speed of 113mph (181kmh) compared with 123mph (197kmh).

'Despite the performance shortfall,' said the *Autocar* report, 'this new roadster retains many of the virtues that have made the MGF the best-selling car in its class for the last three years. The chassis provides sure-footed grip and bags of composure over poorly surfaced B-roads, courtesy of its chunky Goodyear rubber and well-sorted Hydragas suspension.' However, *Autocar* felt that the MGF felt less inspired than the latest Mazda MX-5, blaming the electronic steering – a criticism common to the manual car. 'That said,' *Autocar* conceded, 'the MGF is still a more capable and compelling driver's car than the BMW Z3.'

In conclusion, *Autocar* felt that the CVT transmission was out of place in a sports car: 'Given time to develop the idea, a CVT sports car might make sense, but in this instance the sacrifices are too great and the benefits too few.' Perhaps this conclusion from a basically 'enthusiast' publication was hardly surprising, if a little harsh. My own time behind the wheel had shown that while in terms of a rewarding cross-country drive the Steptronic came some way behind a manual car, for an everyday drive – particularly one involving a commute – it could be just the ticket.

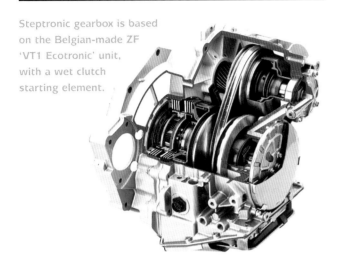

Steptronic gearbox is based on the Belgian-made ZF 'VT1 Ecotronic' unit, with a wet clutch starting element.

The Steptronic transmission

The idea of an automatic transmission in an MG sports car is not quite as new as many suppose. Back in 1968, you could have an automatic gearbox (if you really wanted one) in your MGB or MGC and the shift control was quite a nifty looking chrome lever that looked not a million miles away from the pre-selector mechanism of the pre-war MG K3.

Other than in North America, the automatic transmission has never achieved enormous popularity and even then there has always been something of a stigma attached to a sports car so equipped. Surely Sigmund Freud would have had something to say about it? In recent years, however, there have been many developments: automatic transmissions have improved immensely and have evolved into different types, whilst the expectations of many motorists and – dare I say – the increasing influence of the female driver have made the idea of something other than a traditional manual gearbox easier to contemplate.

Perhaps the biggest influence has come through the adoption of sophisticated clutch control mechanisms and transmissions in the exotic arena of Formula 1 racing and top-flight rallying. So quick are the changes required in these situations that fractions of a second could cost a race placing and so computers now give the professional driver a helping hand. Naturally, the image of these new transmission controls soon spilled over to the more mundane motoring world; a plethora of button- or lever-actuated transmission systems or electronic clutch actuators has appeared, with names like Tiptronic, Seletronic and now Steptronic.

The Steptronic gearbox introduced for the MGF, and subsequently made available on other models in the Rover family, has roots which MG Cars and BMW would probably prefer were forgotten. The eccentric DAF Daffodil, a small Dutch economy car of the 1960s, used a novel type of transmission designed by its makers, Van Doorne. This involved the use of rubber belts operating on movable pulleys

that allowed the ratio between those pulleys – and hence the overall gear ratio – to be varied continuously, rather than selected one step at a time by conventional gears.

The Daffodil was a lightweight car, with a small engine, and while the rubber belts coped reasonably well with small loads, the transmission seemed to have very limited prospects for larger or more powerful applications. Then a new development emerged in the form of precision-machined steel belts, which were able to push rather than pull. These were gradually developed by Van Doorne to the point where they were able to handle mid-range engines and small family saloons. There were problems, however: the belts required very precise (and expensive) machining and unless there was to be a large enough take-up, the necessary investment and future development might not have been forthcoming.

By now the transmission was known generically as CVT (Constantly Variable Transmission) and in addition to the DAF (and subsequently Volvo) applications, others began to begin work on developing CVT systems. Rover's first involvement with the system came about with the face-lift of the Metro to accept the K-series engine. An automatic was deemed important, for sales of the previous generation Metro 1.3 automatic had been quite good in a sector hardly spoilt for choice. For the new Metro, the 1.4-litre (85cu in) K-series was mated to a new CVT transmission and proved to be a very economical, if hardly sparkling, performer. The problem was that the downside of all CVT transmissions tends to

be the peculiarly flat engine note; the fact that the transmission is constantly adjusting the gear ratio makes an attempt at rapid acceleration resemble that of a manual transmission car with bad clutch slip. This might not have worried great-grandma, but for many would-be customers it was undoubtedly a turn-off.

For the MGF application, therefore, Rover worked with Belgian company ZF Getriebe NV Sint-Truiden to develop an integrated engine and transmission management system that allows artificial 'steps' to be introduced within the gear range. Virtually any number of steps could have been chosen but for practical reasons – and also with present fashions in sports gearboxes in mind – the Steptronic was given six ratios. The basic gearbox, known at ZF as the Ecotronic VT1, is capable of transmitting torque up to a limit of 129lb ft (175Nm), which is well within the 122lb ft (165Nm) of the standard 1.8i engine but would be marginal for the 128lb ft (174Nm) of the VVC.

ZF also offers a slightly larger CFT23 Ecotronic gearbox that uses a hydrodynamic torque converter in place of the VT1's wet starting clutch. It is clear that if a more powerful Steptronic is required in future – such as for a production application of the MGF Super Sports – it would be more likely to be based upon the CFT23, which is capable of handling up to 184lb ft (250Nm). For the moment, however, the existing Steptronic provides an interesting alternative for the motorist who likes to have the best of both worlds, offering one of the most flexible transmission arrangements available on any sports car.

Two views of a 2000 model
year MGF in Solar Red: one
distinguishing feature is the
smoked transparent finish
to the front indicators.

The **2000 Model Year** face-lift

The introduction of the MGF Steptronic formed just part of a programme of improvements across the MGF range for the 2000 Model Year.

Other significant changes included a make-over for the interior (promised for some time) including the choice of 'ash' or 'walnut' interior trim plastics. These names were perhaps a little confusing, for rather than referring to types of timber overlay, they were intended to indicate dark grey or light beige respectively. The instrument display came in for attention, losing the cream faces that had been so much admired (or despised, depending on your point of view) back in 1995; some commentators thought that the new silver faces were rather bland if better in other respects.

Other features, long overdue and introduced following customer demand, included: electric door mirror adjustment (considered back in 1995), an adjustable steering column (dramatically improving the driving position for taller drivers), revised interior panel work (which appeared to be made of higher quality materials, with a superior fit and finish) and a neat gear-lever console modelled on the Allen key theme of the fuel filler surround.

Outside, the main changes visible to the casual observer were the smoked 'clear' indicator lenses at the front and a change from the previous black-painted windscreen surround to body colour. The latter change was made sufficiently late in the day, it was confided to me, that the press cars available in July 1999 had had to have their black screen surrounds resprayed to match the body. Inevitably, there were new wheel and tyre combinations, including new 'square-spoke' alloys shared by the VVC and Steptronic that bore a passing resemblance to the wheels fitted to the latest top-of-the-range BMW 3 Series.

During 1999 there were a number of stories in the British motoring press that suggested the imminent demise of the VVC version of the MGF, claiming that there were technical difficulties in getting the high-tech variable valve head version of the K-series through imminent EEC emissions legislation. At Geneva in March 1999, Chris Lee sought to dispel these rumours: 'People keep talking about future problems for the VVC but we are still working very hard to try to find a way of getting through the emissions programme for both the 1.8 (110cu in) base engine and the VVC. If we don't do that, we still have to think about what we will put in the car for the top-of-the-range version – although we would still look at a supercharged version as an extension to the range rather than a substitute for the VVC.'

Also keen to defend the VVC is Ian Elliott. 'When we launched the 1.6, 1.8 (97, 110cu in) and VVC engines at a technical conference in early 1995, we had some emissions

Historic Goodwood circuit was one of the stops on the July 1999 press launch for the revised MGF. Spoked 16in alloy wheels are an optional extra.

Cabin was improved in quality and fittings for the 2000 model year. 'Walnut' interior trim option (the name refers to the beige colour) offers a quite different look from the previous dark grey plastics.

graphs, with HC/CO plotted up one axis and NOx along the other,' he recalled. 'Each K-series engine was plotted in the relevant place, with the best engine very markedly close to the origin, which represented perfection – and that was the VVC. In fact, so good was the VVC that I wondered if it might become the standard engine in time, if only to meet emissions legislation! It really is nonsense to suggest that the VVC is more difficult to get through ECD3,4 than the standard K-series units.'

The VVC engine depended on its continued existence not only on the MGF but also the Rover 200 range and the latter's autumn 1999 face-lift; if it had been an MG-only engine, its future might have been as vulnerable as that of the MGA Twin Cam unit 40 years earlier.

The future for MGF and MG

Many observers were surprised to see an MGF Super Sports making a third appearance at the September 1999 Frankfurt Motor Show – and a month later at the Tokyo Motor Show. This was basically the 1999 Geneva Show car, now resprayed in a dazzling Chromaflair green-gold paint, trimmed with green and black leather inside and with a cockpit generally upgraded to 2000 Model Year specification. Most onlookers hoped that it would be a case of third time lucky; this seemed a clear indication that a green light for the Super Sports was imminent.

According to MG spokesman Mike McHale (speaking in November 1999) there was a good reaction to the Super Sports at Tokyo. 'The people in Japan said it was a winner and there was a lot of interest on the stand: some people even wanted to put down orders there and then. We know that we could sell say 300 per annum but at the end of the day money has to be found and resources made available. The BMW Group is heavily committed to other projects right now and while it is very much on our wish list, we have to weigh up the benefits of spending time and money on Super Sports against other projects.' Sadly, despite a favourable reaction in the motoring press, the Super Sports never seemed to get the attention it deserved within BMW and by the beginning of 2000 it seemed increasingly unlikely that it would ever see production. Sources within BMW later revealed that the company was considering an open MG sports car version of the new front-wheel-drive Mini, slotted below the planned new BMW Z3.

However, unbeknown to McHale (or indeed anyone else outside a very small group) by the time of our conversation, BMW had already been mulling over an approach from Alchemy Partners for a month. Alchemy (one of the top six venture capital companies in the UK) had called Munich with an interesting proposal – effectively to buy Rover – and

cheekily but cannily suggested that BMW should consider selling Land Rover to offset the losses involved. 'We saw an opportunity to resolve somebody's major problem and at the same time to create a big opportunity for ourselves,' explained Alchemy's Managing Partner, Jon Moulton. 'We could see the problem and had the courage of our convictions to call BMW directly and ask them for a meeting.'

The reaction of BMW, which had already pumped billions into the former Rover Group and still talked publicly of turning Rover around, was not easy for Alchemy to predict. Moulton and his colleague Eric Walters were favourably received by BMW's Finance Director, Helmut Panke, made their case and returned to England on the same day, uncertain if their proposal would take root but with the strong feeling that they had interested Panke. Over the next few months, Moulton flew to Munich ten times and nearly always dealt with Panke and his team; BMW Chairman

Third version of Super
Sports, revealed in 1999, is
painted in an eye-catching
'Chromaflair' green/gold
'flip-flop' finish. Distinctive
central 'splitter' remains
under the tail.

Heavily bolstered sports seats feature inside the revised Super Sports.

Joachim Milberg preferred to remain aloof from the discussions. 'I wouldn't have met Professor Milberg at all if I hadn't stumbled into him in a corridor one day; he took no part in the proceedings,' Moulton explained. 'Obviously he preferred to do it at more remote control than perhaps I would have been able to bear if I had been in his shoes!'

What Moulton and his team masterminded was the acquisition of not only the Rover and MG names but also the main car assembly buildings at the Longbridge factory (where the MGF is made) and the brokering of an agreement for BMW to continue supplies of the Rover 75 from its factory at Cowley. The all-new Mini, originally planned for production in new facilities at Longbridge, would shift to Cowley, while BMW would retain a reduced presence at Longbridge in Rover Powertrain. Alchemy devised its bold plan under the corny code-name of Project Crufts. 'That's absolutely true,' said Moulton, laughing. 'One of my partners, Paul Bridges, was responsible for that. It would have been nice to have tied in our announcement to the actual show, but we aren't that clever – actually we hadn't a clue when the dog show was going to take place!'

Buying the MG brand was an essential part of the equation as far as Moulton was concerned: 'It is the strongest name in the Group by a long way and without the MG name we absolutely wouldn't have done the deal. It was the hardest thing to get BMW to part with – they clearly didn't want to let the MG name go; they could clearly see that it had some uses for themselves. But without that, we wouldn't have had

a leg to stand on.' Moulton could see that even though BMW was reluctant to part with the MG name, it had posed some problems for the company. 'They undoubtedly struggled with the fact that it was at least partly competitive with their own BMW brand product,' he believes.

BMW made no mention of the talks with Alchemy, even speaking positively about turning Rover round at the Geneva Motor Show at the end of February 2000. Within a fortnight, however, the rumour mill went into overdrive, sparked by a leaked agenda for the BMW Supervisory Board meeting planned for 15 March. Various 'options' for Rover were tabled at that meeting – their full extent remains undisclosed but is not difficult to fathom – but the Alchemy proposal won through. BMW called what would prove to be a stormy press conference in Munich on Friday 17 March and in the following days and weeks there would be much angry debate about the sequence of events, with dark mutterings of betrayal being expressed in the West Midlands. The fact remained, however, that unless BMW backtracked, no one else seemed to be able to offer a viable alternative to the Alchemy proposal.

For a limited period, during the fortnight after the Alchemy deal had been announced, Jon Moulton and his team remained in exclusive negotiations with BMW, and indeed both parties appeared adamant that a successful outcome to their discussions would be little more than a formality when the deadline for exclusive talks expired on 28 April. At the same time, however, a rival bid began to take shape, before long under the wing of former Rover Group Chairman John

Towers, now a Director at Concentric, a small Midlands firm that numbered BMW Group's British subsidiary as one of its chief customers.

Towers and the partners in his alliance – Nick Stephenson (by now a non-executive director at Lola, the racing car specialist), John Edwards and Peter Beale (both associated with a major Rover dealership) – were concerned at the scale of redundancies that Alchemy proposed, and believed that they could offer a plan that retained far more jobs, and would maintain volume production at Longbridge. The alliance called itself the Phoenix Consortium, echoing the name of the project that had inspired the MGF. 'To a degree the choice of name was coincidental,' Nick Stephenson claims, 'but you could argue that these things are subliminal. John has to take responsibility for the name, and he claims that in the dead of night, while giving thoughts to an alternative to the Alchemy bid, he suddenly recognised that such a project would need a name – and Phoenix was the one that came to mind.'

Towers and Stephenson effectively took the lead roles in the initial fairly informal discussions with BMW, which were conducted with Professor Werner Sämann, the BMW Board member directly responsible for Rover Group affairs. At this stage, however, the talks between Phoenix and BMW, while remaining cordial, had no basis for agreement because Alchemy remained in exclusive negotiations. BMW continued businesslike talks with Alchemy's legal team while at the same time entertaining Phoenix's approach, but publicly expressed doubt about the latter's ability to secure the necessary finances to underpin their more ambitious plan. Alchemy, meanwhile, announced the basis of a bold business plan that included such objectives as a return to US sales, a partnership with Lotus and a dramatic return for MG to the famous Le Mans 24 hour race after a gap of more than 35 years. On 27 April, BMW received a delegation of petition-bearing union officials, who had rallied behind the Phoenix cause and were hoping to persuade BMW to reconsider the Alchemy deal on the eve of the expected completion. BMW issued a press release from Munich that declared: 'During this visit BMW made clear that despite a demand of BMW the financial backing by the [Phoenix] consortium has not been provided yet. On the occasion of the visit of the unions, BMW has once again repeated this fact and pointed out that this does not constitute a basis for entering negotiations with the Phoenix consortium. The negotiations with Alchemy Partners

The MGF SE – for Special Equipment – was launched in July 2000. Distinctive features include Wedgwood Blue paintwork, 16in multi-spoke alloy wheels, a rear spoiler, chromed exterior features and a 'windstop' for open-top comfort.

2000 Model Year **specifications**

Engine	1.8i	1.8i Steptronic	1.8i VVC
Capacity	1,796cc (110cu in)	1,796cc (110cu in)	1,796cc (110cu in)
Bore	80.0mm (3.15in)	80.0mm (3.15in)	80.0mm (3.15in)
Stroke	89.3mm (3.52in)	89.3mm (3.52in)	89.3mm (3.52in)
Ignition	MEMS 1.9	MEMS	MEMS 2J
Maximum power	121bhp (120PS) at 5,500rpm	121bhp (120PS) at 5,500rpm	147bhp (145PS) at 7,000rpm
Maximum torque	165Nm (122lb ft) at 3,000rpm	165Nm (122lb ft) at 3,000rpm	174Nm (128lb ft) at 4,500rpm
Max engine rpm	6,800	6,000	7,100
Power-to-weight ratio			
(bhp/PS per tonne)	114/113	110/109	137/135

Transmission ratios			
First	3.166	2.416	3.166
Second	1.842	1.520	1.842
Third	1.307	1.123	1.307
Fourth	1.033	0.845	1.033
Fifth	0.765	0.681	0.765
Sixth	–	0.518	–
Reverse	3.000	2.658	3.000
Final drive ratio	3.938	4.050	4.200
Transfer gear ratio	–	1.423	–
		25.7 (41.4) CVT mode	

Suspension	
Front	Double wishbones, Hydragas units interconnected front to rear, dampers, anti-roll bar
Rear	Double wishbones, brake reaction rods, Hydragas units interconnected front to rear, dampers, anti-roll bar

Steering			
Type	Rack and pinion with electric power assistance		
Turns lock to lock	3.1	3.1	3.1
Turning circle (kerbs)	10.56m (34ft 8in)	10.56m (34ft 8in)	10.56m (34ft 8in)

Brakes	
ABS type	Bosch 5.3
Front	240mm (9.45in) diameter ventilated discs
Rear	240mm (9.45in) diameter solid discs

will continue in a straightforward manner'. However, Phoenix had garnered help from quarters that Alchemy could not muster. The unions began to mount a legal challenge to BMW, with a threat to sue on behalf of their members for 'improper consultation' on the proposals – a threat that could have exposed BMW or Alchemy to payouts of millions of pounds; the unions obligingly offered to withdraw these should the Phoenix bid be approved, doubtless concentrating Bavarian minds in the process. The British Government, battered by criticism that it had been unaware of proceedings leading up to the deal, also began to offer tacit support for the Phoenix camp. Then, on the very day that everyone expected a deal with Alchemy to be announced, Moulton walked away, claiming that BMW had 'moved the goalposts' by demanding that he underwrite the £100 million compensation talked of by the unions. Celebrations ensued outside the Longbridge factory, where Alchemy's plans for

large-scale redundancies had hardly been popular. With Phoenix's position still not settled, BMW made it clear that Longbridge must be either sold or closed – and wanted a deal brokered before the next BMW Supervisory Board meeting of 16 May.

The motoring world watched with bated breath: Phoenix had only been able to enter formal negotiations after 28 April, and the idea of doing a deal to buy a car business in little over a fortnight seemed an impossible goal. Nevertheless, Towers and his team went to Munich and came back with the bare bones of an agreement, entering into talks with the same BMW negotiating team that had just finished talking to Alchemy. By 9 May, after much burning of midnight oil, the deal had been done – and there was a symbolic exchange of a £10 note as Phoenix bought Longbridge, a licence to use the Rover Group name, outright ownership of the MG, Austin, Morris, Wolseley and Standard marques, and

	1.8i	1.8i Steptronic	1.8i VVC
Tyres			
Front	185/55VR-15	185/55VR-15	215/40ZR-16
Rear	205/50VR-15	205/50VR-15	215/40ZR-16
Spare	175/656T-14	175/656T-14	175/656T-14
Weights			
Kerb weight	1,060kg (2,337lb)	1,100kg (2,425lb)	1,070kg (2,359lb)
Gross vehicle weight	1,320kg (2,910lb)	1,320kg (2,910lb)	1,320kg (2,910lb)
Distribution front/rear	45/55 per cent	45/55 per cent	45/55 per cent
Dimensions (all versions)			
Wheelbase	2,380mm (93.70in)		
Length	3,910mm (153.94in)		
Width, excluding mirrors	1,630mm (64.17in)		
Width, including mirrors	1,780mm (70.08in)		
Height, hood up	1,270mm (50.0in)		
Front track	1,400mm (55.12in)		
Rear track	1,410mm (55.51in)		
Legroom	1,090mm (42.91in)		
Headroom	960mm (37.80in)		
Shoulder room	1,240mm (44.82in)		
Luggage capacity	0.21cu m (7.4cu ft)		
Fuel tank	50.0 litres (11.0 Imperial gallons, 13.21 US gallons)		
Drag coefficients	Cd 0.36, CdA 0.62		
Manufacturer's performance & fuel consumption figures			
0-60mph (0-100kmh)	8.5 (9.0)	9.5 (10.0)	7.0 (7.7)
30-50mph (48-80kmh) in fourth	6.6	–	6.2
50-70mph (80-112kmh) in fourth	7.0	–	6.5
Max speed mph (kmh)	120 (193)	118 (190)	130 (209)
Fuel consumption (Imperial mpg, US mpg, litres/100km)			
Urban	27.8, 23.2, 10.2	24.4, 20.3, 11.6	25.2, 21.0, 11.2
Extra urban	49.3, 41.0, 5.7	43.9, 36.6, 6.4	48.8, 40.7, 5.8
Combined	38.3, 31.9, 7.4	34.0, 28.3, 8.3	36.3, 30.3, 7.8

various related agreements. John Towers and Nick Stephenson were greeted like homecoming heroes when they drove through the gates at Longbridge on the morning the deal was announced. Seven days later, Professor Milberg was able to announce – with undoubted relief – that a deal had been done, and so Rover Group – and MG – were once more back in British ownership, with some old hands on the tiller.

So where does this leave MG, and more specifically the future of the MGF? Nick Stephenson is in no doubt that this is the beginning of an exciting new chapter for the octagon. 'We see MG as having been massively under-exploited, and our vision is that we see it as being a marque that will stand alongside Rover in terms of its physical scale and importance. Historically that hasn't been the case, but we intend to change that.'

There are bold plans for MG under Phoenix's stewardship – new sporting derivatives of Rovers, and ultimately new MG

sports cars and sports saloons – but for the MGF there should be a great future too, possibly taking some inspiration from the Super Sports concept. Within days of the deal, Nick Stephenson had initiated a review of the Super Sports study and other exercises, and assured me that the MGF would have 'a lot more exciting product action applied to it'. Stephenson hopes also to use his connections at Lola to help shape the MGF: 'One of the issues with the MG brand, I believe, is that it needs "sharpening up". The fact is that, if anything, it has become a little "soft" over time, and we are absolutely going to give it a hard edge again. Because it is a very natural fit, and the fact that Lola has very much supported the consortium from day one, I cannot think of anything more natural than to use some of Lola's race-car skills to help put that hard edge back into MG.'

For MG, and particularly the MGF, exciting times are clearly just around the corner…

Index

WASHI

THE ART OF
JAPANESE PAPER

WASHI

THE ART OF JAPANESE PAPER

NANCY BROADBENT CASSERLEY

Kew Publishing
Royal Botanic Gardens, Kew

First published in 2013 by
Royal Botanic Gardens, Kew
Richmond, Surrey, TW9 3AB, UK

www.kew.org

ISBN 978 1 84246 486 1

Distributed on behalf of the Royal Botanic Gardens, Kew in North America by the University of Chicago Press,
1427 East 60th Street, Chicago, IL 60637, USA.

British Library Cataloguing in Publication Data
A catalogue record for this book is available from the British Library.

Cover design: Jeff Eden
Design, typesetting and page layout: Nicola Thompson, Culver Graphics, from an original design by Jeff Eden.

Printed in Great Britain by Ashford Colour Press

Printed on 150gsm Essential Silk which is FSC certified

For information or to purchase all Kew titles please visit
www.kewbooks.com or email publishing@kew.org

Kew's mission is to inspire and deliver science-based plant conservation worldwide, enhancing the quality of life.

Kew receives half of its running costs from Government through the Department for Environment,
Food and Rural Affairs (Defra). All other funding needed to support Kew's vital work comes from members,
foundations, donors and commercial activities including book sales.

CONTENTS

INTRODUCTION

Washi, or handmade Japanese paper, has long held a central role in the domestic, spiritual and cultural life of Japan. Its aesthetic of simplicity, purity and tranquility mirrors a fundamental aspect of Japanese culture itself.

Historically, washi was used in the structure of the home on *shoji* (wooden latticed frames used as windows) and on *fusuma* (paper-covered wooden frames used as sliding partitions). It was used for making decorative screens, umbrellas, clothing, lanterns, fans, kites, dolls, toys, storage boxes, string, hats and raincoats. It was used in the tea ceremony, in Shinto worship and ritual, and for copying Buddhist sutras. It was the dominant support for calligraphy, which held an elevated cultural and philosophical position through its ability to reveal the cultivation and character of the creator. And, of course, as in the West, it had utilitarian uses in correspondence, record-keeping, printing and publishing. While some of the traditional uses have diminished or vanished over the years, washi is still a deeply evocative and significant material, craft and art form in Japan.

The rich history and striking diversity of washi are illustrated in this book through examples from two collections: the portion of the nineteenth century Parkes Collection held in the Economic Botany Collection at the Royal Botanic Gardens, Kew, and a twenty-first century collection assembled by the Washi: The Soul of Japan Committee. The collections have been brought together in an exhibition entitled 'Washi: The Art of Japanese Paper' held at The Gallery at NUA in Norwich, UK, from 12 March to 20 April 2013, and the opportunity for this study has arisen out of that exhibition.

Both of the collections provide a snapshot of washi production at the time of their assembly: the Parkes Collection between 1869 and 1870, and the Washi: the Soul of Japan Collection between 1998 and 2005. The history, significance and content of the collections will be discussed in the subsequent sections of this book.

THE HISTORY OF WASHI

Washi is the commonly-used word for paper which is made by hand in Japan. It is generally made using traditional methods that have changed very little over the centuries. Chinese methods of papermaking were introduced to Kyoto in 610 AD by a Korean priest named Dancho, and the craft spread rapidly to neighbouring provinces. By the beginning of the Nara Period (708–794 AD) nine provinces in Japan were making paper, which was used for census and tax records and for copying Buddhist sutras. The oldest dateable pieces of paper in Japan date from 710 and were used for census records.

During the Heian period (794–1185), each region of the country became known for a particular type of paper, and elaborately decorated and skillfully dyed papers proliferated. Demand for paper grew with the flowering of literary pursuits at court, eventually leading the government to set up its own papermaking centre in Kyoto to supply the needs of the court and governmental agencies. The papermaking technique called *nagashi-zuki*, which is unique to Japan and relates to the method of dispersing the solution of paper pulp on the screen, is believed to have developed here at that time. By the end of the Heian period, papermaking was an important cottage industry throughout Japan. In rural areas, washi joined rice, cloth and coins as an acceptable currency for paying taxes.

The Kamakura period (1185–1333) saw the rise of Zen Buddhism in Japan. Its emphasis on humility, simplicity and aesceticism was reflected in the use of washi to make clothing. The demand for paper expanded further during the Muromachi period (1333–1573), when intense economic growth led to the production of paper for trade as well as for local consumption. The development of a guild system during this period further encouraged the refinement of techniques both for making and decorating paper.

By the beginning of the Edo period (1603–1868), paper was second only to rice as the greatest source of tax income for the Japanese government. While certain villages or areas were famous for their paper, virtually all areas in Japan needed to make paper in order to support their local economy. An additional use for paper arose with the introduction of paper currency during this period, although country-wide standardization was not imposed until the Meiji period (1868–1912).

The Meiji period saw the beginning of the end of Japan's washi culture, as the government encouraged emulation of the West and, specifically, hastened the industrialization of the paper industry. This coincided with the worldwide focus on wood pulp as the raw material for machine-made paper. Production and cost requirements in this new era forced many washi makers to close down, while others tried unsuccessfully to compete with machines by modifying traditional production methods. The number of papermaking households decreased from approximately 70,000 in the early twentieth century to 13,500 in 1941 and to 3,500 in 1962. In the 1960s and 1970s

Fig. 1-1
Washi on interior partitions and walls, Katsura Rikyu Imperial Villa, Kyoto

there was a government effort to support papermaking by creating designations such as Intangible Cultural Asset for certain kinds of washi and papermaking techniques. Nonetheless, the number of recorded papermakers dropped to 886 in 1973, to 446 in 1992, and to approximately 350 in 2010. Now, younger washi makers tend not to be from traditional washi-making families but to have been drawn to the practice from a love of washi and of the process itself.

THE RAW MATERIALS FOR MAKING WASHI

While the Chinese originally used hemp in paper production, from the ninth century onward Japanese papermakers have relied on the fibrous inner bark of three plants: *kōzo, gampi* and *mitsumata*. All are small trees that used to flourish throughout Japan and that, in the case of *kōzo* and *mitsumata*, are now cultivated for papermaking. *Gampi* is very difficult to cultivate and is now scarce in the wild.

Kōzo is the toughest, strongest and most versatile of the Japanese washi fibres. The long, rough fibres neither expand nor contract, which makes *kōzo* paper particularly suitable for printing. There are two species of mulberry plants (family Moraceae) which are referred to as *kōzo: Broussonetia kazinoki* Siebold (formerly *Broussonetia kaempferi*

Siebold), sometimes called *tsurukōzo*, and *Broussonetia papyrifera* (L.) Vent. (sometimes called *kajinoki*).

Gampi fibres, which are long, thin and almost translucent, produce a glossy, smooth washi. *Gampi* was traditionally considered the 'king' of papermaking fibres, and washi made from *gampi* is both resistant to damp and repellent to insects. A member of the family Thymelaeaceae, *gampi* includes numerous species, of which *Wikstroemia sikokiana* Franch. & Sav. (formerly *Diplomorpha sikokiana* (Franch. & Sav.) Nakai) is considered the best for papermaking.

Mitsumata, the third papermaking fibre, is also a member of the family Thymelaeaceae. It has soft, absorbent, rather weak fibres which are usually used in conjunction with *kōzo* or *gampi*. The highest quality of *mitsumata* fibres are bought by the Japanese government each year to use for making banknotes. Like its relative *gampi, mitsumata* (*Edgeworthia chrysantha* Lindl., formerly *E. papyrifera* Siebold & Zucc.) is resistant to insects.

The creation of very fine and thin sheets of washi relies on adding a viscous agent called *neri* to the solution made up of fibre and water. It acts to even out the fibre particles in the solution and to control water drainage while the sheet is being formed. It is usually made from the roots of the *tororo-aoi* plant of the family Malvaceae (*Abelmoschus manihot* (L.) Medik.).

THE PROCESS OF MAKING WASHI

The fibres used for making washi are the bast fibres of the inner bark, which lies under the corky outer bark of the *kōzo, mitsumata* or *gampi* trees. Separating these fibres from the black bark on the outside, and from the woody core on the inside, is labour intensive and time consuming. There is also considerable waste, with one hundred kilograms of branches producing only five kilograms of paper.

The papermaking process usually begins in Japan in November or December with the harvesting of tree shoots and small trees, which are then cut into one-metre lengths and steamed. The steamed sticks are beaten with mallets to facilitate stripping off the several layers of bark by hand. The outer black and green barks are then scraped away from the inner white bark, which will need to be washed in running water, boiled in an alkali, and washed again. It will then be picked over by hand to remove any remaining bits of dark bark or impurities, and beaten just long enough to loosen the fibres. This preparation process is crucial: seventy percent of the total working hours necessary to produce a batch of washi are spent in isolating and preparing the fibres.

Once the fibres have been prepared they are stirred into a vat of cold water, and a viscous agent is added to the mixture to aid even dispersion of the fibres. The papermaker scoops the watery mixture repeatedly onto the flexible screen in the papermaking mould, each time sloshing the excess off in a vigorous motion that throws water off over the front of the mould. This process of building up the fibres of a sheet of washi is called *nagashi-zuki*, and is one of the key distinguishing features of Japanese papermaking.

A finished sheet of washi is added to a stack by removing the flexible bottom portion of the mould, called the *su*, placing it upside-down on the stack and gently peeling it away, leaving the new sheet lying directly on the other sheets. They are left to drain overnight, pressed gently to remove excess water, and then peeled off one by one to be brushed onto traditional wooden boards or onto more modern metal warming racks for drying. Once the sheets are dry and have been removed from the boards or racks, the final steps are to inspect, organise, cut and wrap the sheets for distribution.

WASHI

THE PARKES COLLECTION OF NINETEENTH CENTURY WASHI

THE PARKES COLLECTION

Fig. 2-1
Sir Harry Parkes, from a photograph by S. Suzuki, Tokyo, July 1883, published in Volume I of *The Life of Sir Harry Parkes K.C.B, G.C.M.G., Sometime Her Majesty's Minister to China & Japan*, by Stanley Lane-Poole and Frederick V. Dickens (London, Macmillan and Co., 1894)

Previous page
Blue and white *Paulownia* and tendrils on an ochre ground (detail)
Woodblock-printed onto washi made of *kōzo*
c. 1869
Parkes Collection at the Economic Botany Collection,
Royal Botanic Gardens, Kew

In the summer of 1869 Sir Harry Parkes, the British minister in Tokyo, received a request from the British Foreign Secretary to prepare a report on Japanese paper products and papermaking techniques. The report was to include 'the various forms that paper is made to assume, in some cases even the form, it is said, of wearing apparel. A report on this matter would be curious and instructive.' According to a notation on the letter, it was Prime Minister Gladstone himself who wanted to learn more about Japanese paper. Gladstone's interest had an economic foundation: since the 1840s an increasing shortage of cotton and linen rags, which were then the primary source of fibre for papermaking, had driven European and American papermakers to experiment with various forms of alternative fibres for making paper. In that economic climate, the possibility that Japan had special knowledge about paper and papermaking could have been of great interest to the British government and to British papermakers.

Parkes enlisted the help of the British consuls in the prefectures of Kanagawa, Nagasaki and Osaka, who collected washi samples and wrote reports for him. Over the course of fifteen months, Parkes and his consuls assembled over one thousand samples illustrating 412 types of washi, as well as at least 50 three-dimensional objects made from washi. The consuls' reports relating to Japanese papermaking included lists itemising different types of washi, their uses, their place of purchase and their cost. The samples of washi included translucent, undyed *minowashi*; woodblock-printed, colourful *karakami*; and oiled, textured *kinkarakawakami* which looked like gilded leather. The three-dimensional objects included helmets, telescopes, fans, boxes for letters and toys, and hair ornaments.

In March of 1871, Sir Harry sent his *Reports on the Manufacture of Paper in Japan* and two boxes of washi samples and objects to London, where the Reports were presented to both Houses of Parliament. There was no recorded reaction from the British paper industry to the Parkes Report, as it became known, and later that summer the washi samples and objects were delivered to the South Kensington Museum (now the Victoria and Albert Museum) where the receipt described them merely as '2 cases containing samples of paper from Japan, as per list attached'.

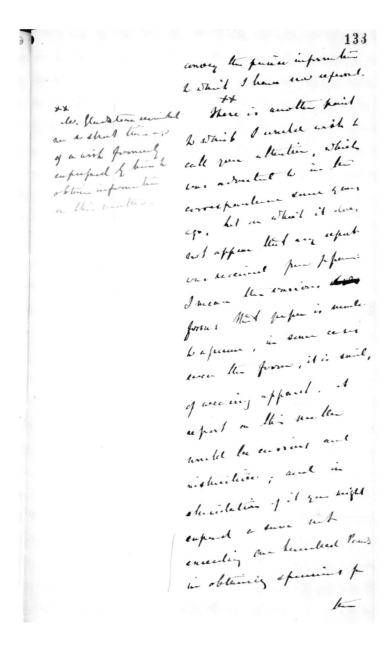

Fig 2-2
Excerpt from letter from Lord Clarendon to Sir Harry Parkes requesting report on Japanese paper (National Archives, FO 46/104)

In 1874 the assemblage of washi came to the attention not of the paper industry but of the botanical community. Dr Joseph Dalton Hooker, the Director of the Royal Botanic Gardens, Kew, learned that the collection was in the South Kensington Museum and requested that it be transferred to Kew, for display in Kew's Museum of Economic Botany, since it was 'exactly fitted to fill a rather important gap in our series of paper materials.' After negotiations, half of the collection was transferred to Kew, which subsequently sent samples to botanical institutions and naturalists in Sydney, Adelaide and Glasgow.

The items that Kew kept are those that form the Parkes Collection in the Economic Botany Collection at Kew today: one hundred and eleven sheets of washi, which are either woodblock-printed in various patterns (karakami) or treated and embossed to look like leather (gikakushi and kinkarakawakami), and seventeen three-dimensional items made of washi. These pieces have never been exhibited in the UK, although they are available in the Economic Botany Collection for use by students and researchers.

Items from the portion of the original Parkes Collection which remained at the South Kensington Museum were exhibited in 1874, but were otherwise uncatalogued and forgotten until paper historians Hans and Tanya Schmoller unearthed them in 1978. The discovery of this part of the Collection caused great excitement in Japan, where the fact of the Collection's creation was well known to historians. The Collection was assumed to have been lost or destroyed over the intervening years, so finding this comprehensive survey of early-Meiji-era washi was a significant event not just for paper historians but for social and cultural historians as well.

As a result of this enthusiasm in Japan for the newly-discovered Parkes Collection, washi samples and objects from both the Kew and V&A portions of the Collection were exhibited in Tokyo in 1994 at the Tobacco and Salt Museum in an exhibition called 'Edo-Period Japanese Paper Sent Overseas: An Exhibition of the Parkes Collection'. The selection of items from Kew included three-dimensional items, samples of washi treated to look like leather, and woodblock-printed karakami.

DECORATED WASHI USED ON SLIDING PARTITIONS (*KARAKAMI*)

Karakami is washi that is applied to the opaque interior sliding partitions (*fusuma*) in a Japanese house or other building. *Karakami* came into use in the late Heian period, when it was first used by the court and subsequently in shrines, temples and aristocratic homes. Production was originally centred in Kyoto, but as *karakami* began to be used on *fusuma* in the homes of the samurai and merchant classes, production shifted to Tokyo. *Karakami* was typically made of strong *kōzo* fibres, often decorated with woodblock-printed patterns incorporating motifs from nature, and glued either to the entire *fusuma* or to its lower half. Nineteenth century visitors to Japan referred to *karakami* as wallpaper, although it was seldom applied to fixed walls. Different *karakami* patterns were favoured by different social groups: palaces, temples and shrines tended to use larger scale designs featuring motifs such as chrysanthemums, *Paulownia* leaves, clouds and cranes; tea ceremony rooms usually used elegant, refined patterns based on flower or vegetative motifs; and private houses tended to use smaller-scale geometric designs or repeated motifs such as cherry or plum blossoms, birds, autumn grasses, or other designs representing the beauty of nature and the seasons.

In order to print designs on the sheets of *karakami* a pigment solution was first applied to the carved surface of a woodblock, usually using a screen made of silk gauze. The sheet of washi was then placed lightly onto the block and rubbed gently with the palm of the hand. The pigment transfer was controlled by the pressure and warmth of the hand, which was a fitting continuation of the labour-intensive process that had begun with the stripping of the bark from the tree cuttings.

Various techniques existed to modify the decoration. To produce richer colours, one half of the washi could be lifted off of the block at a time and pigment reapplied to the block before the washi was pressed gently into place again. For added depth and interest, the washi could be removed and replaced on the block at a ninety-degree angle, either using the same pigment solution on the block or one of a contrasting colour. The washi could be printed first with a small geometric pattern, then printed again on another block with a large, bold design. Powdered oyster shell or mica could be stirred into to the pigment for added lustre, or used alone, in a solution of seaweed and rice starch, to produce a pearlised white effect. After the printing, flakes of gold or silver leaf, or powdered pigment, could be sprinkled or blown over washi that had been brushed with an alum and glue sizing to which the particles could adhere.

The lack of pressure on the block during the printing process meant that the blocks seldom wore out. Some woodblocks dating from the eighteenth century are still in use in Kyoto although many others have been destroyed by fire or thrown away due to space constraints or perceived obsolescence.

The *karakami* in the Parkes Collection was purchased in Nagasaki, although it may have been made elsewhere in Japan. Acting Consul A. A. Annesley sent the *karakami* to Parkes in 1870 and it is listed in Inclosure 5 of the Parkes Report either as 'paper for screens' or 'paper for walls'. These examples of *karakami* were not made to order for the aristocracy but were more likely intended for use in more modest homes, in rooms used for the tea ceremony, or in shrines or temples. In many instances there are three layers of decoration: a painted or dyed ground, a woodblock-printed background pattern, then a larger-scale woodblock-printed design. Each piece measures approximately 470mm x 295mm.

Fig. 2-3
Large-scale silver hollyhock leaves on a white ground

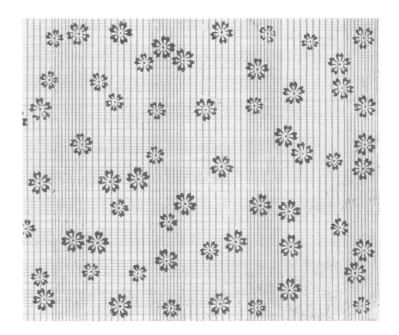

Fig. 2-4
Blue cherry blossoms of varying sizes scattered across an ochre grid on an ochre and white ground (detail)

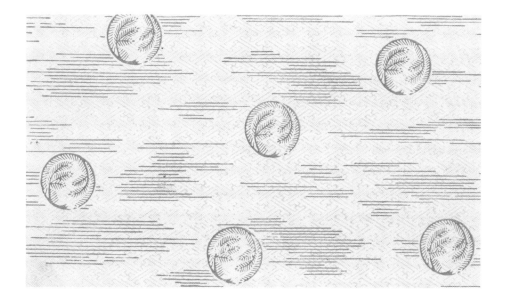

Fig. 2-5
Pine medallions in mist against a key-fret (*sayagata*) motif printed with mica or ground shell

Fig. 2-6
Clematis and arabesques on an ochre ground

Fig. 2-7
Silver *Paulownia* on a white ground

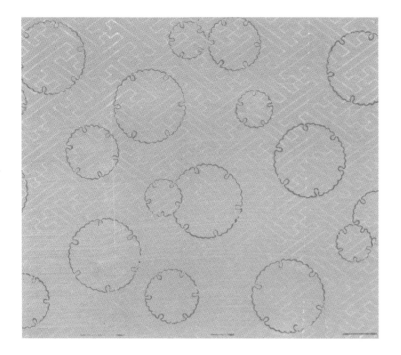

Fig. 2-9
Blue snowflakes on a silver key-fret pattern
(*sayagata*) on a painted mustard ground (detail)

Fig. 2-10
Clematis on a large-scale key-fret pattern
(*sayagata*) printed in mica or ground shell (detail)

Left
Fig. 2-8
White cherry blossoms on
a taupe ground (detail)

Fig. 2-11
Large gold dragon medallion
on a white ground

Fig. 2-12
Floating orchids against a key-fret pattern
(*sayagata*) printed with mica or ground shell

Fig. 2-13
Green pine trees on a grey ground with
blown or sprinkled powdered pigment

Fig. 2-14
Phoenix among arabesques and flowers,
rendered as if stitched (detail)

Fig. 2-15
Large-scale key-fret pattern (*sayagata*), emphasizing the
Buddhist *manji* shape, in gold on a white ground (detail)

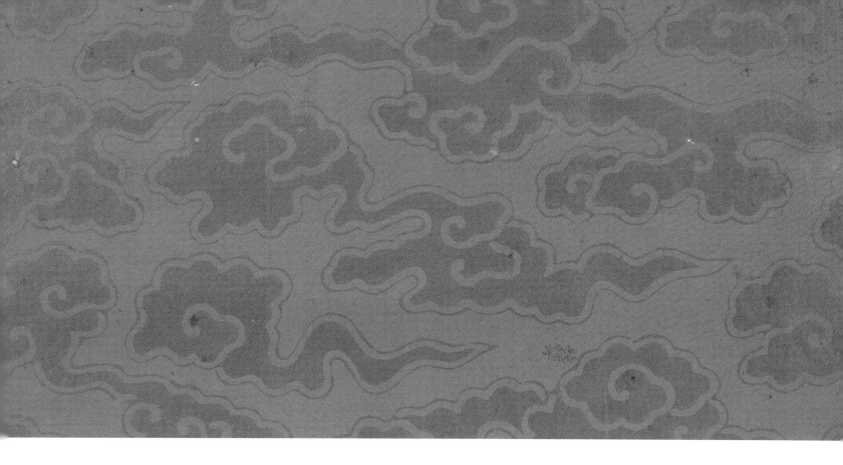

Fig. 2-16
Blue clouds on a
grey ground

Fig. 2-17
Silver bamboo and trellis
on a white ground (detail)

Fig. 2-18
Blue and gold ferns in medallions
on a painted taupe ground (detail)

Fig. 2-19
Blue fans on a grey ground with blown or
sprinkled powdered pigment (detail)

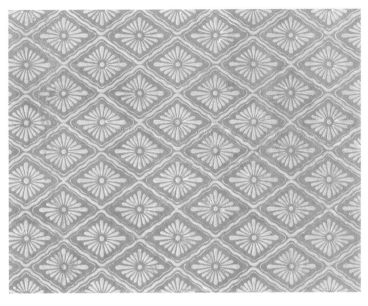

Fig. 2-20
White chrysanthemums in diamond-shaped
lozenges on a grey ground (detail)

Fig. 2-21
Blue key-fret pattern (*sayagata*)
on a white ground (detail)

Fig. 2-22
Blue ferns against a key-fret (*sayagata*) motif printed with mica or ground shell

Fig. 2-23
Taupe and grey
crackle pattern

Fig. 2-24
Blue peonies and wide
ogees on a taupe ground

Fig. 2-25
Leaves, berries and arabesques
in silver on a white ground

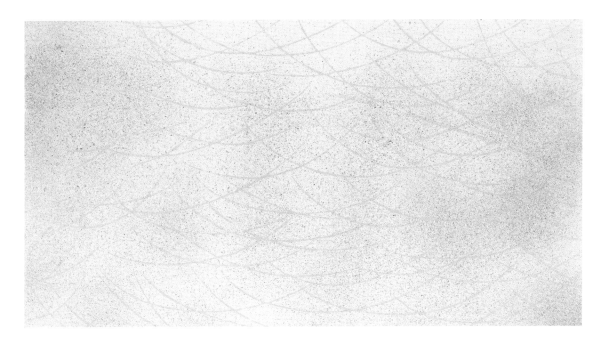

Fig. 2-26
Silver grass on a white ground with blown or sprinkled powdered pigment

Fig. 2-27
Gold chrysanthemums in a Chinese brocade pattern (*shokko*) of octagons and squares on a green ground

Right
Fig. 2-28
Silver floral medallions in squares of blue pine branches (detail)

WASHI TREATED TO LOOK LIKE LEATHER (*GIKAKUSHI* AND *KINKARAKAWAKAMI*)

In the late Edo period (1603–1868), washi treated to look like leather (*gikakushi*) was widely used for making tobacco pouches, containers and bags. This imitation leather was made by gluing two or more pieces of washi together, including a thin dyed piece and a sturdier, often recycled piece for the backing. The resulting piece would be dampened, treated with an oil such as the oil from the Japanese persimmon (*Diospyros kaki* Thunb.), pressed around carved rollers made from cherry wood, and pounded with a special brush in order to make the washi sink into the carved relief and take on the three-dimensional pattern. If a smooth, polished-leather look was desired, the textured surface of the washi, or the surface of treated but non-textured washi, could be rubbed with a wild boar tusk or a piece of earthenware to give a glossy finish to the surface.

This textured imitation-leather washi could also be covered with gold leaf and varnished to make it resemble eighteenth century Spanish leather wallpaper. This kind of washi, called *kinkarakawakami*, was first shown in the West at the London International Exhibition of 1862, and soon architects and designers such as William Burges, E.W.Godwin and Christopher Dresser were using it in interiors. By the Vienna World Exhibition in 1873 its popularity in England and Europe had grown to the extent that retailers like Liberty stocked it for use not only as wallpaper but also for bookbinding, fire screens or as decorative inserts in aesthetic-movement furniture. The British company Rottmann, Strome & Company, which was established in 1883 with offices in London and Yokohama, had Japanese craftsmen make *kinkarakawakami* in 36-inch-wide sheets in order to reduce the number of visible seams in a papered wall. *Kinkarakawakami* was installed in the Royal Institution of Great Britain's lecture hall in the 1880s and in William Morris's Red House while Charles Holmes lived there.

Changes in fashion led to the decline of the industry in the 1920s, and the technique for creating *kinkarakawakami* was lost. Today there is only one active craftsman in Japan, Takashi Ueda, who reinvented the lost technique in the 1980s in order to restore the wall coverings in an early twentieth century building in Hokkaido. He calls his technique *kinkarakami* and acknowledges that it is not an exact replication of the older technique. He has been involved in numerous restorations of *kinkarakawakami* in Japan as well as in new installations and exhibitions of his work.

The pieces of imitation-leather washi in the Parkes Collection were all purchased by Sir Harry Parkes in Tokyo at the shops Takeya and Okuraya. They are listed in Inclosure 9 of the Parkes Report. They range in size from 255mm x 165mm to 580mm x 430mm.

Fig. 2-29
Flower vase and arabesques on book cover made of gilded imitation-leather washi (*kinkarakawakami*)

This piece of *kinkarakawakami* is believed to have been copied directly from a specific 17th century Dutch piece of gold-embossed leather.

Fig. 2-30
Flowers, grapes and leaves on gilded imitation-leather washi (*kinkarakawakami*)

This dense pattern of fruits, leaves and flowers is similar to those seen on Spanish and Dutch leather wallpaper. The grain of the 'leather' is visible as well as the designs themselves, which must have required extreme detail and depth on the carved wooden roller into which the washi was pressed. According to the Parkes Report, this would have been used 'by the upper classes in the various modes of room-decoration, as wall-papers, screen, paneling, covering boxes, &c'.

Fig. 2-31
Clouds on gilded
imitation-leather washi
(*kinkarakawakami*)

The auspicious cloud
pattern that is believed to
have originated in China
two thousand years ago
has been miniaturized on
the gold surface of the
imitation-leather washi.
The possible uses would
have been the same as
for Fig. 2-30.

Fig. 2-32
Diagonal lines of patterns
on gilded imitation-leather
washi (*kinkarakawakami*)

This sampler of geometric motifs
based on birds, flowers and foliage
has a strong sense of movement, and
would have been used for the same
purposes as Figs. 2-30 and 2-31.

Fig. 2-33
Square patchwork of patterns on black
imitation-leather washi (*gikakushi*)

These squares and triangles contain patterns of ogees,
arabesques, flowers, leaves and geometric shapes. This type
of washi would have been used for the same purposes as
Figs. 2-30, 2-31 and 2-32.

Fig. 2-34
Striated black
imitation-leather
washi (*gikakushi*)
(detail)

In order to achieve this gloss and stiffness this washi would
have been painted with black lacquer after it had been
dampened, oiled and pressed into a carved roller. According to
the Parkes Report it would have been used 'largely for making
boxes, purses, pocket-books, tobacco-pouches, &c'.

Fig. 2-35
Burgundy coarse
imitation-leather
washi (*gikakushi*)

Similar to Fig. 2-34, this piece would have
been used for making small containers and
pouches which would have been hard-
wearing and water-resistant.

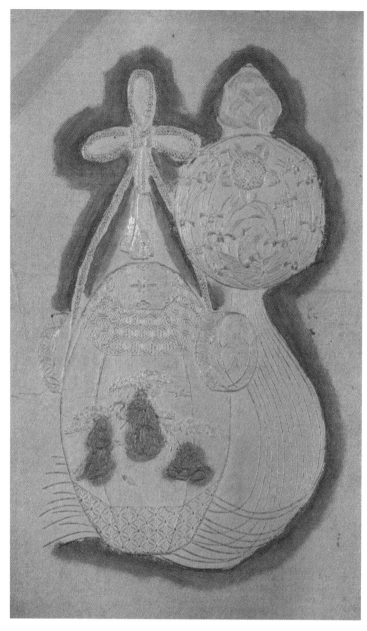

Fig. 2-36
Grey imitation-leather washi (*gikakushi*)
with image of child's toy

The hexagonal toy with strings shown on this
washi was used for hitting balls in a children's
game, and became a typical New Year's
decoration in the Edo period. The Parkes Report
notes that this kind of washi would have been
used for making boxes and pouches. The
centred image might have made this piece of
washi suitable for a decorative box lid.

THREE-DIMENSIONAL OBJECTS MADE FROM WASHI

Seventeen three-dimensional objects have survived in the Kew part of the Parkes Collection, including the original *kōzo* branches, bark and pulp sent to illustrate the papermaking method. There are also a number of items made from the imitation-leather washi (*gikakushi*) described above, including water-resistant shoe covers and a pocketbook.

Other three-dimensional items in the Collection are woven from fine string made from washi (*koyori*), or made from washi that has been shaped and lacquered (*ikkanbari*). Lacquered paper was as strong and durable as wood but had the advantage of being much lighter, so was a popular material in the Edo period for many household and personal items. Lacquered paper items in the Parkes Collection include a helmet and a telescope.

Finally, the other three-dimensional paper items in the Parkes Collection are decorative hair ribbons and hair accessories that flutter and drape as if made of silk. They are mostly made from *chirimenshi*, which is very fine washi that has been compressed around a wooden pole and wrinkled to look like silk crêpe. These are decorated using the resist-paste dyeing techniques of stencil dyeing or tie-dyeing. The three-dimensional items seen here, with the exception of the hair ornaments, were collected in Nagasaki by Acting Consul Annesley and sent to Sir Harry Parkes in 1870. The hair ornaments were bought in Osaka. They are all listed in the Parkes Report in Inclosure 5.

Fig. 2-37
Cut branches from the *kōzo* (*Broussonetia kazinoki*), rough bark and partially-prepared inner bark

These items illustrate the three earliest stages of the papermaking process when the branches are cut, the bark stripped off, and the valuable inner bark removed from the dark outer bark.

Fig. 2-38
Kōzo pulp

An intermediate stage of the papermaking process is the creation of pulp through cooking the inner bark in water until it becomes soft. The long pieces of inner bark are still visible, as the pulp has not yet been beaten into a smoother consistency.

Fig. 2-39
Helmet of a government official
335mm x 320mm x 135mm

Numerous sheets of washi were pressed onto a mould, then shaped by hand to create this light, sturdy and elegant helmet. Black lacquer was applied to the outside of the helmet and red lacquer to the inside in a technique called *ikkanbari*. A family crest and fittings for strings to tie the helmet in place were made out of bronze-coloured metal and attached to the inside and outside of the helmet. The helmet would have belonged to a high-ranking government official.

Fig. 2-40 and Fig. 2-41
Exterior and interior of soldier's helmet
340mm x 300mm x 85mm

Narrow strips of washi were twisted into cords
(*koyori*) which were then woven around a frame
to produce this light, strong helmet. Lacquer
has been applied to both exterior and interior,
and the interior is decorated with scattered gold
foil. Despite its elegantly decorated interior, it
was made for soldiers, not for officers, and was
used in the summer as a sun hat.

Fig. 2-42
Nesting toy boxes
150mm x 110mm x 125mm

Several sheets of damp washi were pressed into a wooden board or roller carved with the pattern of a woven surface, or pressed into a woven surface itself, to create indentations in the washi in the shape of weaving. Once dry, the embossed washi was applied to a bamboo frame and lacquered in the *ikkanbari* technique. Each of the three sets of two nesting boxes has a different family crest on the outside box.

Fig. 2-43
Telescope
295mm x 50mm

This refracting telescope, covered with the *ikkanbari* technique of applying lacquer to washi, is decorated with black and red lacquer and gold foil, and has two lens covers. A piece of newspaper printed in German is attached to the inside of the covers, and Japanese characters are written on the eyepiece. It is not known where the lenses were made.

Fig. 2-44 and Fig. 2-45
Interior and exterior of box for stationery or letters
305mm x 329mm x 100mm

Again made by the *ikkanbari* technique, numerous layers of washi were glued to a frame and lacquered, with a colourful woodblock-printed washi glued to the interior of the box and lid and to the removable tray. The chrysanthemum motif on the interior of the box is reflected on the lid, where the surface of the damp washi was impressed with chrysanthemum shapes before being lacquered.

Fig. 2-46
Small stationery or letter box
190mm x 67mm x 25mm

This narrow box was also made with the *ikkanbari* technique of lacquering several layers of washi that have been applied to a frame. The washi on the lid was embossed with overlapping circular motifs prior to lacquering, and three gold chrysanthemums were impressed on the lid after lacquering.

Fig. 2-47
Rain covers for shoes
132mm x 185mm

These washi covers for Japanese wooden
sandals (*geta*) were used when walking
in mud or rain. They were made by the
gikakushi method of dampening layers
of washi, oiling them, and pressing them
around a wooden roller whose surface was
carved to resemble the grain of leather.
The resulting imitation leather was water-
resistant and durable.

Fig. 2-48
Case for thin washi used
as handkerchiefs
85mm x 195mm

This imitation-leather case was listed in
the Parkes Report as a 'Pocket-book' but
was probably a case for pieces of thin
washi which were used as handkerchiefs.
It was made by the same *gikakushi*
method as the shoe covers in Fig. 2-47.

Fig. 2-49
Fan
255mm x 33mm

This fan was made of washi glued onto a
bamboo frame and shows a woodblock-printed
image of samurais who opposed the Tokugawa
shogunate carrying rifles and gathering around
a cannon. It is a reminder of the political turmoil
in Japan in the late 1860s.

Fig. 2-50
Hair ornaments of crèped washi (*chirimen*)
220mm x 50mm

In the 19th century Japanese women began accessorizing their hairstyles with crèped washi copies of traditional silk ribbons and strips of fabric. These pieces were made of fine washi that was dampened, wrapped around wooden poles and compressed several times in varying directions to make patterns of creases and wrinkles that resembled crèped fabric. These pieces were then stencil-dyed with patterns of flowers, gourds and Chinese characters.

Fig. 2-51
Hair ornaments of tie-dyed washi (*kanokoshibori*)
190mm x 70mm

These hair accessories were tie-dyed after the crèping process described in Fig. 2-50. Tiny knots were tied very tightly in the fine, crèped washi, either in diagonal lines, in meandering lines, or in the pattern of stylised hemp leaves. The washi was then dyed and the knots undone to reveal small dots in the original colour.

Fig. 2-52
Hair ornaments of twisted and pleated crèped washi
310mm x 4mm

Thin pieces of crèped washi, as described in Fig. 2-50, were twisted into loose ropes with strips of foil, or were accordion-pleated into square cords. The use of a starch solution from the *Amorphophallus konjac* K.Koch (*konnyaku*) would help them to keep their shape.

Fig. 2-53
Ornamental hairpins (*kanzashi*)
160mm, 165mm long

These decorative hairpins were worn near the face, where the washi flowers would tremble slightly on wire stems in response to the wearer's movement.

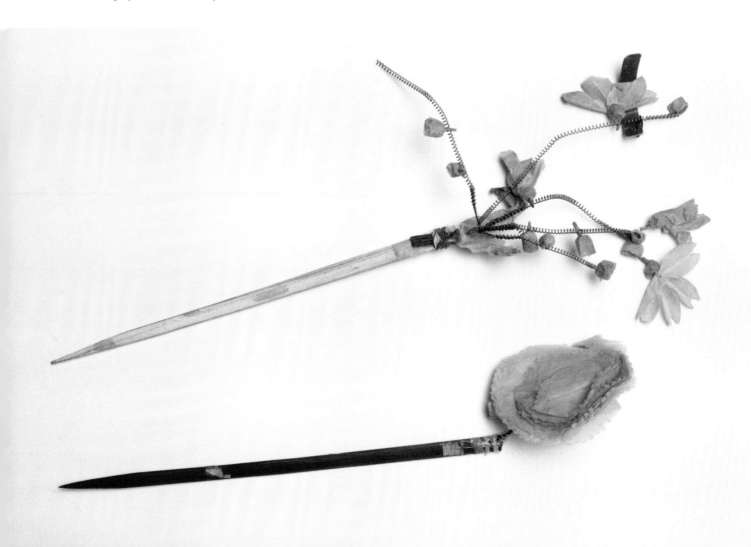

WASHI

THE WASHI: THE SOUL OF JAPAN COLLECTION OF CONTEMPORARY WASHI

THE WASHI: THE SOUL OF JAPAN COLLECTION

This contemporary collection grew out of a plan formulated in the early 1990s between the forerunner to the Washi: The Soul of Japan Committee and a British museum to hold a washi exhibition in the UK. When the exhibition was cancelled in 1998 due to funding problems, the Japanese organising committee decided to call themselves the Washi: The Soul of Japan Committee and to turn their collecting efforts and research towards the production of a multi-volume washi compendium containing washi samples made throughout Japan. The purpose of the compendium would be three-fold: to document the state of washi production in Japan at the turn of the millennium, to act as an inspiration to washi-makers, and to broaden knowledge and access to washi throughout the world.

After two years of collecting washi, three years of preparing the text in Japanese, and five years of translation and editing, the twelve volume compendium was published in 2011. It contains 730 samples and descriptions of plain and decorated washi, along with 320 samples and descriptions of machine-made Japanese paper. The

Committee has kept larger versions of many of the samples included in the compendium to loan for exhibitions. The enormous value of this collection is that it contains a wide variety of contemporary samples from every washi-making prefecture in Japan and provides meticulous description and documentation for each of them in both English and Japanese.

While the surviving washi in the Parkes Collection at Kew falls into only three main categories – decorative washi used on sliding partitions (*karakami*), washi made to resemble leather (*gikakushi* and *kinkarakawakami*), and three-dimensional objects made from washi – the washi collected by the Washi: The Soul of Japan Committee covers scores of categories and sub-categories. The contemporary examples chosen for inclusion in this book are intended to complement the examples from the Parkes Collection in order to provide an overview of various methods of dyeing, treating and decorating washi, as well as to show how the fibres themselves may be manipulated to achieve certain results.

Previous page
Katazomeshi aizome nanbu karakusa sumigiku
Made of *kōzo* by Kuriyama Haruo
Kyoto Prefecture

Chrysanthemums, leaves and arabesques fill the white ground, which would have been protected by the stencil from the indigo dye.

PLAIN WASHI

This term refers to undecorated, undyed washi that contains *kōzo*, *gampi* or *mitsumata* fibres and virtually nothing else. In its unembellished state the quality of the papermaking is particularly evident, as is the nature of the fibres themselves. A stack of white washi may initially look like a pile of identical sheets, but it takes very little time to appreciate the differences in texture, colour, thickness, density and fibre dispersion.

Fig. 3-1
Tokujiwashi kōzo urauchigami
Made of *kōzo* by Chijimatsu Tetsuya
Yamaguchi Prefecture

This washi is cooked in soda ash and soaked in the river, giving it a soft natural colour. The fine but visible fibres give it a liveliness and depth. It is used in conservation projects as well as in *shoji*.

Fig. 3-2
Ogunigami
Made of *kōzo* by Katagiri Saburo
Niigata Prefecture

Washi made in the cold, snowy winter in Niigata is stored, still damp, in the snow until the first sunny days of spring. The washi is then dried on top of the snow, where it is bleached by the sun and the reflected light from the snow. The washi is crisp and thin, with dense fibre distribution.

Fig. 3-3
Tango Futamagami urushikoshi
Made of *kōzo* by Tanaka Masaaki
Kyoto Prefecture

The extreme thinness of this kind of washi makes it a challenge for papermakers. It is soft and drapes well, and the fine, visible fibres give it interest. It is typically used to filter undiluted lacquer and to wrap deluxe Japanese sweets.

Fig. 3-4
Usuminoshi 1.8 momme
Made of *kōzo* by Hasegawa Satoshi
Gifu Prefecture

This is an example of a traditional *minowashi*, which has been designated a Japanese Traditional Craft Product by Japan's Ministry of Economics, Trade and Industry. The town of Mino has been famous for its washi since the 17th century, and at the beginning of the 20th century it was the largest centre of washi production in Japan. *Usuminoshi*, which is extremely fine and soft, is used in the restoration of cultural properties and for various crafts.

WATERMARKED AND WATER-PATTERNED WASHI

A watermark is a faint design or pattern in paper that is usually visible only when the paper is held to the light. A watermark is made in washi by cutting patterns out of treated paper and then placing or sewing these pieces either directly onto the flexible bamboo papermaking screen, or by sewing them onto a piece of silk gauze and then placing or sewing the gauze onto the screen. The film of fibres on top of the applied paper pieces will be thinner than the rest of the sheet, thereby creating the pattern. For a less regular pattern, water can be directly or indirectly sprinkled, sprayed or poured onto the fibres on the screen in order to displace them and create either thinner areas, more like a watermark in concept, or created holes for a lace-like effect. Watermarks have been used in Japan since the 1700s, particularly in connection with providing security for paper money.

Fig. 3-5
Sukashi hanamoy
Made from *kōzo* by Okahisa Mai
Osaka Prefecture

Silk gauze with an applied 8-petal flower design is placed on the papermaking screen during sheet formation, allowing only a partial layer of fibre to accumulate in the blocked areas. This washi is used for collages, tablecloths or other decorative items.

Fig. 3-6
Sukashi ryūsui
Made from 90% *kōzo*, 10% wood pulp by Yamashiro Mutsuko
Kyoto Prefecture

Controlled streams of water are poured over the blue fibres on the papermaking screen, displacing the fibres and creating an irregular watermark in the image of a flowing river. This is used as a background for collages or for calligraphy.

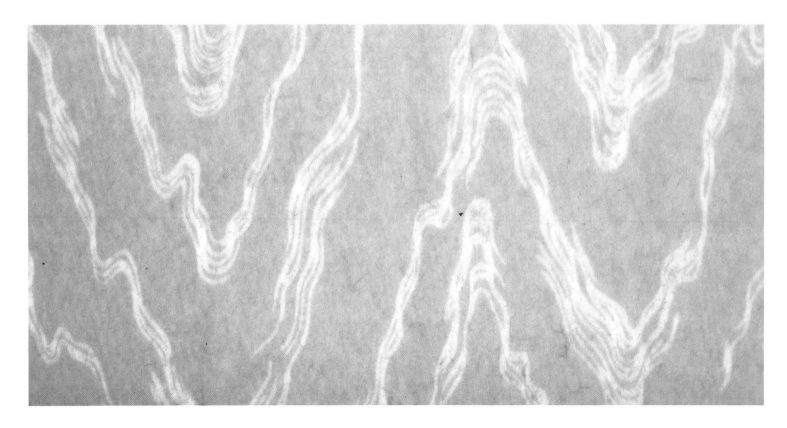

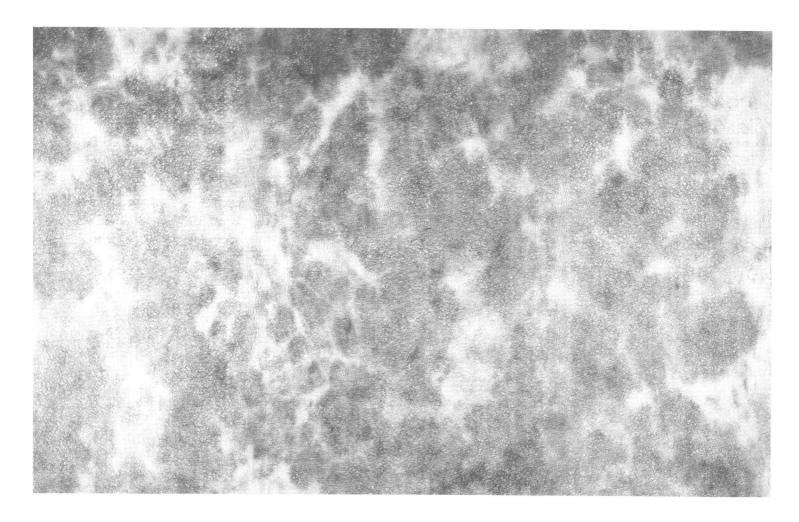

Fig. 3-7
Harusome murazome
Made from *kōzo* by Ichihara Danjaku
Gifu Prefecture

Water is sprinkled onto the thin layer of
fibres on the papermaking screen, creating
tiny holes in an irregular spring rain pattern.
The washi is dyed after the papermaking
process is complete. It is used in hand-torn
collages and other craft projects.

This is another example of
using drops of water to displace
fibres on the papermaking
screen and create a naturalistic
raindrop effect. This is used for
tablecloths, craft projects and
interior design.

Fig. 3-8
Karasuyamawashi kōgeishi
Made from *kōzo* by Fukuda Nagahiro
Tochigi Prefecture

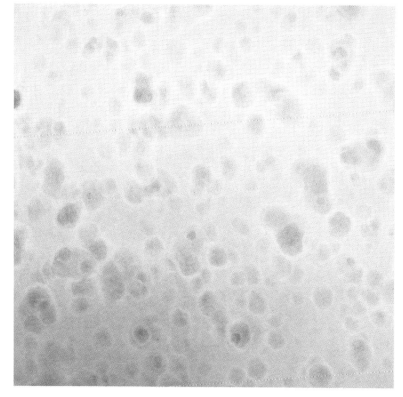

DYED ENTIRE SHEETS OF WASHI

Dyeing washi has been a common practice in Japan since the eighth century. Indigo, red iron oxide and other mineral- and plant-based colours were the most typical ingredients in dyes prior to the introduction of synthetic dyes in the nineteenth century. There are two principal methods of dyeing an entire sheet of washi with one colour: soaking the raw fibres in dye for up to twenty-four hours prior to the papermaking process (*sakizome*), or dipping the finished sheets of washi one or more times into a vat of dye (*atozome*).

Fig. 3-9
Tengu murazome
Made of *kōzo* by Ichihara Danjaku
Gifu Prefecture

This very thin, fine washi is dyed after it has been made, and is available in over thirty colours. It is primarily used for making collages.

Fig. 3-10

Yoshinowashi kusakizome sakura
Made of *kōzo* by Fukunishi Hiroyo
Nara Prefecture

Kōzo pulp is soaked in dye extracted from the bark of cherry trees before the sheets of washi are formed on the screen. This washi is used for calligraphy, painting, and for making paper lanterns.

Narukowashi gampi hon aizome hanadagami
Made itemof *gampi* by Naruko Tetsuro
Shiga Prefecture

Dry washi is dipped three times into a vat of indigo dye to achieve this medium blue colour, then rinsed. This fine washi made of glossy *gampi* fibres is traditionally used for copying out sutras with an ink that is made of gold powder and glue.

Narukowashi gampi hon aizome konshi
Made of *gampi* by Naruko Tetsuro
Shiga Prefecture

This is the same washi as the other indigo-dyed piece in this image but was dipped five times in the vat of indigo dye, resulting in a more intense, darker shade of blue.

TIE-DYED WASHI (*SHIBORIZOME*)

This is a technique that, like many of the resist-dyeing methods in Japan, originated with textile dyeing. Strong, fairly thick washi is generally used so that it will not tear as it is kneaded, pinched and tied into points with thread or string. The tied sheets of washi are soaked and stirred in a vat of dye, then dried and untied to reveal the typical circular patterns softened by dye that has seeped through the wrinkles and knots.

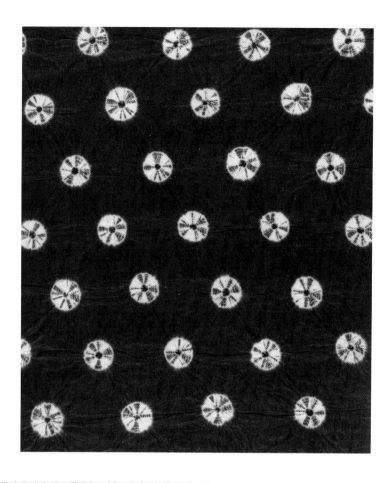

Fig. 3-11
Shiborizome makiage kasa
Made of *kōzo* by Kuriyama Harou
Kyoto Prefecture

The tie-dye technique has been in use in Japan on textiles since the 8th century. This washi is used for clothing and wallpaper, for making various craft items, and on sliding doors.

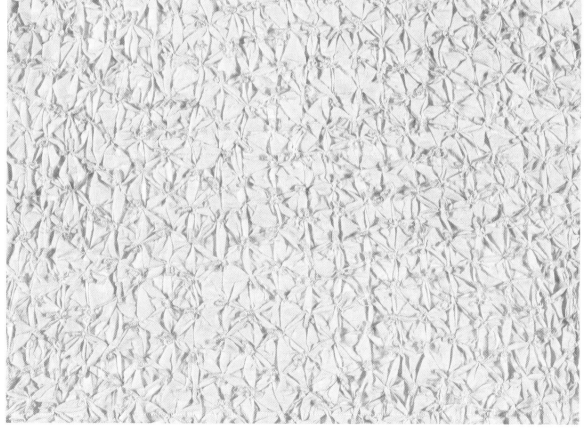

Fig. 3-12
Shibori genshi 1000 shibori urauchi kakōzumi

This is an example of the bound washi before dyeing. This scale of tying would produce washi with 1,000 ties per sheet measuring 61 x 91cm, or 2 x 3 feet. Few craftspeople still produce such densely-knotted washi.

FOLD-DYED WASHI (*ITAJIMEZOME*)

This is a similar resist technique to tie-dyeing in which thin, strong washi is pinched or folded into various patterns which can be held in place with wooden boards, rubber bands, plastic clips or fingers. The folded washi is saturated with water, squeezed out, and dipped by its edges into one or more dyes. It is unfolded while still wet and hung up to dry.

Fig. 3-13
Itajimegami kuchinashi
Made of *kōzo* by
Maezaki Shinya
Toyama Prefecture

Tightly-folded washi can be held in place by hand while it is dipped in dye, although the traditional method would have required wooden boards. The handheld technique may allow for additional bleeding of the dye and a softer appearance.

Fig. 3-14
Sekishū tsukezomegami
tatezome nisanban
Made of *kōzo* by Kubota Akira
Shimane Prefecture

This washi was folded vertically, clamped between boards and dipped into plant dyes. It is used for crafts, interior design and for making collages.

Fig. 3-15
Itajime somegami sekka
Made of *kōzo* by Kuriyama
Haruo
Kyoto Prefecture

After folding and clamping, the corners of the washi folds have been dipped in dye.

WAX-RESIST DYED WASHI (*RŌKETSUZOME*)

This is another method of resist dyeing that has been used in Japan for over a thousand years. Wax is carefully placed or loosely sprinkled onto washi, depending on the nature of the pattern desired, and the washi is then dyed in one or more colours.

In forming these patterns wax has been dropped onto lightly crumpled washi. Some dye was applied to the washi before any of the wax was removed and some applied after part of the wax was removed, in order to create areas of light and shade within the colours. This kind of washi is used for crafts, collage and interior design.

Fig. 3-16
Rōketsuzome
Made of *kōzo* by Takahashi Junichi
Kyoto Prefecture

STENCIL-DYED WASHI (*KATAZOME*)

In this method of dyeing, treated stencil paper is cut into the desired pattern and a thick paste, traditionally made of rice bran, rice flour, salt and lime, is pushed through the stencil and onto the paper. The starch resist covers the negative areas of the pattern, and the stencil covers the positive areas. When the resist has dried, either dyes or pigment solutions can be brushed or soaked into the areas not covered by the resist in order to colour the pattern. When these colours are dry, the paper is soaked in water until the resist falls away or is gently removed, and the pattern is clear against the background. The process can be repeated to add additional colours and patterns. This method of dyeing washi has only been in common use in Japan for the last two centuries, although it has been used in Japan for dyeing textiles for far longer. Stencil-dyed washi is used as wrapping paper, in interior decoration, and for traditional crafts such as doll making.

Fig. 3-18
Katazomegami ainu
Made of *kōzo* and hemp by
Yoshida Yasuki
Toyama Prefecture

This black, brown and ochre pattern represents stylized flowers in a traditional checkerboard grid.

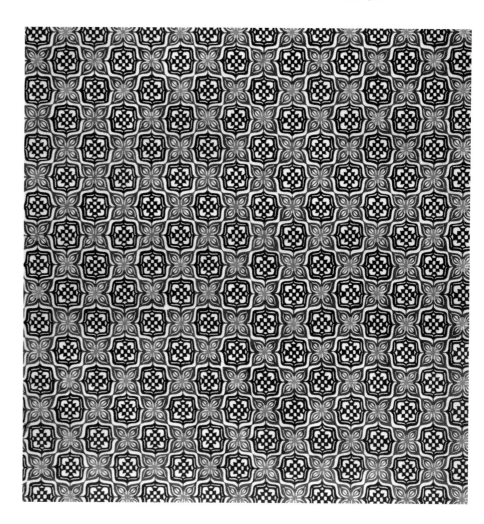

Left
Fig. 3-17
Katazomegami sansui
Made of *kōzo* and hemp by Yoshida Yasuki
Toyama Prefecture

The stencil area for this design would have been relatively large, given the expanse of white background. Depending on which way the washi is viewed, the segments show village scenes or scenes with ships, houses and trees.

Fig. 3-19
Hikizomeji tezurisarasa kusabana
Made of *kōzo* by
Kuriyama Haruo
Kyoto Prefecture

Cherry blossoms, leaves and branches
in muted tones of pink, green
and brown curve gracefully on an
unbleached ground.

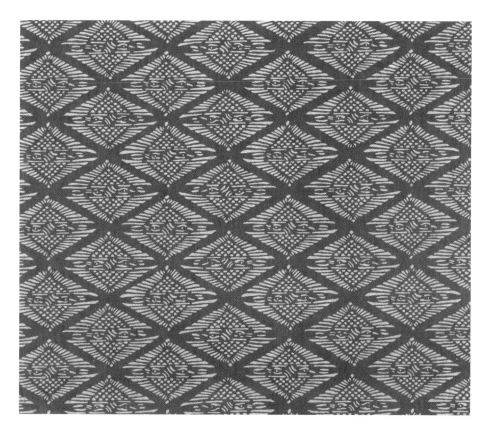

Fig. 3-20
Katozomeshi aizome nanbu hishizuru
Made of *kōzo* by Kuriyama Haruo
Kyoto Prefecture

Two stylised cranes facing in opposite directions form this
sophisticated white diamond pattern on an indigo ground.

Fig. 3-21
Katazomeshi bingatautsushi kachō nami
Made of *kōzo* by Kuriyama Haruo
Kyoto Prefecture

This pattern of birds, flowers and waves is based on a design
from the Okinawan stencil-dyeing tradition of *bingatazome*.

Fig. 3-22
Katazomeshi ryōmenzome
Made of *kōzo* by Kuriyama Haruo
Kyoto Prefecture

This dynamic pattern, dyed in indigo, shows hemp leaves, plum blossoms
and spiky chrysanthemums in a riot of swirling lines and small ogees.

WASHI WITH INCLUSIONS

Embedding flecks of metal foil, contrasting washi fibres, threads and lustrous particles has been common practice since the Heian period (794–1185AD), when papermaking had developed to a high degree of sophistication and technical prowess. Elegantly decorated cards and sheets made from washi were prized as a medium for presenting calligraphy and poetry in the refined, literary society of this period. Adding leaves, grasses and other bits of decorative flowers and plants was a later development.

Fig. 3-23
Matsuzakiwashi konohairi washi
Made of *kōzo* by Koshihara Yasuo
Nagano Prefecture

Leaves were arranged on one thin, damp sheet of washi and covered with another, forming a 'leaf sandwich' when the sheets were couched, pressed together and dried. This is used for stationery, book covers and wallets.

Fig. 3-24
Ōzuwashi tanabatairi haruku
Made of *kōzo* by Numai Mitsuhiro
Ehime Prefecture

Paper confetti and relatively course white fibres were mixed into the dyed pulp solution, and their dispersal throughout the finished sheet creates an illusion of depth in the thin sheet of washi.

Fig. 3-25
Kōgeishi sarashi
Made of *kōzo* by Ichihara Danjaku
Gifu Prefecture

This contemporary version of embedding materials in the pulp solution involves draping thick *kōzo* fibres onto a base layer of damp washi. The thickness of the washi has been varied throughout the sheet by sprinkling water onto the screen during the papermaking process.

Fig. 3-26
Ogawawashi CS paper
Made of 50% *kōzo* and 50% fibreglass by Shimano Toshiaki
Saitama Prefecture

The maker of this washi has been incorporating fibreglass into washi since the 1950s. Although fibreglass is typically used in an industrial setting, this decorative washi is used for stationery and also for lighting, due to its resistance to heat.

TEXTURED AND TREATED WASHI

Washi can be made water-resistant, insect-resistant, more durable and more flexible through the applications of traditional solutions made from the tannin of Japanese persimmon (*Diospyros kaki*) (*kakishibu*) or from *Amorphophallus konjac* root (*konnyaku*). Once treated, the washi can be crumpled or compressed to make wrinkled or crèped paper to use in making clothing, packaging, or small personal items such as bags or wallets, as seen in the Parkes Collection. Two hundred years ago, these washi items could also have been coated in lacquer and used for boxes, dishes and helmets, also as seen in the Parkes Collection. Glued-together sheets of washi that were treated with oil were traditionally used as waterproof coverings for farm equipment and household goods.

Fig. 3-27
Chirimen tateyoko nidoshibori
Made of *kōzo* by Kuriyama Haruo
Kyoto Prefecture

To make washi resemble crèped fabric, several sheets are glued together and scored, then treated with persimmon tannin, wrapped around a wooden pole, and compressed tightly to make fine wrinkles. The washi can be turned at ninety degrees and this process repeated in order to create fine wrinkles in both directions, as seen here. This type of paper was frequently used in the late nineteenth century for pages in books intended for the Western market. Coated with a lacquer solution this washi would have been used as imitation leather, as seen in the Parkes Collection. This particular sheet of washi bears a stenciled pattern of flying birds, leaves and arabesques, and is used for napkins or as cushioned packaging for sake bottles.

Fig. 3-28
Katazome kamiko komon
Made of *kōzo* by Kuriyama Haruo
Kyoto Prefecture

This is an example of 'cloth' made from washi (*kamiko*). It is usually treated with *Amorphophallus konjac* root or persimmon tannin to make it more resilient and durable. After the washi has been pressed, and while it is still damp, it is kneaded thoroughly by hand and dried without being smoothed out. The fibres shrink while drying and become even more interlocked, holding the crumpled texture in place. This washi has a stenciled pattern of flying cranes, leaves and other vegetation.

Figure 3-29
Katazome kamiko bingatautsushi
Made of *kōzo* by Kuriyama Haruo
Kyoto Prefecture

This is another example of washi 'cloth' made in
the same way as Fig. 3-28. It bears a colourful
Okinawan pattern of flowers, leaves and waves.

Fig. 3-30
Somemomi atsukuchi ōban
Made of *kōzo* by Hatano Wataru
Kyoto Prefecture

After this washi was smoothed onto a board
and dried in the sun, it was waterproofed with a
persimmon tannin solution, kneaded by hand to
create its deep wrinkles, and dyed. It is used for
various craft products.

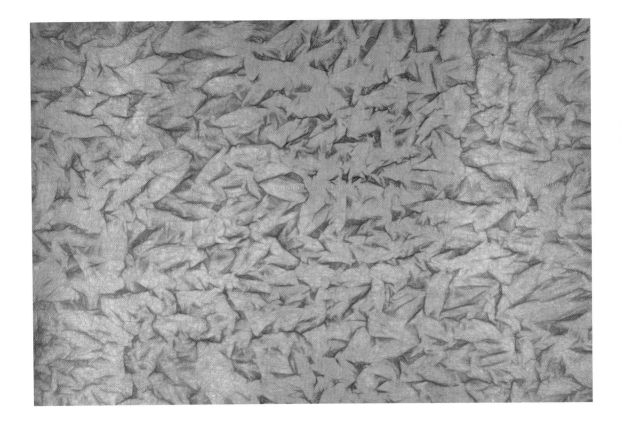

Fig. 3-31
Shiroishiwashi kakishibuzome hinatazome
Made of *kōzo* by Endo Mashiko
Miyagi Prefecture

Washi was dipped into a solution of persimmon tannin, squeezed until partially dry, crumpled by hand and dried in the sun. The tannin pooled in the crevices of the washi, creating a pattern that suggests a greater depth to the washi wrinkles than actually exists. This kind of treated washi was traditionally glued to other sheets of washi and used as a floor covering, or was glued to the outside of baskets used in silkworm cultivation.

Fig. 3-32
Takushi seigaiha aoiro
Made of *kōzo* by Kichimi Teruo
Miyagi Prefecture

This dyed and textured wave design was made by a method similar to the 19th century technique for making washi look like gold embossed leather (*kinkarakawagami*) or like plain leather (*gikakushi*). The laborious process included the following steps: the washi was coated in *Amorphophallus konjac* starch, dried and smoothed, dyed blue, dried, coated in more starch, kneaded by hand, dried, worked into a board with a wave relief carved into it, highlighted with calligraphy ink, flattened, soaked in starch for a third time, dried and pressed. The resulting three-dimensional paper, which is stiff and extremely durable, is used for crafts, for interior design and for making boxes and book covers.

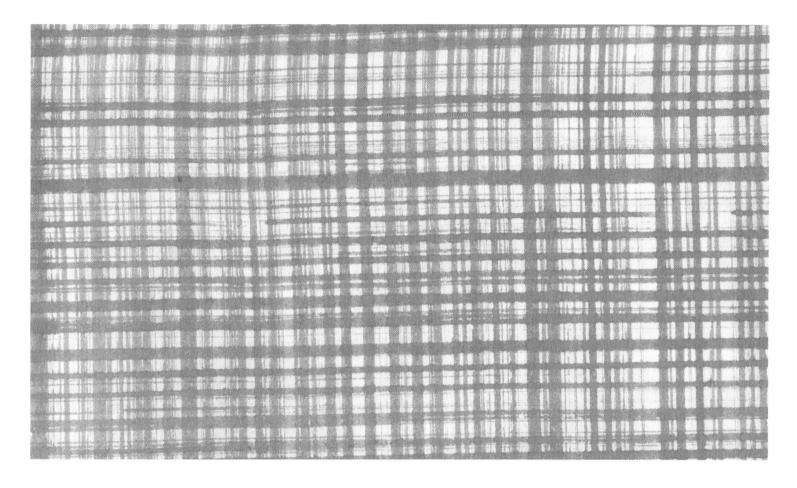

Fig. 3-33
Shikebiki kōshi
Made of *kōzo* by Kuriyama Haruo
Kyoto Prefecture

A sparsely-bristled brush was used to paint lines of persimmon tannin on the washi, resulting in an insect-repellent washi with an appealing pattern. This was traditionally used for wrapping hanging scrolls, bolts of kimono cloth, and sweets.

Fig. 3-34
Aburagami
Made of *kōzo* by Kuriyama Haruo
Kyoto Prefecture

Literally meaning 'oil paper', this washi was treated with linseed oil or perilla oil to make it waterproof. Traditionally it would have been used for any purpose for which plastic sheeting is used today, as well as for umbrellas and raincoats. It is used today for making traditional umbrellas and for wrapping flowers.

OTHER TECHNIQUES FOR DECORATING THE FINISHED SHEET OF WASHI

Various other methods of embellishing the surface of washi, including painting, gluing, woodblock printing and sprinkling shiny or glossy particles, have been in use since as long ago as the eighth century AD. An example of washi that has been torn and glued for an intensely decorative effect can be seen on the inside back flap of this book.

Fig. 3-35
Momikarakami komomi
Made from *kōzo* by
Honjo Takeo
Kyoto Prefecture

The crackled, 'distressed' design on this washi is created by painting two contrasting layers of a pigment and seaweed solution onto the washi. When the sheet is crumpled or kneaded, various different sorts of crazed, crackled and flaking designs appear, revealing the base coat of paint through the fissures in the top coat. Washi with a crackle pattern has been used as mounting paper for hanging scrolls since the seventeenth century. It is frequently used for hanging scrolls in tea ceremony rooms, where its simple and imperfect aesthetic is particularly valued.

Fig. 3-36
Narukowashi kōzeishi iroji karakami
Made of *gampi* and *mitsumata* at Naruko Paper Mill Co., Ltd.
Shiga Prefecture

A diamond, floral and arabesque pattern is woodblock-printed onto the dyed washi. The traditional technique, as seen in the washi in the Parkes Collection, was to apply a mixture of mica, gold powder and glue to a carved wooden block and then press the washi gently onto the block to form the impression. This washi, called *karakami*, is used on the sliding partitions in a Japanese house.

Fig. 3-37
Narukowashi kōzeishi tsurayuki karakami
Made of *gampi* and *mitsumata* at Naruko
Paper Mill Co., Ltd.
Shiga Prefecture

A hexagonal tortoiseshell pattern enclosing
stylized flowers is printed on the dyed washi with
a carved woodblock, as in Fig. 3-36, and mica
is sprinkled over the entire surface of the washi
to create a lustrous sheen. This washi, called
karakami, is used on the sliding partitions in a
Japanese house.

Fig. 3-38
Narukowashi gindamasunago bokashi karazuri ryōshi
Made of *gampi* at Naruko Paper Mill Co., Ltd.
Shiga Prefecture

A subtle wave pattern is woodblock-printed in two corners
of the washi, with fine silver powder and specks of gold foil
sprinkled in circular shapes over the waves. The surface of the
washi has been burnished with the tusk of a wild boar, which
is a traditional method of producing an even higher lustre on
the already glossy *gampi* fibres.

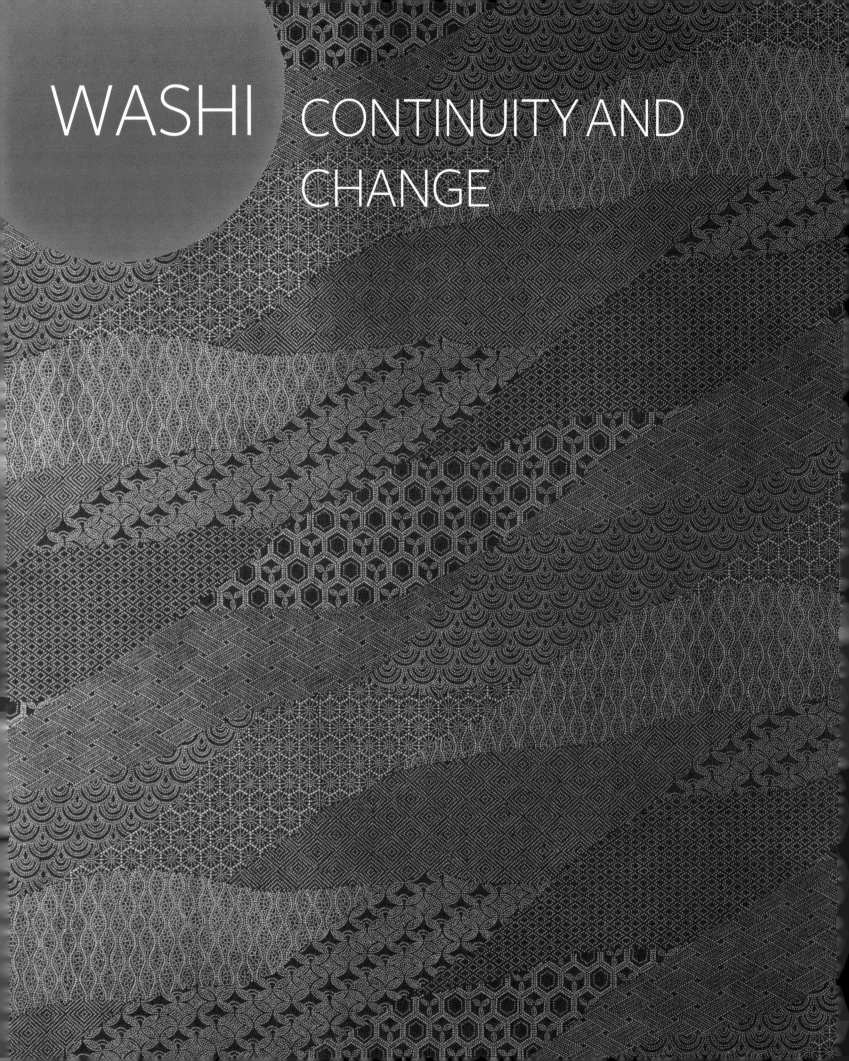

WASHI
CONTINUITY AND CHANGE

CONTINUITY AND CHANGE

A comparison of the washi in the two preceding collections reveals that while hot pink dyes and fibreglass inclusions have expanded the decorative possibilities for the contemporary maker, traditional design motifs based on nature are still flourishing, as are such traditional dyeing techniques as stencils and tie-dyeing. While the nineteenth century practice of treating washi so that it can be used like leather has virtually died out, pieces of contemporary washi with complex watermarks and inclusions are now used for tablecloths and other items of interior design. Technological and lifestyle changes have altered the uses and market for washi at the same time that increased mobility and expanded employment options have dramatically shrunk its labour force, but the world of washi is still compelling and rewarding for those who seek it out today as consumers or practitioners.

At its core, washi is about the papermaking process itself, and that has changed little over the centuries. Although certain labour- or time-saving devices are now available, such as using heated metal drying frames instead of wooden boards and sunshine, or using a machine in certain instances to strip bark off the pre-soaked branches, the process itself can only be mechanised up to a certain point. It is ultimately, as it always has been, about the maker, the fibre solution, and the maker's control of the movements of the papermaking mould. In comparing the washi in these two collections, it is clear that the skill, rigour and devotion of the nineteenth century papermakers is still present in their twenty-first century counterparts.

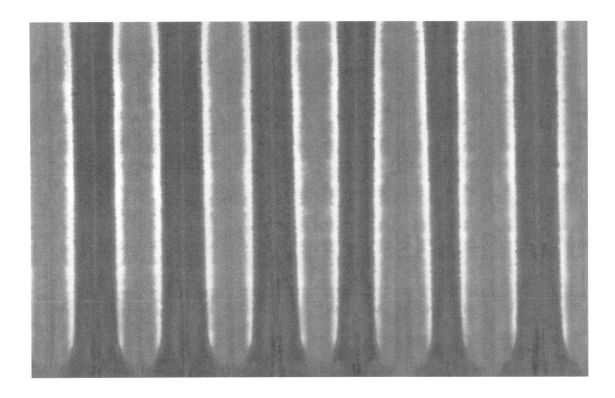

Fig. 4-1
Itajime somegami shima
Made of *kōzo* by Kuriyama Haruo
Kyoto Prefecture

This fold-dyed washi (*itajimezome*) has been accordion-pleated, with the edges of the pleats immersed in dye. It is used for craft projects and interior decoration.

Previous page
Kiribori edokomon samezukushimichinaga
Made of *kōzo* by Takahashi Junichi
Kyoto Prefecture

This patchwork of traditional geometric motifs was created by using an awl to punch tiny holes into a stencil, through which resist paste was pressed before the washi was dyed.

SOURCES AND FURTHER READING

Barrett, Timothy. (1983). *Japanese Papermaking: Traditions, Tools, and Techniques*. Weatherhill Inc., Tokyo. Reprinted (2005), Floating World Editions, Warren, Connecticut.

Hughes, Sukey. (1978). *Washi: The World of Japanese Paper*. Kodansha International Ltd, Tokyo.

Hunter, Dard. (1947). *Papermaking: The History and Technique of an Ancient Craft*. Alfred Knopf, New York. Reprinted (1978), Dover Publications, New York.

Jugaku, Bunshō. (1959). *Paper-Making by Hand in Japan*. Meiji-Shobo Publishers Ltd, Tokyo.

Karacho: Karakami Paper in Kyoto. (2004). DesignEXchange Co., Ltd, Tokyo.

Lane-Poole, Stanley and Frederick V. Dickens. (1894). *The Life of Sir Harry Parkes K.C.B., G.C.M.G., Sometime Her Majesty's Minister to China & Japan*. Macmillan and Co., London.

Parkes, Harry S. (1871). *Reports on the Manufacture of Paper in Japan, Presented to Both Houses of Parliament by Command of Her Majesty*, 1871. Harrison & Sons, London.

Schmoller, Hans. (1984). *Mr. Gladstone's Washi: A Survey of 'Reports on the Manufacture of Paper in Japan'*. Bird & Bull Press, Newtown, PA.

Tindale, Thomas Keith and Harriet Ramsey. (1952). *The Handmade Papers of Japan*. Charles E. Tuttle and Company, Tokyo.

Umi o watatta edo no washi: pakusu korekushon ten ('Edo-Period Japanese Paper Sent Overseas: An Exhibition of the Parkes Collection'). (1994). Tobacco and Salt Museum, Tokyo.

Washi: The Soul of Japan – Fine Japanese Paper in the Second Millennium. (2011). Washi: The Soul of Japan Committee, Kyoto.

PHOTOGRAPHY CREDITS

Figure 1-1, courtesy the author; Figures 1-2, 1-3, 1-4, courtesy Elaine Cooper; Figure 2-1, courtesy the Japan Society of the UK; Figure 2-2, courtesy National Archives, Kew; Figures 2-37 through 2-53, Andrew McRobb/©RBG Kew; all other images, Paul Little/©RBG Kew.

Images and further information on the Parkes Collection in the Economic Botany Collection, Kew can be found at www.kew.org/collections/ecbot

This book was written in connection with the exhibition *Washi: The Art of Japanese Paper*, held at The Gallery at Norwich University of the Arts, 12 March – 20 April 2013.

Front cover
Gold hawk perched on bare branch of pine tree, framed by silver clouds and silhouetted against night sky
Woodblock-printed onto washi treated to look like leather (*gikakushi*), c. 1869

Inside front cover
Silver full moons, black sparrows superimposed on silver snowflakes, and gold cherry blossoms with names of famous cherry-blossom-viewing sites in Tokyo
Woodblock-printed onto washi treated to look like leather (*gikakushi*), c. 1869.

Inside front flap
Silver pine trees on a cream ground
Woodblock-printed onto washi made of *kōzo*, c. 1869.

Title page
Gold clouds and *Paulownia* on a blue ground
Woodblock-printed onto washi made of *kōzo,* c. 1869

All of the above from the Parkes Collection at the
Economic Botany Collection, Royal Botanic Gardens, Kew

Inside back cover
Katozomeshi kikukarakusa
Contemporary washi made of *kōzo* by Kuriyama Haruo
Kyoto Prefecture
Chrysanthemums, which signify longevity and represent the imperial court, combine with leaves and arabesques in a vivid pattern of white, black and red.

Inside back flap
Narukowashi yaburitsugi ryōshi
Contemporary washi made of *gampi* at Naruko Paper Mill Co., Ltd.
Shiga Prefecture
Seven pieces of printed and decorated washi made from *gampi* have been torn and glued together to create a subtle collage that appears to be a single sheet.

ACKNOWLEDGEMENTS

Many thanks go to the following individuals and organisations: Dr Mark Nesbitt of the Economic Botany Collection, Royal Botanic Gardens, Kew; Dr Christine Guth and Dr Sarah Teasley of the Royal College of Art; the Sainsbury Institute for the Study of Japanese Arts and Cultures, including Dr Simon Kaner, Mami Mizutori and Yoko Kishida; Michio Ichikawa, Yoshie Sakata, Yoshizo Uemura and Masuhiro Yamada of the Washi: The Soul of Japan Committee; Neil Powell of Norwich University of the Arts; Great Britain Sasakawa Foundation; Daiwa Anglo-Japanese Foundation; and The Fukui-ken Japanese Paper Industrial Co-operative (Echizen Washi).